EZEKIEL UNMASKED
A REVELATION
OF
YESHUA'S LOVE
JUSTICE
AND
REDEMPTION

Yeshua's Love - Volume I
Chapter 1-24

P. D. DALLING

3G Publishing, Inc.
Loganville, GA 30052
www.3gpublishinginc.com
Phone: 1-888-442-9637

©2015, P.D. Dalling. All rights reserved.

ISBN: 978-1-941247-4-3

All Scripture quotations, unless otherwise indicated, are taken from the King James Version of the Bible.

Scripture quotations identified NKJV are from the New King James Version of the Bible. Copyright 1979, 1980, 1982, 1992 by Thomas Nelson, Inc. All rights reserved. Used by permission.

Scripture quotations identified NASB are from the New American Standard Bible. Copyright 1960, 1962, 1963, 1968, 1971, 1972, 1973, 1975, 1977, 1995 by the Lockman Foundation. All rights reserved. Used by permission.

Scripture quotations identified NIV are from the New International Version of the Bible. Copyright 1973, 1978, 1984, 1995 by Zondervan Publishing House. All rights reserved. Used by permission

Scripture quotations identified NLT are from The New Living Translation. Copyright 1996, 2004, 2007 by Tyndale House Foundation. Used by permission of Tyndale House Publishers, Inc. All rights reserved.

Scripture quoted by permission. Quotations designated (NET) are from the NET Bible® copyright © 1996-2007 by Biblical Studies Press, L.L.C. http://netbible.com. All rights reserved.

Credit to E.W. Bullinger., *Number in Scripture*. Cosimo, Inc. 2005. Brief quotation embodied in review.

Credit to James Strong. Strong's Exhaustive Concordance of the Bible, Massachusetts: Hendrickson Publishers, n.d

Hebrew, Aramaic or Greek words carries an assigned number in brackets which corresponds with its English equivalent to aid the astute reader to a deeper understanding of the broken seal of the book of Ezekiel.

All rights reserved. No part of this publication may be reproduced, stored in a retrieval system, or transmitted in any form or by any means, electronic, mechanical, photocopy, recording, or otherwise, without the prior written permission of the publisher and copyright owner.

Contents

About the Author — vii
Preface — ix

Chapter 1 — 17
Verses 1-4 — 17
Verses 5-9 — 20
Verse 10 — 29
Verse 11 — 33
Verse 12 — 34
Verses 13–14 — 36
Verses 15–21 — 38
Verses 22-25 — 47
Verses 26-28 — 52

Chapter 2 — 57
Verses 1-5 — 57
Verses 6-10 — 58

Chapter 3 — 61
Verses 1-11 — 61
Verses 12-15 — 63
Verses 16-21 — 65
Verses 22-27 — 67

Chapter 4 — 69
Verses 1-3 — 69
Verses 4-8 — 71
Verses 9-17 — 79

Chapter 5 — 97
Verses 1-4 — 97
Verses 5-10 — 99
Verses 11-17 — 101

Chapter 6 — 105
Verses 1–4 — 105
Verses 5-10 — 106
Verses 11-14 — 108

Chapter 7 — 111
Verses 1-4 — 111
Verses 5-16 — 113
Verses 17-22 — 115
Verses 23-27 — 117

Chapter 8 — 119
Verses 1-5 — 119
Verses 6-10 — 121
Verses 11-12 — 125
Verses 13-15 — 126
Verses 16-18 — 126

Chapter 9 — 129
Verses 1-4 — 129
Verses 5-7 — 132
Verses 8-11 — 134

Chapter 10 — 137
Verses 1-7 — 137
Verses 8-17 — 149
Verses 18-22 — 155

Chapter 11 — 159
Verses 1-3 — 159
Verses 4-7 — 160
Verses 8-13 — 161
Verses 14-21 — 162
Verses 22-25 — 164

Chapter 12 — 167
Verses 1-16 — 167

Verses 17-20   172
Verses 21-28   173

Chapter 13   175
Verses 1-10   175
Verses 11-16   178
Verses 17-23   179

Chapter 14   181
Verses 1-11   181
Verses 12-23   183

Chapter 15   189
Verses 1-8   189

Chapter 16   193
Verses 1-10   193
Verses 11-14   199
Verses 15-19   202
Verses 20-34   204
Verses 35-43   210
Verses 44-52   213
Verses 53-63   215

Chapter 17   217
Verses 1-4   217
Verses 5-6   221
Verses 7-21   222
Verses 22-24   225

Chapter 18   229
Verses 1-4; 18-23; 27-28   229
Verses 5-9   231
Verses 10-13   233
Verses 14-17   234
Verses 24-26   236
Verses 29-32   237

Chapter 19 — 241
Verses 1-9 — 241
Verses 10-14 — 244

Chapter 20 — 249
Verses 1-10 — 249
Verses 11-39 — 251
Verses 40-44 — 256
Verses 45-49 — 258

Chapter 21 — 261
Verses 1-7 — 261
Verses 8-13 — 263
Verses 14-17 — 264
Verses 18-27 — 265
Verses 28-32 — 267

Chapter 22 — 271
Verses 1-16 — 271
Verses 17-22 — 275
Verses 23-31 — 282

Chapter 23 — 285
Verses 1-21 — 285
Verses 22-35 — 289
Verses 36-49 — 293

Chapter 24 — 295
Verses 1-14 — 295
Verses 15-27 — 299

About the Author

P.D. Dalling was born on the small island of Jamaica West Indies of both African and Jewish lineage. She was commissioned by the LORD to be a voice to the nations of the world through these inspired writings in these final hours of human history. A student of the Word, P.D Dalling was given several visions and dreams starting from the young age of five. The most intriguing of these visions was one given in consecutive order over a period of seven years showing the construction of an enormous temple from the laying of its foundation until the final stages of it being painted in gold. The author later realized that the vision was to prepare her for this assignment as she neared the completion of a six week teaching on *"The Justice of God."*

Prior to completing this series of teachings, the author once more sought Yeshua as she usually does for the next assignment. A few days later on a hot Saturday afternoon, a call came from a devoted Saint of God and watchman living in the State of Florida, who was unaware of the author's prayer request; this devoted follower of Yeshua Jesus shared a message received from the Lord at 2 A.M. that morning. "Tell My child to teach on the book of Ezekiel, it will be tough." The author accepted the challenge but was met with many obstacles and a wrestling in spirit as to the format for something of this magnitude. Then came the answer in a dream to the author; the Lord wanted this work to be put into writing.

P.D. Dalling had to rely on the leading and inner witness of Holy Spirit to begin and complete this project, as He explicitly spoke: "I will teach you." Indeed this was a very difficult task that took on a whole new meaning of what is meant: to have fellowship with Holy Spirit.

Because this work was commissioned by the LORD, P.D. Dalling refrains from offering any personal credentials or academic scholarship. All glory and honor goes to Abba Father, Yeshua Jesus His Son and my great teacher and friend Holy Spirit who will reward their bondservant in heaven.

Preface

The book of Ezekiel will take you on a prophetic journey from the day the LORD GOD called Ezekiel to be His voice to the nation of Israel in exile, unto these present times. Said to be the most intriguing and mysterious book of the Old Testament, there are two clear themes to its interpretation; the literal and the spiritual-prophetic. Psalm 12:6 states: The words of the LORD are pure words: as silver tried in a furnace of earth, purified seven times. This is a fair description of the depth of the interpretation of the book of Ezekiel, because it is given by inspiration and revelation of Holy Spirit. This work offers no preponderance for replacement theology. The book speaks of GOD'S dealings with Israel His people to the unification of the body of Yeshua with their Jewish brothers as One New Man (Ephesians 3). This work flows with GOD'S grace, mercy, and love for a people who rebelled against Him, worshiped other gods, and suffered at the hands of their oppressors. When they repented, like a loving Father, He forgives and reconcile with His beloved.

In the book of Ezekiel the LORD GOD sometimes spoke by the mouth of His prophet using metaphors, allegories, euphemisms, typologies, prophetic role play, analogies, and coded mysteries, which has frustrated readers of this book for centuries. At this time and by GOD'S own providence, He has broken the seal that clouds the mind to reveal divine truths in these last days. This work is presented in three volumes. Volume one covers chapters 1-24 and addresses Israel's past. Volume two covers chapters 25-39 and address Israel's present state and volume three covers chapters 40-48 unveiling Israel's glorious future and the adoption of the Gentiles into the generation of Yeshua Jesus. Yeshua's love, for His beloved people is revealed in volume one; His justice in laid out in volume two and His redemption in volume three. This compilation unmasks the spiritual prophetic content of the book of Ezekiel; it demonstrates the love of Abba Father for all people whom He created in His image and likeness and gives a final call for all to come out of this sin infested world and find rest in Him.

The LORD addresses both good and evil, shepherds and hirelings, the righteous and the unrighteous; leaders of Israel as well as leaders of other nations. Yeshua's suffering and His coming reign as the Prince of peace among His brethren is reveled in the book of Ezekiel. It will be this Prince; the Son of GOD, who will reunite man with Abba Father not as a god, but as ONE NEW MAN in Yeshua HaMashiach, Jesus the Messiah. Ephesians 2:11-15 and 3:1-6 are principal building block for this review on the forty-eight chapters of Ezekiel: *Wherefore remember, that ye being in time past Gentiles in the flesh, who are called Uncircumcision by that which is called the Circumcision in the flesh made by hands; that at that time ye were without Christ, being aliens from the commonwealth of Israel, and strangers from the covenants of promise, having no hope, and without God in the world: but now in Christ Jesus ye who sometimes were far off are made nigh by the blood of Christ. For He is our peace, who hath made both one, and broken down the middle wall of partition between us; having abolished in His flesh the enmity, even the law of commandments contained in ordinances; for to make in Himself of twain ONE NEW MAN, so making peace. . . . For this cause I Paul, the prisoner of Jesus Christ for you Gentiles, if ye have heard of the dispensation of the grace of God which is given me to you-ward: how that by revelation He made known unto me the mystery; (as I wrote afore in few words, whereby, when ye read, ye may understand my knowledge in the mystery of Christ) which in other ages was not made known unto the sons of men, as it is now revealed unto His holy apostles and prophets by the Spirit; That the Gentiles should be fellow heirs, and of the same body, and partakers of His promise in Christ by the gospel.*

As the construction of the temple of man takes shape in volume three of these writings, we will see the manifold grace of Abba Father unfolding. The tabernacle of Moses is a picture of the law or teachings, but the temple of Yeshua Jesus is all about the grace of His Father, which He extends to all. Romans 6:1-14 states: *What shall we say then? Shall we continue in sin, that grace may abound? God forbid. How shall we, that are dead to sin, live any longer therein? Know ye not, that so many of us as were baptized into Jesus Christ were baptized into His death? Therefore we are buried with Him by baptism into death: that like as Christ was raised up from the dead by the glory of the Father, even so we also should walk in newness of life. For if we have been planted together in the likeness of His death, we shall also be in the likeness of His resurrection: knowing this, that our old man is crucified with him, that the body of sin might be destroyed, that henceforth we should not serve sin. Now if we be dead with Christ, we believe that we shall also live with Him: knowing that Christ being raised from the dead dieth no more; death hath no more dominion over Him. For in that He died, He died unto sin once: but in that He liveth, He liveth unto God. Likewise reckon ye also yourselves to be dead indeed unto sin, but alive unto God through Jesus Christ our Lord. Let not sin therefore reign in your mortal body, that ye should obey it in the lusts thereof. Neither yield ye your members as instruments of unrighteousness unto sin: but yield yourself unto God, as those that are alive from the dead, and your members as instruments of righteousness unto God. For sin shall not have dominion over you: for ye are not under the law, but under grace.* The body of Yeshua Jesus, like Israel, is in spiritual exile, but the day will come as you will see step by step unfolding in the book of Ezekiel, when man will once again enjoy fellowship with God face to face.

The unmasking of the book of Ezekiel will bring about a radical change in the way Believers in Yeshua Jesus view Scriptures. It will rattle the conscience of the skeptic and shake the very foundation of Christian dogma. There are lengths, widths, heights and depths in the Word of God that are yet to be revealed. The LORD is waiting to take those who are willing to travel with Him from the surface of His Word and descend to its greatest depths but the choice is ours. Beneath the surface of the Word of God are wonders to behold, this however will be a lifelong task of total abandonment that comes at a great price. The deeper Yeshua takes us in the Word, will make the crushing greater and the judgment stricter, but in the end the natural man will be regenerated and the attributes of the Living God will radiate from his being thereby changing the lives of others. Ecclesiastes 1:9-10 applying the NKJV states: *That which has been is what will be, that which is done is what will be done, and there is nothing new under the sun. Is there anything of which it may be said, "See, this is new"? It has already been in ancient times before us.* As plans are being made for the third temple to be constructed in Jerusalem, God has already begun a parallel work in mankind by preparing us to be His spiritual abode to enter the kingdom of God and the New Jerusalem that comes down from heaven. This temple is therefore referred to as the fourth temple in these writings because it is not natural but spiritual.

Both Jews and Gentile Believers will understand their divine purpose as God reveals something about Himself and His relationship with mankind as He breaks the seal and reveals astounding truths from the Book of Ezekiel. Ezekiel unmasked is therefore God's message to Jews and Gentiles. He addresses our weaknesses and raises the bar to show our strengths. He places the ball labeled "choice" in our court as He motivates us to choose eternal life over death and lasting fellowship instead of damnation. If we accept His calling; He lifts us out of the mire of sin, declares us holy by His grace, and calls us kings and priests. He speaks of Israel as His firstborn and all those who believe in Yeshua Jesus, as been born-again! One day the body of Yeshua will share in the glorious inheritance of Israel as sons and daughters of the King of all kings and Lord of all lords.

God is building a temple

Not made by human hands

The blueprint designed in heaven

A revelation of ONE NEW MAN

Jews and Gentiles called by God to live in unity

Under the eternal banner of love for all the world to see

Both were bought and paid for at a very dear price

Yeshua's poured out blood became their perfect sacrifice.

P.D.Dalling, "A Temple Not Built By Human Hands."

Volume One

Israel's Present:
Yeshua's Love

Chapter 1

Verses 1-4

Now it came to pass in the thirtieth year, in the fourth month, in the fifth day of the month as I was among the captives by the river Chebar that the heavens were opened, and I saw visions of God. In the fifth day of the month, which was the fifth year of Jehoiachin's captivity, the word of the LORD came expressly unto the priest, the son of Buzi, in the land of the Chaldeans by the river Chebar; and the hand of the LORD was there upon him. And I looked, and, behold, a whirlwind came out of the north, a great cloud, and a fire infolding itself, and a brightness was about it, and out of the midst thereof was the color of amber, out of the midst of the fire.

The opening of the heavens is multifaceted: it validates the spiritual realm, it seals man's instructions, and it changes the way one thinks forever. Ezekiel gives the date, physical location and reigning king of Judah who was also among the captives when he had the first of a series of visions and encounters with the LORD. Here Ezekiel is caught up in a dimension where the heavens were opened and he beheld things that the natural eyes could not have otherwise looked upon. Being the invited guest of Abba Father, the prophet was now chaperoned by Holy Spirit to the throne room of the LORD; the place where GOD reveals His plans and purposes for mankind. Ezekiel was still very young at the time of the exile and his heart was grief stricken as calamity had befallen the beloved city of Jerusalem. Both the righteous and the wicked were carted off to a strange land and a barbarous people. It then became the responsibility of the LORD God to educate this bewildered and grieving young priest sitting among his brethren by the river Chebar. That which will follow Ezekiel's tutelage, would give him peace for the next seventy trying years that were ahead and the assurance that GOD did not punish without a cause. This righteous man was called by the LORD to be His voice of rebuke as well as comfort to the exiles because they too, especially the young, would gain understanding as to the reason why they were being punished and only true repentance would be the antidote by which the favor of the LORD would be appeased.

The exiled priest was now to be ordained as a prophet. One may never understand why the righteous suffers the same fate at times with the wicked, but in the end it will bring him or her to that level of perfection in Yeshua Messiah and intimacy with GOD that could not have been attained otherwise. The LORD'S ways are higher than ours, and at times He will strategically place His people in uncomfortable situations to bring out the best in them and also His ultimate plan. In Ezekiel 1:3 it is stated: *The Word of the LORD came expressly unto Ezekiel.* The word "expressly" is used in the KJV; its Hebrew transliteration is **Hayah** [1961] which refers to the ever living; ever present, and ever knowing I AM THAT I AM. This statement is verifying that the pre-incarnate Son of GOD, Yeshua Jesus, was instructing Ezekiel because He was known as the "Word" before His earthly advent. 1 John 5:7 applying the NKJV states: *For there are three that bear witness in heaven: the Father, the Word, and the Holy Spirit and these three are one* (for further reading, see also Deuteronomy 6:4; Mark 12:29; John 1:1-4; 17:5; Philippians 2:6; Colossians 1:17; 1 John 1:1-2; Revelation 1:2; 19:13).

Awe struck, Ezekiel is overwhelmed as the power of the LORD God rest upon him and he saw a whirlwind engulfed in flames coming from a northerly direction. At a loss for words, Ezekiel described what he was looking at as having the veracity of a whirlwind. Now a whirlwind is a column of air that rotates rapidly; we see these in nature, such as hurricanes, tornadoes, wind storms and typhoons. Ezekiel stands transfixed in wonder, as he watches the unusual cloud approaching from a distance. Psalm 97:1-3 states: *The LORD reigneth; let the earth rejoice; let the multitude of isles be glad thereof. Clouds and darkness are round about Him: righteousness and judgment are the habitation of His throne. A fire goeth before Him, and burneth up His enemies round about.* Arrested by the glory cloud of the presence of GOD, Ezekiel knew that his life would never be the same again.

The Hebrew word used for "cloud" is **Awan** [6051], which means the presence of GOD! This is the same word used in Exodus 24:15-17: *And Moses went up into the mount, and a cloud covered the mount. And the glory of the LORD abode upon Mount Sinai, and the cloud covered it six days: and the seventh day He called unto Moses out of the midst of the cloud. And the sight of the glory of the LORD was like devouring fire on the top of the mount in the eyes of the children of Israel.* Here the LORD uses the natural weather system to reveal the majesty of His power, but also imbedded in this event is a much greater revelation. Ezekiel 1:4 states: *a whirlwind came out of the north*. In Scripture, the north is symbolic of three things: the direction from which rebuke comes, a place of fair weather, and lastly man's delegated authority, which will be explained later. In Job chapter 37:9 and 22 it is stated: *Out of the south cometh the whirlwind and cold out of the north . . . Fair weather cometh out of the north: with God is terrible majesty.* Ezekiel observed the whirlwind coming from the north the place of fair weather, instead of the south and this was not a good sign because it is a picture of the unfolding of the judgment of God.

The massive wall of cloud was accompanied by an engulfing fire which did not consume in its path. This however was no ordinary flame, because it was the glory and majesty of the LORD GOD being revealed. Scriptures record that the LORD hides Himself in darkness (Exodus 20:21; Deuteronomy 4:11, 12), and He appears in fire (Exodus

3:2-6; Deuteronomy 4:24, 36; 5:22; Hebrews 12:29). The prophet, awe stricken, now braces himself, as the great cloud engulfed in billowing flames grew ever closer to him and it became clear to Ezekiel that the LORD was accompanied by His own special envoy of glorious living creatures called the Cherubim. These are the same class of beings commissioned by God to be the security guards of Eden when man was banished from their because of sin. In the dispensation of Yeshua Jesus, man will once again return to his home, the beautiful kingdom of God, the very ground from which he was created to communicate with God like he did before his fall from grace. As we continue our journey through the book of Ezekiel, more will be explained about these living creatures, because God created them in such a way that aspects of their attribute and appearance gives a visual story about man himself and his intrinsic design for worship.

Verses 5-9

Also out of the midst thereof came the likeness of four living creatures. And this was their appearance; they had the likeness of a man. And every one had four faces, and every one had four wings. And their feet were straight feet; and the sole of their feet was like the sole of a calf's foot: and they sparkled like the color of burnish brass. And they had the hands of a man under their wings on their four sides; and they four had their faces and their wings. Their wings were joined one to another; they turned not when they went; they went every one straight forward.

There is so much being revealed here, these creatures are identified as the Cherubim in Ezekiel 10:20-22. The prophet gives a vivid description of every facet of their appearance, and each aspect reveals something about God and His hope for all humanity. With this in mind, the Word of God will be examined from its Hebraic root, to unearth spellbinding truths that we would not have otherwise known. Ezekiel looks on in wonder and expectancy at these angelic creatures. As a priest and minister in the temple at Jerusalem, the prophet knew of the presence of replicas of these awesome creatures affixed on the Mercy Seat, but now he is granted the unique opportunity of seeing these living creatures for the first time. Their appearance is beyond intrigue, as there is something much more spectacular about their features that will grip our soul. In great wonder and absorbed in deep thoughts and curiosity, the first thing Ezekiel observed about these living creatures was their four faces in the likeness of man.

The LORD GOD did not comission an angel to deliver a message to the prophet, He came Himself, and the direction He was seen approaching was cause for concern. What did the house of Israel do to warrant a personal visit from the Creator of the universe? And why was the first four of their sixteen faces that of man? Let's examine some facts that could have easily been missed. The living creatures' faces being four in number are a total of sixteen. In Scripture the number four speaks of God's completed creative works, Genesis 1:14-19 reads: *And God said, Let there be lights in the firmament of the heaven to divide the day from the night; and let them be for signs, and for seasons, and for days, and years: and let them be for lights in the firmament of the heaven to give light upon the earth: and it was so. And God made two great lights; the greater light to rule the day, and the lesser light to rule the night: He made the stars also. And God set them in the firmament of the heaven to give light upon the earth, and to rule over the day and night, and to divide the light from the darkness: and God saw that it was good. And the evening and the morning were the fourth day.* That which the Lord has spoken He has upheld by the word of His power (Hebrews 1:3), times, seasons, days, years, lights etc., are an eternal witness of His infinite wisdom and a permanent testimony of His eternal existence.

Now remember one of the sets of faces of the living creature is that of man, and these beings are before the throne of

GOD in rhetorical worship (Revelation 4:8). The massage that the LORD was sending to us here is this: the face of man speaks of leadership, authority, fellowship, and worship; (see Genesis 1 and 2). We are created to worship Abba Father; and a time is coming when fellowship between GOD and man will be restored and man will worship his Creator in spirit and in truth once again (John 4:23-24). There were four sets of faces, and each set is telling us that the ultimate goal of man is to rise to completeness and perfection in God because he was created for worship.

Each Cherub had four faces and each one had four wings, which is a total of sixteen faces and sixteen wings. Their feet or legs were straight and the soles of their feet were like that of a calf, which sparkled like burnish copper. The Hebrew word used for "straight" is **Yashar** [3474], it means just, right, upright, moral, lawful, or honest, therefore having one's approval or blessing. Psalm 1:1-3 states: *Blessed is the man that walketh not in the counsel of the ungodly nor standeth in the way of sinners, nor sitteth in the seat of the scornful. But his delight is in the Law of the LORD; and in His Law doth he meditate day and night. And he shall be like a tree planted by the rivers of water, that bringeth forth his fruit in his season; whatsoever he doeth shall prosper*. We see the creation of a new man unfolding; being just, moral, lawful and honest.

Next the soles of their feet were described as that of calf's feet. Calf's feet are symbolic of strength (Proverbs 14:4). In Hebrew "sole" is **Kaph** [3709], it compares to the eleventh letter of the Hebrew alphabet *Kaf/Khaf,* which shape like the letter "C" turned backwards; it means to turn upward, to expose the inside, which is to say; all things are revealed, there is nothing to hide, no secrets to keep; it bares its sole as it does its soul. Here we see the design of these living creatures telling a story of the future restoration and reconciliation of man with his Creator. A time is coming when we will no longer have to hide ourselves; for all things will be restored as they were before Adam sinned and condemned mankind to death. This process began when man voluntarily gave up his right of self rule and made Yeshua his Lord and Savior (Romans 10:9).

In the book of Ezekiel the LORD at times spoke to the prophet using euphemism, idioms, metaphors, and prophetic roll play. Always bear in mind that the LORD'S intention was never to confuse us, but to draw us closer to Himself because we will understand their meaning as we grow spiritually. God dearly loves us, and wants to share His plans with us; therefore, we must come into a pure relationship with Him so that He delights in sharing His truths that are veiled to the world. Next the feet of the Cherubim is said to sparkle like the color of burnt copper. Anything that is destroyed by fire undergoes a type of transformation; the process necessary for the new man in Yeshua Jesus. Incidentally the Hebrew word for "color" is translated "eye" and since the design of the Cherubim is a visual story of the new man in Yeshua, the "eye" is symbolically speaking of man's new found understanding of his purpose, identity and destiny, which is Yeshua Messiah in him the hope of glory (Ephesians 1:18; Colossians 1:27).

The feet of these living creatures were brass or copper, which speaks of judgment or justice against sin, and because they were described as being burnt, the spiritual man in Yeshua Jesus is judged and his sins completely forgiven. 1 Peter 4:5-6 states: *Who shall give account to Him that is ready to judge the quick and the dead? For this cause was the gospel preached also to them that are dead, that they might be judged according to men in the flesh, but live according to God in the spirit.* Man as a restored being is hereby depicted by the many facets and attributes of these living creatures and there is still more to come.

As silver symbolically refers to Yeshua Jesus our Redeemer, burned copper speaks of His judgment and our reconciliation and fellowship with Him through grace. 1 Corinthians 3:11-17 explains this quite clearly: *For other foundation can no man lay that is laid, which is Jesus Christ. Now if any man build upon this foundation gold, silver, precious stones, wood, hay, stubble; every man's work shall be made manifest: for the day shall declare it, because it shall be revealed by fire; and the fire shall try every man's work of what sort it is. If any man's work abides which he hath built thereupon, he shall receive a reward. If any man's work shall be burned, he shall suffer loss: but he himself shall be saved; yet so as by fire. Know ye not that ye are the temple of God, and that the Spirit of God dwelleth in you? If any man defile the temple of God, him shall God destroy; for the temple of God is holy, which temple ye are.*

Sin became our death sentence, but we were made alive in Yeshua Jesus because of the Father's grace and desire to fellowship with us, the crown of His creation. What remains of our identity will be sparkling burnish or burned copper because our deeds have been purified. Man's life will one day be pleasing to the LORD, as nothing will be found in him that will be at enmity with Abba Father; he will be holy, righteous, and pure like Yeshua Jesus. These are His words in John 14:30b: "*For the prince of this world cometh, and hath nothing in Me.*" When we see Yeshua we will be just like Him. 1 John 3:2-3 states: *Beloved, now are we the sons of God, and it doth not yet appear what we shall be: but we know that, when He shall appear, we shall be like Him; for we shall see Him as He is. And every man that hath this hope in Him purifieth himself, even as He is pure.*

Let's pause for a moment to discuss the hands of man that are under the wings of these living creatures, because the wings are the abiding secret place of protection and security of man in Abba Father. Psalm 91:1-4 states: *He that dwelleth in the secret place of the Most High shall abide under the shadow of the Almighty. I will say of the LORD, He is my refuge and my fortress: my God in Him will I trust. Surely He will deliver thee from the snare of the fowler, and from the noisome pestilence. He shall cover thee with His feathers, and under His wings shalt thou trust: His truth shall be thy shield and buckler.* God will one day restore man, old things will pass away, and the new will come. The hands speak of our works, which must be in

Yeshua Jesus as they will follow us into the next life of God's glorious kingdom (Revelation 14:13). The Hebrew word for "hands" is **Yad** [3027]; although **Yad** speaks of work(s), it can also symbolize power or strength, possession or submission. When **Yad** is used as an idiom, it refers to the act of placing something into someone's hand, otherwise, to delegate authority, responsibility, care or dominion. The new man in Yeshua is here being prepared to rule with Yeshua. Ezekiel 1:8 holds the key to something special to be revealed in verse 9. Man must first willingly accept his own cross and follow Yeshua; he suffers like He suffered and he will rule like He rules, over principalities, thrones and dominions. These are the hands that are seen extended from under the wings of the Cherubim that symbolically expresses man being sheltered by the Almighty and ruling with Him in authority.

The man in Yeshua Jesus follows his Messiah's blood line; he is then said to experience re-gene-ration, when broken down in this manner we are able to see a deeper revelation, as there is a spiritual exchange which takes place in man's gene pool and that is: he is now identified in Yeshua by a new blood line! Man now rules with Yeshua as kings and priests. Israel belongs to the LORD God, and the church is the body of Yeshua because she has been bought by the precious blood of the LAMB. In his vision, Ezekiel sees four living creatures with four faces of man that is used in the collective sense as a representation of all mankind; both male and female. The Hebrew word used here for "man" is **Adam** [120], it differs from [119], **Adham**, which means "ruddy" or "reddish brown." Four of the creatures' faces are that of man [*Adam*], which is a representation of all of humanity. Man was once given control over all that the LORD God created. Through deception by the great serpent the devil, man sinned, thereby forfeiting his authority to have dominion over the earth. In Yeshua, the Believer's authority was restored because of the Messiah's finished work on the Cross. Yeshua Jesus regained the authority for us by being the perfect sacrifice of His Father; defeating sin for all and for all times. Yeshua said, *"Behold, I give* *you the authority to trample on serpents and scorpions, and over **all** the power of the enemy, and **nothing** shall by any means hurt you"* (Luke 10:19 NKJV).

Being the crown of God's creation, man was mentioned first of all the faces of these living creatures. Man holds this place of authority as these glorious beings not only looked like man but had the hands of man under their wings. The features of these living creatures were dominated by the number four. Four is the symbolic number of completion and restoration of God's creative works, thereby culminating with man's redemption and these beings are a living witness of the coming completion of man who is the crowning glory of all the Lord's creation (Genesis 1:26-27). Lastly we will discover that Abba Father is about to reveal to us the preparation for the consummation of the marriage of Yeshua Messiah and His Bride and for this reason Ezekiel 1:9 will be discussed in two parts as the mysteries of the Lord continues to be revealed to this generation.

Part A

Their wings were joined One to Another

One to another - the Hebrew word used here for "*one*" is **Ishshah** [802], it is a feminine noun interpreted woman, a wife, or a bride. Its basic meaning describes a female as opposed to a male **Ish** [376]. In Genesis 2:23-24 we read: *And Adam said, This is now bone of my bones, and flesh of my flesh: she shall be called woman [**Ishshah**], because she was taken out of man [**Ish**]. Therefore shall a man leave his father and his mother, and shall cleave unto his wife [**Ishshah**]: and they shall be one flesh.* **"Ishshah"** is translated "woman" or "wife," a concept first described in the book of Genesis. This was the first marriage, the pure bride, the virgin bride, before Adam and Eve sinned. This is a picture of the future bride of Yeshua Jesus, and one day He will consummate this relationship (Revelation 21:5). As previously stated, the designs of the living creatures are relating a story; every aspect of their form is revealing a divine truth to all mankind. The Lord God placed information about Himself and His dealings with mankind in the creation of these beings. Psalm 19:1-5 NKJV states: *The heavens declare the glory of God; and the firmament shows His handiwork. Day unto day utters speech, and night unto night reveals knowledge. There is no speech nor language where their voice is not heard. Their line has gone out through all the earth and their words to the end of the world. In them He has set a tabernacle for the sun, which is like a bridegroom coming out of his chamber, and rejoices like a strong man to run its race.* The Lord has placed signs in both heaven and earth, to inform us about past, present and future events.

The living creatures (Cherubim) of Ezekiel 1:9 are depicting a story of marriage, "their wings were joined one to another." Adam sinned, but the second Adam; Yeshua Jesus became our living sacrifice and brought us back from damnation to have dominion; reconciling us unto Abba Father. Yeshua Jesus is our Advocate before His Father and those who believe in Him will not experience a second death and permanent separation from His presence. Believers are joined to Yeshua by being born again into the family and household of GOD, and will one day share in the inheritance of His first born Israel! The Hebrew word translated "one" is **Ishshah**, meaning woman, wife, or bride. The Hebrew word for "another" is **Achoth** [269], this word comes from the same root as "brother" [251], it means a sister of full blood or a spouse, betrothed or engaged to be married. We are betrothed to Yeshua and must prepare ourselves to be received by Him.

Part B

*They turned not when they went; they went **every one** straight forward.*

The word "every one" used in the second part of Ezekiel 1:9 means something quite different. To reiterate verse 9a; *"there wings were joined one to another;* the Hebrew word for "one," is **Ishshah**, meaning woman, wife, or bride. In the second portion of verse 9, "one" is used a second time, *"They went every one straight forward,"* the Hebrew word used here is *"**Ish**,"* [376]. **Ish** refers to the husband, as *Ishshah* [802] refers to the wife. Ezekiel 1:9 is therefore revealing a betrothal between a man and a woman. Betrothal speaks of engagement for marriage. God designed these beings to tell the whole world a story that He is preparing a bride for His Son. *"Their wings were joined one to another,"* is a picture of betrothal. These things were prophesied by Hosea in chapter 2:19-23 which states: *And I will betroth thee unto Me forever; yea, I will betroth thee unto Me in righteousness, and in judgment, and in lovingkindness, and in mercies. I will even betroth thee unto Me in faithfulness: and thou shalt know the LORD. And it shall come to pass in that day, I will hear, saith the LORD, I will hear the heavens, and they shall hear the earth; and the earth shall hear the corn, and the wine, and the oil; and they shall hear Jezreel. And I will sow her unto Me in the earth; and I will have mercy upon her that had not obtained mercy; and I will say to them which are not My people, Thou art My people; and they shall say, Thou art my GOD.* Israel is the inheritance of Abba Father (Joel 3:1-2; Isaiah 19:25; Psalm 78:71; Jeremiah 12:14). The LORD God speaks not only unto Israel, but to all Gentile Believers in Yeshua Jesus.

Verse 10

As for the likeness of their faces, they four had the face of a man, and the face of a lion, on the right side: and they four had the face of an ox on the left side; they four also had the face of an eagle.

Ezekiel describes the living creature's faces; the first was that of man, the second sets of faces were that of a lion on the right side, the third sets of faces were that of an ox [oxen] on the left side, and the fourth sets of faces had the appearance of an eagle. These living creatures are associated with the presence of God, as the glory of the LORD is enthroned upon them; 1 Chronicles 13:16. If the number four speaks of God's creative works, then the number sixteen (4x4), refers to the completion of its perfection. Abba Father continues to unfold more about Himself and His relationship with His creation. The face of man was mentioned first, which is a picture of him as ruler through delegated authority by God (Genesis 1:26-28). The second set of faces was that of a young lion, which is a picture of man in Yeshua (1 Corinthians 3:16; Romans 6:3-11; 8:29; Ephesians 2:1-10). The third set of faces were that of an ox [oxen], which speaks of man as a bondservant (Acts 8:27-39; Matthew 28:18-20; 1 Corinthians 9:9-19). Lastly the fourth set of faces were that of an eagle; a picture of man as a watchman or prophet of the Lord, (Proverbs 23:5; 30:18, 19; Isaiah 40:31; Ephesians 1:15-23).

There are more truths to be revealed as God strategically placed the faces of the living creatures north, east, west, and south. The first position given was the right (Ezekiel 1:10), which corresponds with east the positions of the faces of the lion. The Word of God tells us that Yeshua is seated at the right hand of God, (Mark 16:19; Acts 2:33; Romans 8:34; Colossians 3:1; Hebrews 10:12; 1 Peter 3:22). When Yeshua returns, He will be seen coming from the east, (Matthew 24:27). This position is speaking of the new man in Yeshua, not that he is or ever will be God, but this picture reveals that like Yeshua, he is the son of God, for the Spirit of Yeshua lives in him making him an Overcomer.

The next position identified is that of the bondservant, the left or west. It is stated in Ezekiel 1:10 that the faces of the ox, [oxen] were to the left. Man is next seen as ruling with Yeshua the Lion of the tribe of Judah in his role as a bondservant. Man must first prove himself as a bondservant, before he is given the authority to rule and reign with Yeshua as kings and priests. For this reason man is first introduced as an Overcomer in Yeshua (the lion), and next as a bondservant (the oxen). The oxen is a domesticated animal that has been castrated; it is a type of eunuch, having been deprived of its ability to reproduce of itself and is solely used for the purpose of servitude. The message given here is that man is called to serve, he cannot preach his own gospel and he cannot claim ownership to anyone because he, too, needs a Savior. Like the oxen, man is totally dependent upon the Lord. For this reason, oxen are never offered as temple sacrifice as they are laborers in the vineyard of GOD.

To assign the next two positions north and south, Ezekiel 1:5 offers a clue. The living creatures' faces first mentioned were that of man, but as we notice his position was not yet assigned; having forfeited his legal right to rule the earth through God's delegated authority that was given to him. For this reason man is assigned to the north, which is counterclockwise from east. Here we see a type of rebellion being presented. Let's take for example a clock, if its hands move backward instead of forward, its rotation is called counterclockwise, which is to say: it is moving in a direction opposite to that which it was designed. This is the likely reason why the first set of faces mentioned were that of man, although it was the lion and oxen positions that was given. Man had to be reconciled unto Abba Father first, before he could take his rightful place as a leader.

The new man in Yeshua has to live a progressively sanctified life in the service of his Lord, thereby exercising sovereign power with Yeshua Jesus. Although north is counterclockwise from east, it lies at a ninety degree angle from it, which is the coming unveiling of unity, perfection and oneness of the new man in the kingdom age of Yeshua Messiah. Man must first pass the test of following, before he is granted the honor to lead. King David puts it this way in Psalm 8:3-6: *When I consider thy heavens, the work of thy fingers, the moon and the stars, which thou hast ordained; what is man that Thou art mindful of him? And the son of man, that thou visitest him? For thou hast made him a little lower than the angels, and hast crowned him with glory and honor. Thou madest him to have dominion over the works of Thy hands: Thou hast put all things under his feet.*

This brings us to the eagle, the place in the south; it is a picture of man as prophet or watchman; he sees from a vantage point far above. His spirit is heightened as he is taken to a place in God where he sees things holistically not because of natural sight, but because of insight. If we are at ground level, that is the level at which we view things, but as we move higher in God, we are able to see things much clearer, and the higher we go the greater we are able to see and this is the way of the eagle. The eagle is said to have acute vision and the ability to soar at great heights using updrafts of wind. The eagle is not afraid of any atmospheric disturbances and is said to be the only bird that flies directly into a thunderstorm. This is a picture of the prophet or watchman of God; he or she is fearless as they deliver God's messages of hope or rebuke. The eagle occupies the south while man is in the north; a straight line without any curve in his visual depth or perception. Man as the prophet or watchman of God will wear the mantle of a priest when Yeshua Jesus reigns on earth (1 Corinthians 13:9-10). This belief will be justified as the hidden treasures of the book of Ezekiel are revealed.

There is so much more to the Hebrew Text of the Old Covenant that reveals greater depths of truth and the LORD God wants us to search them deeply and laboriously with the patience and tenacity of an archeologist for by doing so great truths are reveled. More will be explored as we continue our journey through the book of Ezekiel. These are only the foundational principles of God's dealing with man; soon we will see a greater picture unfolding as we explore these awesome truths.

Verse 10 has shown the four attributes of man:

- Man as a ruler – the main faces of the living creatures
- Man in Yeshua – the young lion
- Man as bondservant or minister – the ox/oxen
- Man as a watchman or prophet – the eagle

Verse 11

Thus were their faces: and their wings were stretched upward; two wings of every one were joined one to another, and two covered their bodies.

The first portion of this verse was covered in Ezekiel 1:9. In verse 11 however, the wings of the living creatures are "stretched upward," which is an act of complete surrender, worship, adoration and praise. This is a total of six wings, which is the number connected to man. On the first day of creation God separated light from darkness, and at the second coming of Yeshua; He will also separate light from darkness, saints from sinners, wheat from weed, and sheep from goats; this will echo the beginning of renewed worship unto our Maker as the Bride of Yeshua Jesus as seen portrayed by the joining of the wings of living creatures one to another.

The wings of the Cherubim were stretched upward. Two wings covered their body; **Kasah** [3680] is the Hebrew word transliterated "covered," some of its meanings are; to conceal, hide, to clothe, to cover sin, to forgive, or to keep secret. Hebrews 2:16-17 applying the NKJV states: *For indeed He does not give aid to angels, but He does give aid to the seed of Abraham. Therefore, in all things He had to be made like His brethren, that He might be a merciful and faithful High Priest in things pertaining to God, to make propitiation for the sins of the people.* This is a picture of man in Yeshua Jesus being covered and his sins forgiven, therefore, we must be shining examples of Yeshua. Man in Yeshua must seek peace and make a lifelong commitment of pursuing it, because it is a reflection and demonstration of our love for one another and our God given attribute to forgive. The creative designs of these creatures tell the story of God's love for all mankind. These Cherubim also called living creatures, stands in the presence of God in a continued act of worship and one day we will also do the same.

The next pair of wings covered the bodies of the Cherubim and the Hebrew **Ghwiyah** [1472] is used here for "bodies," it infers that which is either dead or alive. 1 Corinthians 15:20-24 states: *But now is Christ risen from the dead, and become the firstfruits of them that slept. For since by man came death, by man came also the resurrection of the dead. For as in Adam all die, even so in Christ shall all be made alive. But every man in his own order: Christ the firstfruits; afterward they that are Christ's at His coming. Then commeth the end, when He shall have delivered up the kingdom of God, even the Father; when He shall have put down all rule and all authority and power.* Man will once again lift holy hands in worship to God, because of the finished work of Yeshua on the tree where His innocent blood was poured out for the sins of all mankind; forgiving, because the Father loved us so much. Abba Father offered all that He had in the person of His only Son, that one day we will stand before His throne and worship Him with all the host of heaven as though we never sinned.

Verse 12

And they went every one straight forward: whither the spirit was to go, they went; and they turned not when they went.

The word "spirit" is referring to the breath of God. Isaiah 11:4 used the same Hebrew word **Ruach** [7307]: *But with righteousness shall He judge the poor, and reprove with equity for the meek of the earth: and He shall smite the earth with the rod of His mouth, and with the breath of His lips shall He slay the wicked.* Breath or its Hebrew counterpart *"Ruach"* is not referring to the spirit of these creatures, but the very essence of the creative life giving power of the Almighty; His divine breath, which sustains all. Job in his distress said, "*All the while my breath is in me, and the Spirit is in my nostril.*" (Job 27:3). Psalm 146:3, 4 states: *Put not your trust in princes, nor in the son of man, in whom there is no help. His breath goeth forth, he returneth to his earth; in that very day his thoughts perish.*

It is the breath of God, His *Ruach* that sustains the life of both the just and the unjust.

The living creatures were led by the Spirit of God, which shows their act of devotion and obedience. The apostle Paul under the inspiration of Holy Spirit our great Teacher penned these words in Romans 8:14-17 quoting the NASB: *For all who are being led by the Spirit of God, these are sons of God. For you have not received a spirit of slavery leading to fear again, but you have received a spirit of adoption as sons by which we cry out, "Abba! Father!" The Spirit Himself testifies with our spirit that we are children of God, and if children, heirs also, heirs of God and fellow heirs with Christ, if indeed we suffer with Him so that we may also be glorified with Him.* We too, must follow the examples of these living creatures, being led by the Spirit of God and if we are not led by the Spirit of God, we are walking in carnality and rebellion.

The Cherubim followed the Spirit; wherever He went they pursued. As new creation in Yeshua Messiah, our Father is patiently waiting for us to come back home. He so lovingly creates these creatures to tell a story of His love for all mankind, and His desire to have sweet fellowship with us once again. The living creatures are a picture of man as we will one day become perfect and lacking nothing; a pure body of Saints made up of people from every nation, tribe and language. The body of Yeshua Jesus is a collective group of born again Believers who will share in the inheritance of Israel. The quest of the Believer is therefore his continued growth in perfection, purity and holiness. All who call upon Yeshua HaMashiach, whom Gentile Believers call Jesus, are sanctified in Him when we accept Him as Savior and Lord. At this point we take little baby steps, until we become mature in the things of the Spirit. Ephesians 4:13 states: *Till we all come in the unity of the faith, and of the knowledge of the Son of God, unto a perfect man, unto the measure of the stature of the fullness of Christ.*

Verses 13–14

As for the likeness of the living creatures, their appearance was like burning coals of fire, and like the appearance of lamps: it went up and down among the living creatures; and the fire was bright, and out of the fire went forth lightening. And the living creatures ran and returned as the appearance of a flash of lightening.

The Hebrew transliteration of the Word of God is quite detailed and holds vital keys to the true understanding of its contents and thoughts being conveyed in many languages. A research of the Hebrew Text sheds a brighter and more revelatory light on Scripture that is not for the book of Ezekiel alone but for all of the Old Covenant. Ezekiel 1:13 opens with the statement: *"As for the likeness of the living creatures."* The Hebrew word transliterated for "living creatures" is **Chay** [2416]; it is taken from another Hebrew word **Chayah** [2421], which carries the thought of life and restoration. Without God we are truly nothing; we have no life, no existence, and no hope of redemption. Romans 8:11 states: *But if the Spirit of Him that raised up Jesus from the dead dwell in you, He that raised up Christ from the dead shall also quicken your mortal bodies by His Spirit that dwelleth in you.* This is the hope of the Believer. Ezekiel 1:13 continues to describe the appearance of the living creatures as resembling that of burning coals of fire and lamps. Here we see the prophet searching for words to explain what he saw because what he was viewing and attempting to describe, was nothing that he had ever seen before. Ezekiel described their likeness as flames darting up and down. The term *"up and down"* is the Hebrew **Halakh** [1980], when used metaphorically it is conveying the thought of one's personal and continued relationship. It speaks of our "walk" which is a life driven by a divine purpose of connection and association with Abba Father who is greater than us.

The prophet observed that the lightening accompanying these living creatures was darting out of the fire itself. Ironically, lightening is the Hebrew word **Baraq** [1300], it conveys the idea of a sword that is flashing, which is symbolically speaking of the protective nature of the LORD. Psalm 121 applying the NKJV states: *I will lift up my eyes to the hills from whence comes my help? My help comes from the LORD, who made heaven and earth. He will not allow your foot to be moved; He who keeps you will not slumber. Behold, He who keeps Israel shall neither slumber nor sleep. The LORD is your shade at your right hand. The sun shall not strike you by day, nor the moon by night. The LORD shall preserve you from all evil; He shall preserve your soul. The LORD shall preserve your going out and your coming in from this time forth, and even forevermore.* These awesome creatures were the Cherubim that were created as worshipers and also protectors and their appearance is telling us a story about Abba Father and His relationship with mankind. Being in the presence of GOD, the Cherubim or living creatures as they are referred to here, carries His glory and Ezekiel describes it as being burning fire, lamps and lightening.

The living creatures are said to be in great motion, they *"ran and returned as the appearance of a flash of lightening,"* (vs.14). What the prophet was viewing was like that of a pantomime as another story is being unveiled by the movements of these creatures. The Hebrew **Shuv** [7725] is used here for *"returned,"* it is explained as the act of turning back, turning around as in coming back to Abba Father or being converted. **Shuv** conveys this thought in a figurative sense demonstrating man being reconciled with the GOD.

Verses 15–21

Now as I beheld the living creatures, behold one wheel upon the earth by the living creatures, with his four faces. The appearance of the wheels and their work was like unto the colour beryl: and they four had one likeness: and their appearance and their work was as it were a wheel in the middle of a wheel. When they went, they went upon their four sides: and they turned not when they went. As for their rings, they were so high that they were dreadful; and their rings were full of eyes round about them four. And when the living creatures went, the wheels went by them: and when the living creatures were lifted up from the earth, the wheels were lifted up. Whithersoever the Spirit was to go, they went, thither was their spirit to go; and the wheels were lifted up over against them: for the spirit of the living creature was in the wheels. When those went, these went; and when those stood, these stood; and when those were lifted up from the earth, the wheels were lifted up over against them: for the spirit of the living creature was in the wheels.

Brace yourself for a mighty revelation; remember the living creatures are telling a story about man in his reconciled state of holiness as we were before sin severed our face to face fellowship with God. The living creatures became the substitutionary overseers over Eden following this catastrophic event as man could no longer continue to reside there in his fallen state. Just as Adam and Eve disobeyed God and became aware of good and evil; God knew that they would be tempted to disobey Him yet again and eat of the tree of life, thereby living eternally in a condemned state of sin without any hope of reconciliation.

1 Corinthians 15:22 states: *For as in Adam all die, even so in Christ shall all be made alive.* Adam and his wife had to leave Eden so that the second Adam Yeshua Jesus would be our bridge and hope of reconciliation with the Father once more. The all knowing Father had a solution for the problem before this devastating sin was committed; making it clear to mankind that we are created with the innate ability to choose right from wrong; to accept His offer of atonement or reject it. The LORD so loved us that our reconciliation unto Himself, was the reason why Yeshua had to come into this world. 2 Corinthians 5:18-21 states: *And all things*

are of God, who hath reconciled us to Himself by Jesus Christ, and hath given to us the ministry of reconciliation; to wit, that God was in Christ, reconciling the world unto Himself, not imputing their trespasses unto them; and hath committed unto us the word of reconciliation. Now then we are ambassadors for Christ, as though God did beseech you by us: we pray you in Christ stead, be ye reconciled to God. For He hath made Him to be sin for us, who knew no sin; that we might be made the righteousness of God in Him. We would have no hope of salvation if it were not for Yeshua Jesus; man would therefore not be redeemable.

To remove Adam and Eve from the garden was an act of great love and grace. God has given us all both a choice and a chance to return to Him voluntarily through His freewill offering of Yeshua. Genesis 3:22-24 states: *And the LORD GOD said, Behold, the man is become one of us, to know good and evil: and now, lest he put forth his hand, and take also of the tree of life, and eat, and live forever: therefore the LORD GOD sent him forth from the garden of Eden, to till the ground from whence he was taken. So He drove out the man; and He placed at the east of the garden of Eden Cherubim, and a flaming sword which turned every way, to keep the way of the tree of life.* These same classes of living creatures are the guards of Eden until the return of Yeshua, when all things will be made new.

The prophet Ezekiel was obviously mystified by what he was looking at, for not only did these living creatures have four sets of faces depicting that of man, a lion, an ox and an eagle, they were borne by a wheel that was within a much larger wheel with rings that were high and awesome to look at. In Ezekiel 1:14 the word **Shuv** was used figuratively to describe the fact that the living creatures were role playing the final state of man as he returns unto Abba Father in repentance; having his spirit, soul, and body, finally recreated, renewed, and reconciled unto God. Ezekiel declared, "*Behold one wheel upon the earth,*" the wheel Ezekiel saw was the WORD of GOD moving over the face of the earth. Psalm 147:15 states: *He sendeth forth*

His commandment upon the earth: His word runneth very swiftly.

The Word of God is described as a wheel, which makes a revolution of 360 degrees; going back to the point from which it originated, therefore making a circuit and this can be proven. Isaiah 55:6-11 is a key verse: *Seek ye the LORD while He may be found, call ye upon Him while He is near: let the wicked forsake his way, and the unrighteous man his thoughts: and let him return unto the LORD, and He will have mercy upon him; and to our GOD, for He will abundantly pardon. For My thoughts are not your thoughts, neither are your ways My ways, saith the LORD. For as the heavens are higher than the earth, so are My ways higher than your ways, and My thoughts than your thoughts. For as the rain commeth down, and the snow from heaven, and returneth not thither, but watereth the earth, and maketh it bring forth and bud, that it may give seed to the sower, and bread to the eater: so shall My word be that goeth forth out of My mouth: it shall not return unto Me void, but it shall accomplish that which I please, and it shall prosper in the thing whereto I sent it.*

The Word of God is described as a revolving wheel, it completes a circuit. The point at which it leaves is the point at which it returns. Take for example sound waves, they vibrate and is transmitted in three ways: solid, liquid or gas, at ranges that may or may not be perceptible by the human ear. With this note we must be very cautious because every word that leaves our mouth are transmitted by vibrations and in many case we need to repent because of our spoken words (Proverbs 18:21; Matthew 12:37).

The Word of God revolves like a wheel, and the wheel within the wheel is the Word of God in us which He watches over and protects! It is the Word of God in us that keep us from falling into sinful acts, Psalm 119:11 states: *Thy word have I hid in my heart, that I might not sin against Thee.* It is the Word of God in us that matures us spiritually. As it revolves in us we become aware of the things that are not pleasing to Abba Father. The Spirit of God lives in the spirit of man, He is the One who guides, teaches, and renews the mind through the Word.

Because the LORD God has given us a conscience to know right from wrong, no one in this earth can accuse Him of any wrongdoing. If our conscience is scorched by sin, it dries up and withers away because we have made the decision to reject God and His Word. Therefore the question reverberates, who can accuse the LORD GOD of any wrongdoing? The LORD uses people, life lessons, and even dreams and visions to get the attention of the rebellious; and if these wooing are rejected, He is left with no other choice, but to walk away to the grief of His heart. John 3:16-17 states: *For God so loved the world, that He gave his only begotten Son, that whosoever believeth in Him should not perish but have everlasting life. For God sent not His Son into the world to condemn the world; but that the world through Him might be saved.*

Let's look at one more key Scripture, which validates that the wheel within the wheel is the Word of God in us. Proverbs 25:11 states: *A word fitly spoken is like apples of gold in pictures of silver.* This Scripture is literally translated, "Spoken upon wheels," the Hebrew word used in this verse for "*fitly*" is **Ophen** [655], it literally means; that which revolves or turns; it can also mean that which occurs in its appointed season. Isaiah spoke of the suffering of Yeshua, *The Lord GOD hath given me the tongue of the learned, that I should know how to speak a word in season to him that is weary: He wakeneth morning by morning He wakeneth mine ear to hear as the learned. The Lord GOD hath opened mine ear, and I was not rebellious, neither turned away back,* (50:4-5). There is an appointed time or season for the Word of God to be fulfilled. The spoken Word is described as a revolving wheel, which creates and makes us a unified whole and at peace even during times of upheaval, turmoil, or unrest. It gives us the assurance and unshakable hope that all is well in spite of discouraging circumstances. The Word of God must be within us; the ever flowing river(s) of living water: saving, healing, and restoring.

Ezekiel describes the appearance of the wheel and their function, which he likened unto the color beryl (or the eye of beryl). The Hebrew word **Ayin** [5869] is translated "color," it can also be used to describe suffering, distress or pain, caused by the direct influence of an external source, as well as the influence that one has over another which is not arbitrary or dogmatic, but yielding freely. It can also be interpreted "eye," used metaphorically to express the attitude of watching over something or someone. The all seeing eye of God watches over those who belong to Him (Psalm 32:8).

Next we examine the beryl, which is also called the tarshish stone. It is placed in the class of precious stone and is somewhat yellow or amber in color. The tarshish stone was first mentioned in Exodus 28:15-20. As part of the design of the priestly garment, the beryl or tarshish stone was the first stone on the fourth row of the breastplate known in the Old Covenant as the breastplate of judgment, which is worn by the high priest. Each stone was engraved with the names of the twelve tribes of Israel. The high priest under the Old Covenant was a typology of Yeshua but we see in the New Covenant (*B'rit Chadashah*), Yeshua Jesus taking His rightful place as our true High Priest, whom the breastplate of judgment is kept in reserve. The high priest of the Old Covenant was a natural man while the High Priest of the New Testament is Spiritual: the Man Yeshua HaMashiach; Jesus the Christ. Hebrews 5:1-5 reminds us: *For every high priest taken from among men is ordained for men in things pertaining to God, that he may offer both gifts and sacrifices for sins: who can have compassion on the ignorant, and on them that are out of the way; for that he himself also is compassed with infirmity. And by reason hereof he ought, as for the people, so also for himself, to offer for sins. And no man taketh this honor unto himself, but he that is called of God, as was Aaron. So also Christ glorified not Himself to be made an High Priest; but He that said unto Him, Thou art My Son, today have I begotten thee.* Under the Old Covenant, man was in Yeshua by the Law but under the New Covenant Yeshua Jesus resides in man by grace!

Ezekiel goes on to say that the living creatures were all similar and acted alike. These beings demonstrated complete unity in purpose, there was no jostling for supremacy; they worked as a unified body. Every thought and action was a reflection of the working of the Word; the Living Word, which is Yeshua Jesus. These beings did nothing that was self gratifying or self-promoting; all was done to bring glory and honor to God and we too, like these living creatures, are created with the same purpose in mind. The Spirit must be given full control of our lives; this is not to say that we will not be tempted or live a life that is completely free from sin, but we are behooved to resist temptation and if we fall, we have an Advocate with the Father, the Man Yeshua Jesus our Lord (Proverbs 24:16; 1 John 2:1). The interpretation here is: the appearance and function of the wheels was an act of God watching over His Word to perform its utterance. Holy Spirit identifies with us, that we are heirs of salvation and breathes the Word of God from our lips that His will be done in earth as it is in heaven, (Matthew 6:9-10).

The wheel is therefore described as the living, active and all powerful Word of God, that He watches over to do mighty and glorious things in our behalf. 1 John 1:1-3 states: *That which was from the beginning, which we have heard, which we have seen with our eyes, which we have looked upon, and our hands have handled, of the Word of life; (For the life was manifested, and we have seen it, and bear witness, and shew unto you that eternal life, which was with the Father, and was manifested unto us;) that which we have seen and heard declare we unto you, that ye also may have fellowship with us: and truly our fellowship is with the Father, and with His Son Jesus Christ.* All things exist by the Word of His power (Hebrews 1:3) and His Word is a revolving wheel. Have you ever wondered at the awe of God? All that He creates in the cosmos revolves on its axis.

Man hates the notion that there is an intelligent designer behind creation and for this reason he rebels and seeks to destroy anything and everything that is associated with God. Have you ever asked yourself the question, if someone does not believe that God exists, why is there so much tenacious fighting and lobbying to remove the evidence of something they do not believe? Man is earth and was created by God and this is the bottom line. The wheel within the wheel is therefore Yeshua Himself through eternal Holy Spirit working on behalf of mankind, reconciling us unto Abba Father. Yeshua is both the Living Word as well as the spoken Word of God and both are eternally One.

Ezekiel continues to describe the unity in purpose of these beings, *"They turned not when they went."* This phrase is metaphorically speaking of the new man in Yeshua Jesus. The endless working of the Spirit of God in man washing his soul with the Word of God, thereby creating in him a clean heart and renewing a right spirit within him, not by force but by choice as he yields himself to his Maker. 2 Corinthians 4:7 speaks of Holy Spirit as a treasure in our bodies: *But we have this treasure in earthen vessels, that the excellency of the power may be of God, and not of us.* The new man in Yeshua is governed by the Spirit who resides in our spirit and this is the way God intended it to be.

Next, Ezekiel 1:18 describes the rings as being *"full of eyes."* "Full" is the Hebrew **Male** pronounced *maw-lay* [4392], which speaks of one who is worthy and when mentioned along with "eye," **Ayin** [5869]; we observe a very personal and intimate message from Abba Father to humanity. The understanding and interpretation of "eye" when transliterated speaks of the suffering or affliction of a person at the hands of another. This is the portrayal of Yeshua's affliction upon the tree which became our Cross of redemption (for further reading see Isaiah 53; Matthew

26:38-27:1-50; Mark 15:37; Luke 23:1-46; Acts 2:22-36). There is hope for those who walk uprightly because this promise was made possible because Yeshua Jesus was found worthy by the Father to be afflicted for all.

As the heavens declare the glory of God, these living creatures also tells a story of what the LORD has done for us and also what we must do for Him as our act of surrendered worship. When Yeshua reigns, we will not be sitting by drinking milk and eating honey, but we will be active participants in the eternal worship of the LORD being the recipients of His grace. The cosmos harmoniously revolves on its axis and so does the Word of God. The spoken Word creates vibrations; and the Word of God is the first voice recognition system to grace the universe; not only does it recognize the spoken Word, but it also knows its source in a personal way. Psalm 91:14-15 gives a good example of the genius of our heavenly Father: *Because He hath set His love upon Me, therefore will I deliver him: I will set him on high, because he hath known My name. He shall call upon Me, and I will answer him: I will be with him in trouble; I will deliver him, and honor him.*

The wheel within the outer wheel is a picture of man in Yeshua Jesus, living and growing in the Word of God and having his life transformed by it through the inner witness of Holy Spirit. His life is guided by Holy Spirit therefore his actions are a mirror image of the Spirit within. Holy Spirit is our firewall of protection wherever we go, He goes (Ezekiel 1:19). The next thing we see in the coming cohesiveness between man and God is demonstrated by the living creatures: when they were lifted up from the earth, the wheels were lifted up also. The term "were lifted up" is the Hebrew **Nasa** [5375]; embedded in its meaning is the act of worship to raise the voice up towards heaven, to lift up the eyes and hands in reverence and the soul in holy adoration to GOD Most High, which is a true reflection of Psalm 24. Not only do we lift our heads, but our spirit, soul and body is in total rapturous worship unto Abba Father.

It is therefore said that we are "lifted up" and our entire being is soaked in worship in the presence of God.

Ezekiel was shown through the actions of these living creatures the final stages of man's completion in Yeshua. This is a picture of man breaking free from all the cares of the earth in spite of many distractions, difficulties, heartache and pain, that are likely to keep him earth bound and look unto Yeshua, the Author and Finisher of his faith. He soars in the realm of the spirit and his rocket booster is his worship; lifting him higher and higher in praise until the gravity of earth and all its cares can't hold him any longer. He now soars on this worship, into the very presence of Almighty God, this is what **Nasa** is all about; this is what "to be lifted up" means.

Ezekiel 1:20-21 states: *Whithersoever the Spirit was to go, they went, thither was their spirit to go; and the wheels were lifted up over against them: for the spirit of the living creature was in the wheels. When those went, these went; and when those stood, these stood; and when those were lifted up from the earth, the wheels were lifted up over against them: for the spirit of the living creature was in the wheels.* Here we see a picture of pure devotion, and that is to say, their actions were not forced or bound by time restrictions. They were sensitive to Holy Spirit, therefore they moved in harmony with Him. This is a picture of the continued growth and maturation of man in Yeshua Jesus, being sustained by his Helper: Holy Spirit.

Verses 22-25

And the likeness of the firmament upon the heads of the living creature was as the color of the terrible crystal, stretched forth over their heads above. And under the firmament were their wings straight, the one toward the other: every one had two, which covered on this side, and every one had two, which covered on that side, their bodies. And when they went, I heard the noise of their wings, like the noise of great waters, as the voice of the Almighty, the voice of speech, as the noise of an host: when they stood, they let down their wings. And there was a voice from the firmament that was over their heads, when they stood, and had let down their wings.

The prophet's vision takes momentum; he sees what appears to resemble the expanse of the sky but in fact it was deep space. Much like what is viewed by astronauts; it is the place where the gravitational pull of earth has no control. Here again we see a play on words, because the firmament being described by the prophet has nothing to do with stars planets, galaxies, or such likes, but a dwelling place in God where man is free from the pressures and pull of the enticements of this earth as it is a place where man asks nothing from God, because it is not a place of supplication or intercession but a place of thanksgiving, praise and worship, as man basks in the presence of the Living God. This is not only the hope of man but also the home of man. A place where Yeshua Jesus presents us to the Father as a chosen generation, a royal priesthood, and a holy nation of a very special people to display our praise unto Him who called us out of darkness into His marvelous light. In times past, we were not a people, but are now the people of God: which had not obtained mercy, but now has obtained mercy (see 1 Peter 2:9-10). The prophet viewed that under the place transliterated *"firmament,"* in many versions of the Bible is actually *"space,"* which metaphorically is used to describe our new uninhibited freedom in God, being positioned and also clothed in His righteousness and grace.

Ezekiel described the firmament (space), which he saw as being upon the heads of the living creatures. The Hebrew word for heads is **Rosh** [7218] and among its meanings are: elected or an appointed person. Saints of God, we are the elect, and the appointed ones. The Apostle Paul states in Romans 8:28-39 under the inspiration of Holy Spirit: *And we know that all things work together for good to them that love God, to them who are the called according to His* *purpose. For who He did foreknow, He also did predestinate to conform to the image of His Son, that He might be the firstborn among many brethren. Moreover whom He did predestinate, them He also called: and whom He called, them He also justified: and whom He justified, them He also glorified. What shall we then say to these things? If God be for us, who can be against us? He that spared not His own Son, but delivered Him up for us all, how shall He not with Him freely give us all things? Who shall lay any thing to the charge of God's elect? It is God that justifieth. Who is he that condemneth? It is Christ that died, yea rather, that is risen again, who is even at the right hand of God, who also maketh intercession for us. Who shall separate us from the love of Christ? Shall tribulation, or distress, or persecution, or famine, or nakedness, or peril, or sword? As it is written, for thy sake we are killed all the day long; we are accounted as sheep for the slaughter. Nay, in all these things we are more than conquerors through Him that loved us. For I am persuaded, that neither death, nor life, nor angels, nor principalities, nor powers, nor things present, nor things to come, nor height, nor depth, nor any other creature, shall be able to separate us from the love of God, which is in Christ Jesus our Lord.* This is a picture of Believers who have broken free from all the cares of the world, because their hope is in Yeshua alone; the earth and its trappings have no power over their lives. During periods of tribulation they remain focused, firm and unmovable, because anchored deep within, is the knowledge that nothing can or ever will separate them from the love of God.

Believers will one day be lifted up and work in complete unity with Holy Spirit. Jesus prayed to the Father: *Sanctify them by Your truth. Your word is truth. As you sent Me into the world, I also have sent them into the world. And for their sakes I sanctify Myself, that they also may be sanctified by the truth. "I do not pray for these alone, but also for those who will believe in Me through their word; that they all may be one, as You, Father, are in Me, and I in You; that they also may be one in Us, that the world may believe that you sent Me. And the glory which You gave Me I have given them, that they may be one just as We are one: I in them, and you in Me; that they may be made perfect in one, and that the world may know that you have sent Me, and have loved them as You have loved Me. "Father, I desire that they also whom You gave Me may be with Me where I am, that they may behold My glory which You have given Me; for you loved Me before the foundation of the world. O righteous Father! The world has not known You, but I have known You; and these have known that You sent Me. And I have declared to them Your name, and will declare it, that the love with which You loved Me may be in them, and I in them,"* John 17:15-26 NKJV. What a blessed assurance we have as the elect of God. We are the hands, feet, and voice of our Savior in these trying times. As we work with Holy Spirit, we must learn to work with others and be a ray of hope for unbelievers. We must embrace others with pure love for such love is perfect and cast out fear ((1 John 4:18). The prophet described the firmament as being upon the heads of these living creatures (Cherubim). This is a metaphor describing the liberation of the Saints who broke free from all earthly distractions, worries, and cares and taking authority over them all. This is the reason why the firmament or space was not over their heads but on their heads; therefore giving us a picture of what the triumphant Saint will look like.

Ezekiel's gaze is now centered on what appears to be an awesome (terrible) crystal stretched over the heads of the Cherubim. The Hebrew word used to describe the word "terrible" is **Yare** [3372]; it speaks of reverential fear or dread, trembling and jubilant worship. The prophet was experiencing an outpouring of emotions much like Peter's on the Mount of Transfiguration. The priest called to be a prophet to the exiled Hebrews, whose name means "God strengthens," was about to enter the very presence of God. Notice that the firmament or space was upon the heads of the living creatures, while the magnificent crystal stretched above their heads. The Cherubim are teaching us what true worship is all about, as we too, like they, were created for worship.

Let's go to the book of Revelation where the Apostle John had a similar vision: *After that I looked, and, behold, a door was opened in heaven: and the first voice which I heard was as it were a trumpet talking with me; which said, come up hither, and I will shew thee things which must be hereafter. And immediately I was in the spirit: and, behold, a throne was set in heaven, and one sat on the throne. And He that sat was to look upon like a jasper and a sardine stone: and there was a rainbow round about the throne, in sight like unto a emerald. And round about the throne were four and twenty seats: and upon the seats I saw four and twenty elders sitting, clothed in white raiment; and they had on their heads crowns of gold. And out of the throne proceeded lightnings and thunderings and voices: and there were seven lamps of fire burning before the throne, which are the seven Spirits of God. And before the throne there was a sea of glass like unto crystal: and in the midst of the throne, and round about the throne, were four beasts full of eyes before and behind. And the first beast was like a lion, and the second beast like a calf, and the third beast had a face as a man, and the fourth beast was like a flying eagle. And the four beast had each of them six wings about him; and they were full of eyes within: and they rest not day and night, saying, Holy, holy, holy, Lord God Almighty, which was, and is, and is to come. And when those beasts give glory and honor and thanks to Him that sat on the throne, who liveth for ever, the four and twenty elders fall down before Him that sat on the throne, and worship Him that liveth forever and ever, and cast their crowns before the throne, saying, Thou art worthy, O, Lord, to receive glory and honor and power: for Thou hast created all things, and for thy pleasure they are and were created,* 4:2-11. Crystal speaks of our transparency shining forth. To say something is "*crystal clear,*" means it is absolutely understood; therefore God's elect, will see and understand things as clearly as God does. Man will one day with this new revelation fully grasp his passion, pursuit, purpose, and praise, because when he comes face to face with his risen Lord he will be just like Him; seated in heavenly places and that which was once puzzling, will be clearly understood.

In Ezekiel 1:23 the wings of the living creatures are described as being "straight," the Hebrew word used here is **Yashar** [3477], which describes their character as being upright, just, righteous, pleasing and their actions justified thereby obtaining approval from God. Next we see their wings covering their body and the Hebrew for "covered" is **Kasah** [3680]: a picture of keeping a secret, to cover sin, to forgive. It points to the act of God the Father forgiving our sins and teaches us that we should follow this intrinsic attribute, ready to protect rather than to expose; forgive rather than taking revenge. As the living creatures approached the throne of God the prophet heard the sound of their mighty wings.

In Ezekiel 1:24 the prophet states: *"And when they went I heard the noise of their wings.*" The word *"heard"* is the Hebrew **Shama** [8085]. These magnificent creatures had massive wings because they created waves of deafening vibrations, which the prophet heard in the spiritual realm. They must have sounded like a mighty waterfall thundering over the cleft of a rock; or the familiar sound of the voice of the Almighty for the heavens were opened and Ezekiel saw visions of God while he pondered his fate, and that also of the other Hebrew settlers in exile by the river Chebar. Not being able to fully describe the sound he heard in the throne room, the prophet continued; the wings of the Cherubim sounded like the eternal melody, resonating in words: *"SHAMA;"* which is the same salutation given when a court is called to order and the presiding Honorable Chief Justice name is announced. Suddenly there was a hush in heaven, a reverential silence filled the air; nothing moved; a pin drop could be heard as the wings of the living creatures made its final crescendo and came to rest at their sides in honor to the LORD God. Ezekiel looks on as a silhouette of the presiding Judge appears; THE LORD GOD ALMIGHTY!

Verses 26-28

And above the firmament that was over their heads was the likeness of a throne, as the appearance of a sapphire stone: and upon the likeness of the throne was the likeness as the appearance of a man above it. And I saw as the colour of amber, as the appearance of fire round about within it, from the appearance of His loins even upward, and from the appearance of His loins even downward, I saw as it were the appearance of fire, and it had brightness round about. As the appearance of the bow that is in the cloud in the day of rain, so was the appearance of the brightness roundabout. This was the appearance of the likeness of the glory of the LORD. And when I saw it, I fell upon my face, and I heard a voice of one that spake.

Awe struck, Ezekiel once again searches for the right words to describe the appearance of the throne room of God. In his mind's eye he described it as resembling a precious stone and came to the conclusion that the awesome structure gleamed like sapphire. Sapphires are composed of colors that sparkle with great brilliance and clarity of an intense transparent deep blue with iridescences as clear as glass; they also display spectrums of yellow, and purple, green, pink and orange. Ezekiel being a priest, knew what the sapphire stone looked like, as it was the second precious stone on the Breastplate of Judgment on the high priest garment (Exodus 28:18).

There is a much deeper story however being told here. Ezekiel did not say that the throne was a sapphire stone, but instead, it looked like one because of its luster. What then is the story behind this precious stone? With the exception of red, sapphire stones are the same color of the rainbow. Job 28:5-7 and Isaiah 54:5-14, are key Scriptures that will unlock the door to this revelation: "*The earth, from it comes food, and underneath it is turned up fire. Its rocks are the source of sapphires, and its dust contains gold. The path no bird of prey knows, nor has the falcon's eye caught sight of it . . . .* "*For your husband is your Maker, whose name is the LORD of hosts; and your Redeemer is the Holy One of Israel, who is called the God of all the earth. For the LORD has called you, like a wife forsaken and grieved in spirit, even like a wife of one's youth when she is rejected," says your God. "For a brief moment I forsook you, but with great compassion I will gather you. In an outburst of anger I hid My face from you for a moment, but with everlasting lovingkindness I will have compassion on you," says the LORD your Redeemer. "For this is like the days of Noah to Me, when I swore that the waters of Noah would not flood the earth again: so I have sworn that I will not be angry with you nor will I rebuke you. For the mountains may be removed and the hills may shake, but My lovingkindness will not be removed from you, and My covenant of peace will not be shaken," says the LORD who has compassion on you. "O afflicted one, storm-tossed, and not comforted,* **Behold, I will set your stones in antimony, and your foundations I will lay in sapphires.** *"Moreover, I will make your battlements of rubies, and your gates of crystal, and your entire wall of precious stones. All your sons will be taught of the LORD; and the well-being of your sons will be great. In righteousness you will be established; you will be far from oppression, for you will not fear; and from terror, for it will not come near you," NASB.* Sapphires, like rubies, are quite special to God and there are many mentions of these precious stones in the Bible used literally, figuratively, and also metaphorically to describe things associated with or created by God.

The book of Job speaks of the source from which sapphires are made, which is the tremendous heat of the earth's crust. Because of this same fact we can truly say that the sapphire spoken of in the Word of God is created by intense heat. Fire is also associated with the presence of God, which is a picture of the covering of His unfailing mercy, justice, righteousness and covenant with mankind, (for further reading see Exodus 13:22; Numbers 9:16; 14:14; Deuteronomy 1:33; Nehemiah 9:19; Isaiah 4:5). Isaiah 21:19-20 concurs with John in the book of Revelation because the sapphire is seen as an important aspect of the twelve foundations of the wall of the New Jerusalem. Based on the symbolism of the sapphire stone the message being conveyed is a reminder to the world that the LORD sits on a throne which reminds Him of His love for mankind and those who draw near to Him will receive the covering of His mercy, justice, righteousness and grace. Whom the Lord has purified, He will find pleasure and delight. Therefore, like the throne of God, His people will also shine forth as the sapphire. We will re-examine this precious stone once again in chapter ten as it relates to the Believer.

Ezekiel eyes are focused on the silhouette of a figure seated on the throne. From his description, the prophet likened His appearance to that of consuming fire from head to toe, as bolts of His exuberant brilliance explodes around Him. Daniel said: *I beheld till the thrones were cast down, and the Ancient of days did sit, whose garment was white as snow, and the hair of His head like the pure wool: His throne was like the fiery flame, and His wheels as burning fire* (7:9). Like Daniel, Ezekiel is now face to face with the awesome presence of the glory of Abba Father. He once more searches for words to describe the LORD's glory which he likens to that of a rainbow. A fitting description, as the rainbow speaks of God's covenant with all the descendants of Noah; Genesis 9:13-17 states: *I do set My bow in the cloud, and it shall be for a token of a covenant between Me and the earth. And it shall come to pass, when I bring a cloud over the earth, that the bow shall be seen in the cloud: and I will remember My covenant, which is between Me and you and every living creature of all flesh; and the waters shall no more become a flood to destroy all flesh. And the bow shall be in the cloud; and I will look upon it, that I may remember the everlasting covenant between God and every living creature of all flesh that is upon the earth. And God said unto Noah, This is the token of the covenant, which I have established between Me and all flesh that is upon the earth.* This covenant metaphorically displayed in an array of colors is more than a reminder to the LORD, because He never forgets. It is however a reminder to us that He is merciful and full of grace; Ezekiel being overwhelmed by the spectacular presence of the Almighty could no longer stand. As the prophet's human frame succumbed to the glory and majesty of the LORD; he sinks to his knees and fell prostrate upon his face; just then the air reverberates with the voice of Abba Father.

Chapter 2

Verses 1-5

And He said unto me, stand upon thy feet, and I will speak unto thee. And the Spirit entered into me when He spake unto me, and set me upon my feet, that I heard Him that spake unto me. And He said unto me, I send thee to the children of Israel, to a rebellious nation that rebelled against Me; they and their fathers have transgressed against Me, even unto this very day. For they are impudent children and stiffhearted. I do send thee unto them; and thou shalt say unto them, Thus saith the LORD GOD. And they, whether they will hear, or whether they will forbear, (for they are a rebellious house,) yet shall know that there hath been a prophet among them.

These verses are a continuation from Ezekiel 1:28. The prophet lays prostrate in the presence of God Almighty, too weak to stand upright on his own; the Helper Holy Spirit steps in yet again to strengthen him. Ezekiel is now officially commissioned as a prophet unto the children of Israel. Not only did they and their forefathers break the teachings and commandments of God, but they divorced themselves from Him. They were bold an unashamed of their apostasy yet a loving Father instead of removing Himself completely from among them, appoint a prophet to be His voice because of His covenant and this is a reflection of His lovingkindness to His beloved Israel. Psalm 135:4 applying the NKJV states: *For the LORD has chosen Jacob for Himself, Israel for His special treasure.* Ezekiel was encouraged by the LORD to speak to Israel whether they choose to listen or not because he is now God's ambassador to that nation and they would know without a shadow of doubt that the Spirit of the LORD GOD rested upon him.

Verses 6-10

And thou, son of man, be not afraid of them, neither be afraid of their words, though briers and thorns be with thee, and thou dost dwell among scorpions: be not afraid of their words, nor dismayed at their looks, though they be a rebellious house. And thou shall speak My words unto them, whether they will hear, or whether they will forbear: for they are most rebellious. But thou, son of man, hear what I say unto thee; Be not thou rebellious like that rebellious house: open thy mouth, and eat that I give thee. And when I looked, behold, an hand was sent unto me; and, lo, a roll of a book was therein; and He spread it before me; and it was written within and without: and there was written therein lamentations, and mourning, and woe.

Once more the LORD encourages Ezekiel not to be afraid to deliver His rebuke to his brethren. Chastisement was necessary, and it was coming. The LORD GOD describes the people whom Ezekiel lived among as being scorpions, which was an unflattering term to address their hypocrisy. They professed one thing, yet their actions were the direct opposite, in reality they resented the truth although pretending to be in agreement. The people believed GOD had winked at their sins because He withheld judgment, not knowing that His love and mercy constrained His ruling. God repeatedly warned Israel but His extended mercy returned to Him rejected and He was left with no alternative but to withdraw Himself from them for a season.

The prophet also received a warning from God to deliver His messages exactly the way He gave it and not to be afraid of the consequences of retribution because the words were not his own, he was only an envoy. The prophet knew that his judgment would be more severe if he sugar coated the Word of God or be a people pleaser. With his commission settled in his heart, Ezekiel resigns himself to do exactly as he had been told. The newly appointed prophet is given a scroll (book), which had writings on both sides. This scroll was not pleasant to either look upon or read, as its inscriptions were lamentations, mourning, and woes.

What really did Ezekiel see? Was it the destruction of the temple by the Romans? Was it the dispersion of the Hebrew people outside of Israel called the Diaspora? Was it the concentration camps of the Nazis? Or was it the relentless persecution and constant threat of annihilation which followed them to every corner of the earth where they subsequently settled? What Ezekiel eyes observed written on both sides of the scroll was definitely not good news.

Chapter 3

Verses 1-11

Moreover He said unto me, Son of man, eat that thou findest; eat this roll, and go speak unto the house of Israel. So I opened my mouth, and He caused me to eat that roll. And He said unto me, Son of man, cause thy belly to eat, and fill thy bowels with this roll that I give thee. Then did I eat it; and it was in my mouth as honey for sweetness. And He said unto me, Son of man, go, get thee unto the house of Israel, and speak with My words unto them. For thou art not sent to a people of a strange speech and of an hard language, but to the house of Israel; not to many people of a strange speech and of a hard language, whose words thou canst not understand. Surely, had I sent thee to them, they would have hearkened unto thee. But the house of Israel will not hearken unto thee; for they will not hearken unto Me: for all the house of Israel are impudent and hardhearted. Behold, I have made thy face strong against their faces, and thy forehead strong against their foreheads. As an adamant harder than flint have I made thy forehead: fear them not, neither be dismayed at their looks, though they be a rebellious house. Moreover He said unto me, Son of man, all My words that I shall speak unto thee receive in thine heart, and hear with thine ears. And go, get thee to them of the captivity, unto the children of thy people, and speak unto them, and tell them, Thus saith the LORD GOD; whether they will hear, or whether they will forbear.

We see a radical change here; what Ezekiel saw written on both sides of the scroll was the judgment of God upon a rebellious people and the prescribed remedy for their restoration. As instructed, the prophet ingested and digested the scroll and it became as sweet as honey. Here is the unfolding of a picture of the future hope for Israel's redemption. The prophet gained strength and confidence knowing that although Israel suffered much for their rebellion against Abba Father, the day would come when the LORD'S favor would once again be extended to them, which was also the hope of the foreigners who dwell among them and by faith, lived righteously before their God.

The book of Ezekiel being filled with idioms, metaphors, allegories, and typologies, paints a picture of the coming rule and reign of Yeshua Jesus the Messiah over all His people; these are the words of Yeshua in John 10:14-16: *I am the good Shepherd, and know My sheep, and am known of Mine. As the Father knoweth Me, even so know I the Father: and I lay down My life for the sheep. And other sheep I have, which are not of this fold: them also I must bring, and they shall hear My voice; and there shall be one fold, and one Shepherd.* We will see this concept clearer and in greater detail in volume two and three of the these writings, because embedded in the Hebrew and symbolic language of the book, are messages about Yeshua Jesus, Israel and the body of Christ, which are its signature features.

Ezekiel's task was to meditate upon the Word of God, as Holy Spirit would be his Teacher and Interpreter of the great mysteries of the visions and encounters that he would experience. Ezekiel had to totally place his trust in God, because He was about to use him in such a way that many would ridicule him and deem him a lunatic. Without drawing any attention to his inadequacies, Ezekiel willing surrendered his agenda for a higher calling, because only then, would he be an effective prophet unto the LORD, and a man regarded as righteous among his brethren living in Babylon.

Psalm 119:96-107 is more than beautiful words, but a fitting reflection of the priest who is now being commissioned as prophet to Israel during a time when the nation was in exile: *I have seen an end of all perfection: but thy commandments is exceeding broad. O how I love thy law! It is my meditation all the day. Thou through thy commandments hast made me wiser than my enemies: for they are ever with me. I have more understanding than all my teachers: for Thy testimonies are my meditation. I understand more than the ancients, because I keep Thy precepts. I have refrained my feet from every evil way, that I might keep Thy word. I have not departed from Thy judgments: for Thou hast taught me. How sweet are Thy words unto my taste! Yea, sweeter than honey to my mouth! Through Thy precepts I get understanding: therefore I hate every false way. Thy word is a lamp unto my feet, and a light unto my path. I have sworn, and I will perform it, that I will keep thy righteous judgments. I am afflicted very much: quicken me, O LORD, according unto Thy word.* With the Word of God settled in the prophet's heart, Ezekiel boldly goes forth to the exiled house of Israel to both speak and demonstrate God's Words in power without fear of intimidation or ridicule.

Verses 12-15

Then the Spirit took me up, and I heard behind me a voice of a great rushing, saying, Blessed be the glory of the LORD from His place. I heard also the noise of the wings of the living creatures that touched one another, and the noise of the wheels over against them, and a noise of a great rushing. So the Spirit lifted me up, and took me away, and I went in bitterness, in the heat of my spirit; but the hand of the LORD was strong upon me. Then I came to them of the captivity at Tel-abib, that dwelt by the river of Chebar, and I sat where they sat, and remained there astonished among them seven days.

The Spirit of God now lifts Ezekiel as in flight; this is the same encounter experienced by Philip in the New Covenant (Acts 8:35-40). The power of the Spirit of the Almighty picks up the newly instated prophet. Being filled with the Spirit of God, Ezekiel heard the praises of the living creatures, saying, *"Blessed be the glory of the LORD from this place."* What jubilation and honor to Him who lives eternally, the Most High, the LORD GOD. The KJV states that the prophet heard what sounded *"like a noise of a great rushing,"* which is to say; the magnitude of the voices of the host of heaven, reverberated with perfect harmony.

The prophet must have been passing by the living creatures as the Spirit takes him back to the river Chebar. Here he caught yet another glimpse of the dress rehearsal of the marriage supper of the Lamb of God, because he said he heard the noise of the wings of the living creatures as they touched one another. This is the same scene the prophet spoke of in Ezekiel 1:9; the Hebrew word for "one," **Ishshah** [802] is rendered "wife" while the word for "another" is **Achoth** [269], which is the same as spouse. On exiting the dimension of the spiritual realm, the final thing Ezekiel caught a glimpse of; was a picture of hope, and redemption, knowing that one day Yeshua Jesus would present His bride to Abba Father being purified.

Ezekiel whisks pass the ever living wheel of the Word of God making its eternal circuit over against the living creatures, which is a description of the revealed Word of God to mankind by the Spirit of God. Yeshua Jesus said in John 16:13-14 quoting the NASB: *"But when He, the Spirit of truth, comes, He will guide you into all truth; for He will not speak on His own initiative, but whatever He hears, He will speak; and He will disclose to you what is to come. He will glorify Me, for He will take of Mine and will disclose it to you."* At this point Holy Spirit is the wheel [Word] within mankind; transforming us into the image of Yeshua Jesus, thereby preparing us for our regenerated bodies. The Overcomers are those who will defeat the carnal man that wages war against the spirit and triumph over the constant battle with sin, to soar in the presence of the Almighty God on wings of worship.

The newly appointed prophet was so saturated with the presence of GOD that as the Spirit transported him back to the natural realm filled with chaos, disappointments and the reality of the loss of freedom; he became heartbroken and overwhelmed with sadness and grief. The temple was razed by fire and for seventy years the residents of the city of Jerusalem would be subjected to religious oppression in Babylon. Ezekiel's mind is flooded with mixed emotions, being a righteous man who longed to see the day when Israel would once again be a nation living in peace and harmony and basking in the goodness of God. The prophet clung to the hope he had for God is not like man who deceives; that which He had both showed and spoken to Ezekiel, He would perform. The Word of the living God was bedrock in the prophet's soul and this was his flag of hope. For seven days Ezekiel sat among his exiled brethren along the Chebar River, near Nippur in Babylon; all clueless to the prophet's meeting with the LORD. Very soon they would realize that Ezekiel was not the same, because he had a life changing encounter that would profoundly affect Israel's past, present and future generations.

Verses 16-21

And it came to pass at the end of seven days, that the word of the LORD came unto me, saying, Son of man, I have made thee a watchman unto the house of Israel: therefore hear the word at My mouth, and give them warning from Me. When I say unto the wicked, Thou shalt surely die; and thou givest him not warning, nor speakest to warn the wicked from his wicked way, to save his life; the same wicked man shall die in his iniquity; but his blood will be required at thine hand. Yet if thou warn the wicked, and he turn not from his wickedness, nor from his wicked way, he shall die in his iniquity; but thou hast delivered thy soul. Again when a righteous man doth turn from his righteousness, and commit iniquity, and I lay a stumblingblock before him, he shall die: because thou hast not given him warning, he shall die in his sin, and his righteousness which he hath done shalt not be remembered; but his blood will I require at thine hand. Nevertheless if thou warn the righteous man, that the righteous sin not, and he doth not sin, he shall surely live, because he is warned; also thou hast delivered thy soul.

Ezekiel continues to ponder the glorious vision and its revelation. Still bewildered, his thoughts drifts back and forth; he was quite aware of the current predicament facing his brethren as well as himself, but etched in his mind, was a brilliant flame called "hope." The time had now come for this priest to lay aside his priestly garment, because the LORD GOD had personally mantled him with the new office of a watchman (prophet). Ezekiel ingested and digested the Word of God, and the Spirit of the Living God would never leave him; Ezekiel is now officially inaugurated as God's voice to His exiled people. Those who once occupied the city of Jerusalem were now caught between a rock and a hard place because of their rebellious ways and those who were godly were also faced with the same dilemma. This may seem unfair but in reality it is not. How would the wicked turn from doing evil if they had no one in their midst to guide them? What might seem as being painful to the godly will one day bring glory and rich rewards. The godly who suffer with the wicked are God's instrument of mercy to those who continue to do evil.

As commanded by the LORD, Ezekiel had to warn both the wicked as well as the righteous. Those who professed righteousness but traded their righteousness to practice wickedness; in that day when gross sin blemished their acts of righteousness and the rebuke of the prophet of the Lord goes unheeded; past acts of righteousness will not be a redeemable ticket. All wonderful humanitarian deeds that were accredited to their account will be made null and void. This same principle also applies to the wicked, but if one should repent of all their evil ways, the LORD would not hold culpable, but exonerate him. The office of a prophet is a very strict one; for these servants of God are speaking directly under the anointing of Holy Spirit, if we speak lies; it is not Holy Spirit speaking, but man or the spirit of anti-Christ. Wickedness as well as righteousness will be rewarded by the LORD.

Verses 22-27

And the hand of the LORD was there upon me; and He said unto me, Arise, go forth into the plain, and I will there talk with thee. And I arose, and went forth into the plain: and, behold, the glory of the LORD stood there, as the glory which I saw by the river of Chebar: and I fell on my face. Then the Spirit entered into me, and set me upon my feet, and spake with me, and said unto me, Go shut thyself within thine house. But thou, O son of man, behold, they shall put bands upon thee, and shall bind thee with them, and thou shalt not go out among them: and I will make thy tongue cleave to the roof of thy mouth, and thou shalt be dumb, and shalt not be to them a reprover: for they are a rebellious house. But when I speak with thee, I will open thy mouth, and thou shalt say unto them, Thus saith the LORD GOD; He that heareth, let him hear; and he that forbeareth, let him forbear: for they are a rebellious house.

Once again Ezekiel clearly hears the LORD speaking to him, so he got up and went to the designated place of meeting out in the plain away from the other exiles. To his utter amazement the glory of the LORD was there; the same overwhelming presence that the prophet experienced in his earlier vision consumes him once again. Ezekiel is completely overwhelmed at the wonder and splendor of the Almighty God. Drained of all natural strength, the prophet falls prostrate as he did before at this amazing and glorious sight; unable to rise on his own; once again, Holy Spirit steps in.

Holy Spirit enters the prophet giving him supernatural strength and he stands up; just then he hears the familiar voice of the LORD, *"Go, shut thyself within thine house."* This is a call of separation; Ezekiel must comply, and remove himself from his fellow brethren. When the hand of God rests upon a servant, He calls them into a unique type of fellowship that even their closest family or friends are unable to fully grasp. In exile some degree of self government still existed and for this reason Ezekiel's message of rebuke to his brethren, would leave him in chains and under house arrest. This was bad news; but what the wicked meant for evil, God would use in Ezekiel's favor. Holy Spirit was about to use this period of solitary confinement to fulfill Abba Father's divine purpose. With the Spirit's help, the prophet embarks on a long fast, one in which his speech would be incapacitated and his voice would only be heard when the Spirit of the Living God desired to address them.

Chapter 4

Verses 1-3

Thou also, son of man, take thee a tile, and lay it before thee, and portray upon it the city, even Jerusalem: and lay siege against it, and build a fort against it, and cast a mount against it; set the camp also against it, and set battering rams against it round about. Moreover take unto thee an iron pan, and set it for a wall of iron between thee and the city: and set thy face against it, and it shall be besieged, and thou shalt lay siege against it. This shall be a sign unto the house of Israel.

Curiously the Babylonian guards must have watched Ezekiel as he gathers bits and pieces together to perform his wordless story telling. Some probably laughed, thinking the prophet had lost his mind, but those to whom this pantomime was intended would clearly understand the message behind the madness. In Ezekiel 4:2-3, the LORD said *"against it"* seven times in reference to the destruction of Jerusalem and the number seven in Scripture is the symbolic mark of completion and spiritual perfection. The LORD'S repeated warnings to Israel were finally over and it was now time for His judgment. The sins of the people had now come up for a determination of action and the justice of God was about to be seen, felt and heard. This was a punishment that would last seventy years and the city of Jerusalem would never be the same for many generations to come, when all Israel will shout with one accord: *"Baruch Haba B'Shem Adoni,"* that is: "Blessed is He who comes in the name of the LORD."

The prophet was told to:

1. Lay a siege against it (vs. 2):

   The portrayal of Jerusalem being surrounded by their enemies: **to contain**

2. Build a fort against it (vs. 2):

   A secondary wall built by their enemies surrounding the city: **to confine**

3. Cast a mount against it (vs. 2):

   A depiction of the nation that would subdue Jerusalem (mount/mountain, is metaphorically speaking of a nation): **to control**

4. Set the camp also against it (vs. 2):

   The settlements of the enemy outside the city walls: **to constrain**

5. Set battering rams against it round about (vs. 2):

   The gates of Jerusalem being breached by force: **to conquer**

6. Set thy face against it (vs. 3):

   Pronounce judgment upon Jerusalem as the LORD orders: **to condemn**

7. You shall lay siege against it (vs. 3):

   A surety that the destruction of Jerusalem by the Babylonians would be accomplished as stated in the first order: **to conclude**

Ezekiel, without saying a single word, dramatizes the Word of the LORD to exiled Judah. He takes a tablet made of clay; places it before him and engraved upon it the city Jerusalem. Even the method of dramatization was a sign unto the people, as engraving was done on a surface that had already hardened; therefore, the inscription had to be chiseled as a demonstration of Israel's rebellion against GOD. Israel designed a pathway for themselves, which lead them away from the covering and protection of Abba Father. A memorial of Israel's descent from righteousness was necessary to show them that the predicament they now found themselves was by their own doing and only national repentance, which was a sign of contrition, would move the hand of GOD in their behalf. The next seventy years would be one of anarchy, religious antagonism and deep distress.

Verses 4-8

Lie thou also upon thy left side, and lay the iniquity of the house of Israel upon it: according to the number of the days that thou shalt lie upon it thou shalt bear their iniquity. For I have laid upon thee the years of their iniquity, according to the number of the days, three hundred and ninety days: so shalt thou bear the iniquity of the house of Israel. And when thou hast accomplished them, lie again on thy right side, and thou shalt bear the iniquity of the house of Judah forty days: I have appointed thee each day for a year. Therefore thou shalt set thy face toward the siege of Jerusalem, and thine arms shall be uncovered, and thou shalt prophesy against it. And, behold, I will lay bands upon thee, and thou shalt not turn thee from one side to another, till thou hast ended the days of thy siege.

One might consider these orders as being crude and rather strange, but the LORD viewed them as mercy and grace. 1 Corinthians 1:20-29 states: *Where is the wise? Where is the disputer of this age? Has not God made foolish the wisdom of this world? For since, in the wisdom of God, the world through wisdom did not know God, it pleased God through the foolishness of the message preached to save those who believe. For Jews request a sign, and Greeks seek after wisdom; but we preach Christ crucified, to the Jews a stumbling block and to the Greeks foolishness, but to those who are called, both Jews and Greeks, Christ the power of God and the wisdom of God. Because the foolishness of God is wiser than men, and the weakness of God is stronger than men. For you see your calling, brethren, that not many wise according to the flesh, not many mighty, not many noble, are called. But God has chosen the foolish things of the world to put to shame the wise, and God has chosen the weak things of the world to put to shame the things which are mighty; and the base things of the world and the things which are despised God has chosen, and the things which are not, to bring to nothing the things that are, that no flesh may glory in His presence,* NKJV. Keeping these verses of Scripture in mind, we will gain a better understanding why these instructions were given in the first place. The people were bent on doing things their way and the LORD being all-knowing knew that these messages would be understood by the wise in heart but regarded as foolishness to those who walked in rebellion.

Ezekiel proved that he feared the LORD and this was reflected in his obedience to do as was instructed to do despite the ridicule. Proven to be both faithful and humble, Ezekiel embarked on a prophetic pantomime in which he lies on his left side for three hundred and ninety days; a day for each year, in intercession for the house of Israel. This act of penitence on behalf of the house of Israel of lying on the left side, tells yet another story of GOD'S infinite lovingkindness and tender mercies towards His people. He calls Israel His firstborn (Exodus 4:22); He inscribes them in the palms of His hands (Isaiah 49:16); He is their Maker, Redeemer and Husband (Isaiah 54:5). He became a Father unto them by separating them from the sons of Adam. He is their portion and their inheritance and we must never forget that Israel is the apple of His eyes (Deuteronomy 32:1-10; Zechariah 2:8).

Abba Father is the best role model for His children. He must address waywardness and rebellion, otherwise such behavior would ultimately lead to lawlessness; making its lasting effects irreparable as subsequent generations would be worst than their predecessors. Three hundred and ninety days was allotted by the LORD for Israel's unrepentant heart; a day for each year. The Father waited patiently to see if Israel would turn from their iniquity but they did not. The divided northern and southern kingdoms of Israel walked contrary to the LORD'S teachings. Both rebelled and both were judged: Israel under King Jeroboam (1 Kings 12:25-33) and Judah under King Manasseh (see 2 Kings 21:1-9; 2 Chronicles 33:1-9). The LORD God used a prophet named Ahijah to demonstrate in prophetic role play of the coming division of Israel (1 Kings 11:26-40). The downward spirals of both Kingdoms are recorded in 2 Chronicles Chapter 10 and 1 Kings Chapter 12. Judah and Benjamin, the two tribes making up the smaller southern kingdom received a lesser punishment of forty days; a day for each year, because they refused to participate in an insurrection against King Rehoboam. Abba Father now uses the Babylonians as His rod of punishment for His people (2 Kings 17:7-22; 2 Chronicles 36:11-20).

Ezekiel lays restricted on his left side for three hundred and ninety days for Israel, and at the end of this appointed time; he turns to his right side and intercedes for Judah forty days. These are special numbers used repeatedly in Scriptures because they carry a much deeper interpretation; an encrypted message; a revelation that lies dormant until its appointed time to be made known by the LORD. Let us examine the spiritual significance of the sum of both numbers: 390+40=430 (days). The Jewish calendar is the calendar of God's timing; no other calendar holds this prestigious status. The number of days of this calendar year is 360. To subtract 360 from 430 we get to another very important number, 70 (430-360=70); its significance and relationship with 390 and 40 will astound you and the book of Genesis is our starting point.

In the first chapter of Genesis God repeatedly states: the evening and the morning completed one day which gives a total of seven days. He identified each day numerically unlike the pagan names such as Saturday, Sunday Monday etc., which came much later; this same principle applies also to the naming of the months. The next important thing to note is that the moon is God's clock and faithful witness of dividing time and seasons, and He alone has the authority to establish its accuracy, in that, He does not have to either add or subtract a day from His calendar to balance it. Genesis 1:14 states: *And GOD said, Let there be lights in the firmament of the heaven to divide the day from the night; and **let them be for signs,** and for **seasons,** and for **days,** and **years:*** and again in Psalm 89:30-37, God makes a covenant with the house of David: *If his children forsake My Law, and walk not in My judgments; if they break My statutes, and keep not My commandments; then will I visit their transgression with the rod, and their iniquities with stripes. Nevertheless My lovingkindness will I not utterly take from him, nor suffer My faithfulness to fail. My covenant will I not break, nor alter the thing that is gone out of My lips. Once have I sworn by My holiness that I will not lie unto David. His seed shall endure forever, and his throne as the sun before Me. It shall be established forever as the moon, and as a faithful witness in heaven. Selah* and 104:19: *He appointed the moon for seasons: the sun knoweth his going down.*

The Hebrew word for "season" is **moed** or **moadah**, some of its interpretations include gathering, appointment and signal; a determined time or place; it can also mean a congregation. The word moon **yareach**, means month or moon; from which we get lunar, a precise month of thirty days. Here below are clues for a 360 day year:

- Genesis 7:11: *In the **second month**, the **seventeenth day of the month**, the same day were all the fountains of the great deep broken up*

- Genesis 8:3: *And the waters returned from off the earth continually: and after the end of the **hundred and fifty days** the waters were abated* (150÷30=5), which is five months later.

- Genesis 8:4: *And **the ark rested** in **the seventh month**, and on the **seventeenth day of the month**, upon the mountains of Ararat.* Exactly five months from the second month to the fifth month, consisting of thirty days since the fountains of the great deep was broken up; Genesis 7:11, or a hundred and fifty days Genesis 8:3.

- Genesis 8:5: *And the waters decreased continually until the **tenth month**: in the tenth month, on the first day of the month, were the tops of the mountains seen.* From Genesis 7:11 to 8:5 we can clearly see the total of ten thirty day months. Documentation for an eleventh month is mentioned in Deuteronomy 1:3 and a twelfth in 2 Kings 25:27; proving that God's calendar consists of 360 days; each month having thirty days: 12x30=360; a 365/366 day calendar is manmade and therefore inaccurate, time is farther along than we truly realize.

Ezekiel's total time of intercession for the whole house of Israel, was over the span of one lunar year, two lunar months, and ten lunar days; that is fourteen months and ten days lying on his side. Thirteen months on his left side for Israel, (the number thirteen is associated with rebellion and is first mentioned in Genesis 14:); and forty days or one month and ten days for Judah on his right side (the number forty is associated with chastisement). The number of days for both Israel and Judah's punishment totaled 430 and when subtracted from 360 (a day for each Hebrew calendar year) we arrive at the number 70 (430-360=70); the number of years prescribed by the LORD GOD for Judah's Babylonian Exile. Jeremiah 25:1-13 states: *The word that came to Jeremiah concerning all the people of Judah in the fourth year of Jehoiakim the son of Josiah king of Judah, that was the first year of Nebuchadnezzar king of Babylon; The which Jeremiah the prophet spake unto all the people of Judah, and all the inhabitants of Jerusalem, saying, From the thirteenth year of Josiah the son of Amon king of Judah, even unto this day, that is the* *three and twentieth year, the word of the LORD hath come unto me, and I have spoken unto you, rising early and speaking; but you have not hearkened. And the LORD hath sent unto you all His servants the prophets, rising early and sending them; but ye have not hearkened, nor inclined your ear to hear. They said turn ye again now every one from his evil way, and from the evil of your doings, and dwell in the land that the LORD hath given unto you and to your fathers forever and ever: and go not after other gods to serve them, and provoke Me not to anger with the works of your hands; and I will do you no hurt. Yet ye have not hearkened unto Me, saith the LORD; that ye might provoke Me to anger with the works of your hands to your own hurt. Therefore thus saith the LORD of hosts; Because ye have not heard My words, behold, I will send and take all the families of the north, saith the LORD, and Nebuchadnezzar the king of Babylon, My servant, and will bring them against this land, and against the inhabitants thereof, and against all these nations round about, and will utterly destroy them, and make them an astonishment, and a hissing, and perpetual desolations. Moreover I will take from them the voice of mirth, and the voice of gladness, the voice of the bridegroom, and the voice of the bride, the sound of the millstones, and the light of the candle. And this whole land shall be a desolation, and an astonishment; and these nations shall serve the king of Babylon **seventy years.** And it shall come to pass, when **seventy years** are accomplished, that I will punish the king of Babylon, and that nation, saith the LORD, for their iniquity, and the land of the Chaldeans, and will make it perpetual desolations. And I will bring upon that land all My words which I have pronounced against it, even all that is written in this book, which Jeremiah hath prophesied against all the nations,* (for further references, see also Jeremiah 29:8-15; Ezra 1:1; 2 Chronicles 36;21,22; Daniel 9:2). Israel's rebellion and Judah's chastisement for unbelief was finally being addressed. We will examine another revelation that will explain the reason behind Ezekiel's instructions to lay on his left side first and then on his right. What appears as foolishness at first glance Holy Spirit removes the veil revealing divine truths.

On examination of the human anatomy, it was observed that the most important organ located in the thoracic cavity, with its apex extending a little to the left is the heart. Synonymously references to the heart allude to the center of the emotions and our capacity for good or evil. The heart can be spoken of as being good, broken or callous. Some other references to the heart are: loyalty, love and devotion. Jeremiah 17:9-10 states: *The heart is deceitful above all things, and desperately wicked: who can know it? I the LORD search the heart, I try the reins, even to give every man according to his ways, and according to the fruit of his doings.* The ever loving Father looks upon Israel and weeps over them because they have rejected Him. For three hundred and ninety years, the LORD sends His prophets to warn Israel, but their rebellious heart became even more callous; instead of giving them exactly what they truly deserve, as a good Father and Israel's Righteous Judge, He reduces their sentence to three hundred and ninety days. It is said that justice is blind, but in this case justice is mercy and grace. Psalm 107:8-12 states: *Oh, that men would give thanks to the LORD for His goodness, and for His wonderful works to the children of men! For He satisfies the longing soul, and fills the hungry soul with goodness. Those who sat in darkness and in the shadow of death, bound in afflictions and iron because they rebelled against the words of God, and despised the counsel of the Most High, therefore He brought down their heart with labor; they fell down, and there was none to help,* NKJV. Three hundred and ninety days is equivalent to thirteen lunar months, Israel's sentence for their rebellion.

One man, God's chosen priest and prophet amongst rebels and a few righteous; bound to bear the sins of a nation. God's man of the hour; as a priest he performed temple duties, but now living with his captive brethren and banned from such ceremonial practices, he obediently lays before the LORD on his left side and intercedes for Israel as a prophet. Thirteen months went by and Ezekiel now turns on his right side still bound, and offer pleas for Judah for the next forty days.

This takes us to the next revelation: the most important organ in the right side of the body is the liver and just like the heart, we cannot survive without it. Located just below the diaphragm, most of the liver can be found tucked under the protection of the ribs in the upper right portion of the abdominal cavity. An amazing fact about this vitally important organ; is its ability to regenerate itself. How amazing is our God, He created the liver with the ability to repair itself following injury, now He uses this important organ as a symbol of the regeneration and renewal of Judah that is to come. GOD has therefore given Judah a trial period to correct their wrongdoings both spiritually and morally. The heart is the most important organ on the left side, while the liver is the most important on the right; both expressly points to the grace of GOD towards the house of Israel and although He had to punish them for their unrepentant sins, as a Father His love for them never ceased. Judah will see their freedom in seventy years and a remnant will return to Jerusalem to rebuild the temple and broken down walls. For three hundred and ninety days Ezekiel laid restricted on his left side, which was immediately followed by forty more days on his right side bearing the iniquities of his brethrens before God. Next, the prophet sets his face towards the city of Jerusalem, which now lies desolate and in ruins, and prophesy against that great city with uncovered arms, which is a sign of utter shame and disgrace.

Verses 9-17

Take thou also unto thee wheat, and barley, and beans, and lentils, and millet, and fitches, and put them in one vessel, and make thee bread thereof, according to the number of the days that thou shalt lie upon thy side, three hundred and ninety days shalt thou eat thereof. And thy meat which thou shalt eat shall be by weight, twenty shekels a day: from time to time shalt thou eat it. Thou shalt drink also water by measure, the sixth part of an hin: from time to time shalt thou drink. And thou shalt eat it as barley cakes, and thou shalt bake it with dung that cometh out of man, in their sight. And the LORD said, Even thus shall the children of Israel eat their defiled bread among the Gentiles, whither I will drive them. Then said I, Ah Lord GOD! Behold, my soul hath not been polluted: for from my youth up even till now have I not eaten of that which dieth of itself, or is torn in pieces; neither came there abominable flesh into my mouth. Then He said unto me, Lo, I have given thee cow's dung for man's dung, and thou shalt prepare the bread therewith. Moreover He said unto me, Son of man, behold, I will break the staff of bread in Jerusalem: and they shall eat bread by weight, and with care; and they shall drink water by measure, and with astonishment: that they may want bread and water, and be astonied one with another, and consume away for their iniquity.

Ezekiel is given a prescribed diet of wheat, barley, beans, lentils, millet and fitches (spilt), for his three hundred and ninety day intercession for the house of Israel. These six cereal grains and seeds were the ingredients for the bread of adversity. Holy Spirit also revealed that there was more to these cereal grains and seeds, which revealed great truths about the grace of Abba Father towards His people. This unusual bread recipe must have had an unpleasant taste but this was the intent for which it was prescribed. Now let's examine the bread recipe; first of all, the grains and seeds were six in number and this number is assigned to man who was formed from the dust of the earth on the sixth day in the image and likeness of God (Genesis 1:26-31). The all knowing Creator being familiar with the propensities of man knew that he would have fallen short of His glory and perfection because of sin. What can we learn from these six plant sources the chief ingredients for this unusual bread recipe? What message is God trying to convey to us regarding His relationship with His people? With these questions in mind let's examine each plant source as each is a symbol and message of love from Abba Father, not only to His chosen people but also to all mankind.

1. **Wheat**

Wheat is considered to be the most common of all cereal grains so it took first place on the list. It speaks of that which is worth harvesting and also the act of humility. Unlike other grains, wheat is cultivated by broadcasting, plowing, and treading into the soil using domesticated farm animals. Yeshua Jesus gave this parable about wheat recorded in Matthew 13:24-30, that will help to establish its worth and relationship to His people. *Another parable put He forth unto them, saying, The kingdom of heaven is likened unto a man which sowed good seed in his field: but while men slept, his enemy came and sowed tares among the wheat, and went his way. But when the blade was sprung up, and brought forth fruit, then appeared the tares also. So the servant of the householder came and said unto him, Sir, didst not thou sow good seed in thy field? From whence then hath it tares? He said unto them, An enemy hath done this. The servant said unto him, Wilt thou then that we go and gather them up? But he said, Nay; lest while ye gather up the tares, ye root up also the wheat with them. Let both grow together until the harvest: and in the time of harvest I will say to the reapers, Gather ye together first the tares, and bind them in bundles to burn them: but gather the wheat into my barn.* The first observation noted here is the fact that the wheat belongs to God.

Those who cultivate wheat know it is very difficult to differentiate between wheat from weed (tares). Being very similar in appearance, farmers had to wait until the time of harvesting when the bowing heads of the mature wheat grain is clearly evident. At this point the farmer is able to identify and harvest the wheat because the weeds stand tall. The wheat grain is symbolic of humility as all believers ought to be. The worthless tares also known as weeds are separated from the useful wheat through a process called winnowing. This procedure entails tossing the grain into the air, which helps to separates the grains from the chaff. All the undesirable portions of the wheat are blown away by the wind while the grain falls to the ground. Another fact about wheat is seen in Christ's intercession for one of His closest disciples; *And the Lord said, Simon, Simon, behold, Satan hath desired to have you, that he may sift you as wheat: But I have prayed for thee, that thy faith fail not: and when thou art converted, strengthen thy brethren* (Luke 22:31-32). As the Lord justly punishes sin; Satan's unjustly desires to sift us through open doors of sin in our lives. The difference however between both is the fact that the LORD'S punishment brings about separation, salvation and sanctification; while Satan's sifting brings about accusation, humiliation and condemnation.

Here we can clearly see that it is Satan, the accuser of the brethren, who desires to put us through the rigor of temptation and persecution to test our true loyalty unto the LORD and to expose our sins and weaknesses. Simon is behooved to encourage his fellow brethren, knowing that the testing of his faith would make him stronger, bolder and more mature; this is the way all Believers in Yeshua Jesus should view trials: counting them all joy. Israel is here typed as wheat; dispersed, plowed, and trodden under foot, yet this was not to destroy them but to separate them from the weeds of sin that drove a wedge between them and God. This relationship however, was not completely severed, for His bruising was to arouse a sense of righteousness and holiness within them. God has a wonderful plan for Israel; Psalm 126 states: *When the LORD brought back the captivity of Zion, we were like those who dream. Then our mouth was filled with laughter, and our tongue with singing, then they said among the nations, "The LORD has done great things for them." The LORD has done great things for us, and we are glad. Bring back our captivity, O LORD, as the streams in the South. Those who sow in tears shall reap in joy. He who continually goes forth weeping, bearing seeds for sowing, shall doubtless come again with rejoicing, bringing his sheaves with him,* NKJV. Wheat is the first ingredient of this bread for it is God's message of **Reconciliation**.

2. **Barley**

Barley has several uses; from feeding of livestock, to brewing and distilling malt, as well as a cereal. This is what is generally known about barley, but the message that the LORD is conveying here is quite different. We will look at a few Scriptures that will help us to understand the message that the LORD is conveying. He was quite careful when choosing barley as the second cereal grain, because in Scripture it is offered unto the LORD as the jealousy offering (Numbers 5: 14-31). Let us look at some other Scriptures where the word "jealous" was used. Exodus 20:4-6 was its first appearance and it was the LORD who said: *Thou shalt not make unto thee any graven image, or any likeness of any thing that is in heaven above, or that is in the earth beneath, or that is in the water under the earth: thou shalt not bow down thyself to them, nor serve them: for I the LORD thy GOD am a jealous GOD, visiting the iniquity of the fathers upon the children unto the third and fourth generation of them that hate Me; and shewing mercy unto thousands of them that love Me, and keep My commandments.* The LORD is jealous for His people, and worshiping any other is an act of unfaithfulness and whoredom.

An oracle of Jeremiah the prophet: *Turn, O, backsliding children, saith the LORD; for I am married unto you: and I will take you one of a city, and two of a family, and I will bring you to Zion: and I will give you pastors according to Mine heart, which shall feed you with knowledge and understanding. And it shall come to pass, when ye be multiplied and increase in the land, in those days, saith the LORD, they shall say no more, The ark of the covenant of the LORD: neither shall it come to mind: neither shall they remember it; neither shall they visit it; neither shall that be done any more. At that time they shall call Jerusalem the throne of the LORD; and all the nations shall be gathered unto it, to the name of the LORD, to Jerusalem: neither shall they walk any more after the imagination of their evil heart. In those days the house of Judah shall walk with the house of Israel, and they shall come together out of the land of the north to the land that I have given for an inheritance unto your fathers. But I said, How shall I put thee among the children, and give thee a pleasant land, a goodly heritage of the hosts of nations? And I said, Thou shalt call Me, My Father; and shalt not turn away from Me. Surely as a wife treacherously departeth from her husband, so have ye dealt treacherously with Me, O, house of Israel, saith the LORD,* 3:14-20. A faithful remnant will be saved, and they will be a royal and pure people who have not gone a whoring after other gods, neither have they despised their first and only true love. The LORD has emotions, which He wove into our genetic design, did He not say: "*Let us make man in Our image, after our likeness* (Genesis 1:26); therefore we were created with emotions, because the LORD God gave His emotions to us. It's His divine emotions that make us humans and not animals.

As we come to the most important fact about barley, you will see clearly that this cereal is also an offering called "jealousy," as it is offered to bring an awareness of the gross immorality and sin of God's people; a name so given by the LORD GOD Himself. Numbers 5:11-15 states: *And the LORD spake unto Moses, saying, Speak unto the children of Israel, and say unto them, if any man's wife go aside, and commit a trespass against him, and a man lie with her carnally, and it be hid from the eyes of her husband, and be kept close, and she be defiled, and there be no witness against her, neither she be taken with the manner; and the spirit of jealousy come upon him, and he be jealous of his wife, and she be defiled: or if the spirit of jealousy come upon him, and he be jealous of his wife, and she be not defiled: then shall the man bring his wife unto the priest, and* **he shall bring her offering for her, the tenth part of an ephah of barley meal;** *he shall pour no oil upon it, nor put frankincense thereon; for* **it is an offering of Jealousy, an offering of memorial, bringing iniquity to**

remembrance. This was required by Abba Father for the gross sins of the people. The message that barley convey is: we have gone astray, trespassed and committed iniquity against a holy GOD and barley meal is the offering taken to the priest by the guilty as atonement for their whoredom, which is accepted by Abba Father as a memorial.

Ezekiel never considered his orders to be irrational; he obediently gathers the ingredients for this very strange bread knowing that there must be a reason for this unusual diet. Was Ezekiel aware that each ingredient had such depth of meaning and interpretation? God's jealousy was aroused when His people were unfaithful. Like a husband to the children of Israel, it is the LORD that prescribes the required offerings as a token of their repentance. The basic truth and spiritual implication of barley addresses God's backslidden and wondering children who are in bondage; recognizing and repenting of their trespasses; as Jeremiah 3:14a states: *Turn, O, backsliding children, saith the LORD; for I am married unto you.* Barley is the required offering of **Jealousy**; it is God's message to His people to return unto Him and be redeemed.

3. **Beans**

Beans are not classified as a cereal but a legume like the pea; it is mentioned only twice in the Bible, Ezekiel 4:9 and 2 Samuel 17:28. To grasp a clear understanding we will read from 2 Samuel 17: 24-29: *Then David came to Mahanaim. And Absalom passed over Jordan, he and all the men of Israel with him. And Absalom made Amasa captain of the host instead of Joab: which Amasa was a man's son, whose name was Ithra an Israelite, that went into Abigail the daughter of Nahash, sister of Zeruiah Joab's mother. So Israel and Absolam pitched in the land of Gilead. And it came to pass, when David was come to Mahanaim, that Shobi the son of Nahash of Rabbah of the children of Ammon, and Machir the son of Lodebar, and Barzillai the Gileadite of Rogelim, brought beds, and basins, and earthen vessels, and wheat, and barley, and flour,* *and parched corn, and **beans**, and lentils, and parched pulse, and honey, and butter, and sheep, and cheese of kine, for David, and for the people that were with him, to eat: for they said, The people is hungry, and weary, and thirsty, in the wilderness.* Now let us examine the story in the above verses, thereby extracting the symbolism of the third ingredient: beans.

King David was on the run because of an attempted coup d'état by his own son Absolam. While in hiding, Shobi son of King Nahash, brought food and other provisions for David and his faithful men. Included in the ration brought for the King and his friends were beans. In both instances where beans are mentioned in Scripture it is associated with the prevention of hunger and starvation. 2 Samuel 17:29 says that the King and his men were hungry, weary, and thirsty, in the wilderness, which is a barren place devoid of vegetation, but for grace the heart of Shobi was moved to prevent the whole lot from perishing in the wilderness. There is no doubt that the Lord sent Shobi a non-Jew, whose name means *"Captive,"* to their rescue. Psalm 130 is one of many that points to the mercy of GOD, it states: *Out of the depths I have cried to You, O LORD; Lord hear my voice! Let Your ears be attentive to the voice of my supplications. If You, LORD, should mark iniquities, O Lord, who could stand? But there is forgiveness with You, that you may be feared. I wait for the LORD, my soul waits, and in His word I do hope. My soul waits for the Lord more than those who watch for the morning yes, more than those who watch for the morning. O Israel, hope in the LORD; for with the LORD there is mercy, and with Him is abundant redemption. And He shall redeem Israel from all his iniquities,* NKJV. What reassurance we have in the Godhead as Psalm 136 repeatedly echoes, *"His mercy endures forever."* Beans; the third ingredient is the symbol and message of **Mercy**.

4. **Lentils**

Lentils are quite resilient, because this grain grows well even in the poorest of soil. Like wheat the grain is beaten to remove the husk from the straw. Lentils are also mentioned in Genesis 25:34; 2 Samuel 17:28 and 23:11. Let's once more examine the Scriptures to see the stories surrounding this grain and the message it contains. Genesis 25:34 states: *Then Jacob gave Esau bread and pottage of lentils; and he did eat and drink, and rose up, and went his way:* **thus Esau despised his birthright.** This is the first place in the Bible where lentils are mentioned, and here we see Esau desiring lentils, and despising his birthright. The birthright is very important, because it can only be given to the first born son. The Lord God gave this remarkable message to Moses for Pharaoh in Exodus 4:22; *And thou shalt say unto Pharaoh, Thus saith the LORD, Israel is My son, even My firstborn; which concurs with* Hebrews 12:16-17; *Lest there be any fornicator or profane person, as Esau, who for a morsel of meat sold his birthright, for ye know that afterward, when he would have inherited the blessing, he was rejected: for he found no place of repentance, though he sought it carefully with tears.* The birthright was a coveted gift from the father to the firstborn son, to reject such an auspicious gift was in effect dishonoring the father and the place of prestige placed upon the firstborn male. This was an awful time for Israel, they despised their heritage as sons; exiled Israel forfeited their inheritance; the lentils is therefore the symbol and memorial of their sins and God's message to them that being under Babylonian captivity was the fine for their offense because they forsook their **Birthright**.

5. **Millet**

Millet is a very fine seed also known by the name pannag, used mainly by the poor of the land as part of their dietary intake. The refined seed is boiled in water or milk to make a soft and creamy mixture, much like food blended for toddlers. Not much is said about millet because it is only found in Ezekiel 4:9. What then is the significance of millet? The millet, approximately the size of the mustard seed, is said to be a unique type of grain because each shoot or stalk contain an enumerable amount of edible seeds.

But how is the millet related to the nation of Israel? Holy Spirit spoke softly: "My covenant with Abraham." Turning to Genesis 22:15-18 we read: *And the angel of the LORD called unto Abraham out of heaven the second time, and said, By Myself have I sworn, saith the LORD, for because thou hast done this thing, and hast not withheld thy son, thine only son: that in blessing I will bless thee, and in multiplying I will multiply thy seed as the stars of the heaven, and as the sand which is upon the sea shore; and thy seed shall possess the gate of his enemies; and in thy seed shall all the nations of the earth be blessed; because thou hast obeyed My voice.* Millet, unlike any other seed or grain contains in each of its mature stalk, millions of seed, which is symbolic of the covenant that the LORD made with His servant Abraham. This very special seed was one of the ingredients for this unusual bread that would be a part of Ezekiel's diet for the next thirteen lunar months (390 days). The whole house of Israel sinned greatly and their sentence was seventy years hard labor under King Nebuchadnezzar, but a loving God will never forget His people or His covenant with them. Remember, the Lord is not returning for a perfect people, but a people who through His Son will be perfected because of His finished work on a tree that became our Cross of redemption, therefore we are presented to the Father as if we never sinned. Knowing this fact; never forget that willful sin will be judged. James 4:17 clearly states: *Therefore, to him who knows to do good and does not do it, to him it is sin.*

As we meditate upon these things Hebrews 6:10-20 is worth mentioning here as well: *For God is not unrighteous to forget your work and labor of love, which ye have showed toward His name, in that ye have ministered to the saints, and do minister. And we desire that every one of you do shew the same diligence to the full assurance of hope unto the end: that ye be not slothful, but followers of them who through faith and patience inherit the promises. For when God made promise to Abraham, because He could swear by no greater, He swore by Himself, saying, Surely blessing I will bless thee, and multiplying I will multiply thee. And so, after he had patiently endured, he obtained the promise. For men verily swear by the greater: and an oath for confirmation is to them an end of all strife. Wherein God, willingly more abundantly to shew unto the heirs of promise the immutability of His counsel, confirmed it by an oath: that by two immutable things, in which it was impossible for God to lie, we might have a strong consolation, who have fled for refuge to lay hold upon hope set before us: which hope we have as an anchor of the soul, both sure and steadfast, and which entereth into that within the veil; whither the forerunner is for us entered, even Jesus, made an High Priest for ever after the order of Melchisedec.* Like the millet (pannag) seed, so is Israel, multiplied as the stars of heaven and like the sand on the sea shore and mightily blessed by Almighty GOD. Through them all nations of the earth will be blessed and this is not a thought to be frowned upon. The covenant words of Abba Father to His beloved children will never be revoked and a time will come upon this earth, when all mankind will admit that he who fights against Israel are indeed fighting against the Supreme God who calls Israel His own special people. The Jewish people have retained their unique cultural identity although scattered over the face of the earth. The millet in its uniqueness is symbolic of covenant and this special seed in its own extraordinary way, points to the LORD'S promise to Abraham. No other nation in the whole earth has been blessed by the LORD as the nation of Israel and for this reason; the millet seed is symbolic of the LORD'S message of **Covenant.**

6. **Fitches/Spelt**

This is the last ingredient for the bread prescribed to be eaten by the prophet during his time of intercession before the LORD for Israel. Fitches, also known as spelt, must not to be confused with the fitches mentioned in Isaiah 28:25-27, because it is derived from an entirely different Hebrew word. The NKJV was more accurate in its translation by using the word "spelt" instead. Spelt, like millet, also have unique features. Although this grain is of a poor quality for human consumption, two important features were identified that is of great spiritual significance. Spelt, like the wheat cereal, are closely related both in appearance and physical characteristics. At a glance this grain is covered in a protective dry outer covering called a "hull." The hull is resistant to the invasion of insects thereby protecting and preserving its nutritive value and natural flavor. The Symbolic revelation of the hull of the spelt, points to the protection and preservation of the LORD GOD over the small nation of Israel. The LORD has been Israel's ally; giving them miraculous victories over their enemies time and time again throughout history, when all believed they would have been defeated. Psalm 121:1-8 states: *I will lift up mine eyes unto the hills, from whence commeth my help. My help commeth from the LORD, which made heaven and earth. He will not suffer thy foot to be moved: He that keepeth thee will not slumber. Behold, He that keepeth Israel shall neither slumber nor sleep. The LORD is thy keeper: the LORD is thy shade upon thy right hand. The sun shall not smite thee by day, nor the moon by night. The LORD shall preserve thee from all evil: He shall preserve thy soul. The LORD shall preserve thy going out and thy coming in from this time forth, and even for evermore.* The protective hull of the spelt is only removed before it is pulverized into flour; therefore it preserves the grain from the invasion of insects. Like the hull, the LORD GOD in His unbroken covenant with Israel, continue to be their bulwark and wall of protection and preservation. The symbolic meaning of the spelt is God's message of **Protection** and **Preservation**.

A three hundred and ninety years sentence reduced to three hundred and ninety days; is an act of mercy and grace, which speaks of the infinite love of God. The LORD continues to love an imperfect people, who will one day be reconciled unto Him forever. Abba Father sent His perfect Son, which is His perfect sacrifice, who will present a perfected people unto Himself as His perfect bride. The days are close at hand, when the house of Israel and those who have joined themselves unto her will cry to the Lord and be offered **reconciliation** by the God of Abraham, Isaac, and Jacob, who is **jealous** for his people to return unto Him in repentance that He might show them **mercy** and remind them of their **birthright** given to them as an everlasting **covenant**, which He made with their forefathers; for it is only in the LORD their GOD, will they find **protection** and **preservation** from the constant threats of extinction purported by their enemies who surrounds them.

The 6 ingredients of Ezekiel's bread and their symbolic meaning:

Wheat – **Reconciliation**

Barley – **Jealousy**

Beans – **Mercy**

Lentils – **Birthright**

Millet – **Covenant**

Fitches/Spelt – **Protection** and **Preservation**.

The LORD continues His instructions by informing Ezekiel that his diet during this period of intercession for Israel would be by weight: twenty shekels per day. The book of Ezekiel, just like the book of Revelation, is filled with symbolic language that might appear difficult to understand; this in itself is a type of sealing, which only Holy Spirit can shed the truth and light. Every drop of God's Word has infinite depth to it. As we read the Holy Scriptures, Holy Spirit may take a single verse and reveal depths and dimensions, which we could not have known otherwise. Every time we meditate upon the Word of God, we are in fact, meditating upon Yeshua Jesus Himself who reveals unto us divine truths by His Spirit. The LORD'S instructions for Ezekiel's daily ration were twenty shekels which is about 8.4 ounces. Not only was this amount just enough to sustain his life, but the number reveals the imperfection of Israel spiritual growth. They had fallen short of twenty one, another perfect number in the series of sevens, yet sustained by the completion of His grace (5x4=20). Genesis 2:1-3 states: *Thus the heavens and the earth were finished, and all the host of them. And on the seventh day God ended His work which He had made; and He rested on the seventh day from all His work which He had made. And God blessed the seventh day, and sanctified it: because that in it He had rested from all His work which God created and made.* As a matter of information; wherever you see "GOD" or "LORD GOD" written in the Old Testament, it is speaking of Abba Father, and where you see "God" or "Lord God," is referring to Yeshua Jesus the Son, where both are combined "LORD God," it is referring to both Father and Son; keep this in mind as we continue our journey through the Word of God.

Numbers that are equally divided in series of seven is speaking of the completion of perfection and as we continue our exploration of the book of Ezekiel this fact will be greatly emphasized. Twenty when divided by seven will be fractionalized to reveal its imperfection. Let us look at it another way 7+7+6=20; six is the scriptural symbol of man instead of 7+7+7=21 or 3x7=21 or 7x3=21 which points to perfection. The number six is one less than its perfect next level of seven; therefore, the number twenty although possessing some degree of perfection, is a mark of God's grace and for this reason Ezekiel's food was twenty shekels, as opposed to twenty one shekels. Ezekiel's small meal is a picture of God's grace upon the house of Israel until the allotted seventy year sentence had expired. In Ezekiel 4:11, the LORD instructs the prophet that even the water he drank should be by measure, which was also a very small quantity, one sixth of a hin. The hin is associated with offerings in the Old Covenant and is used for measuring liquids such as, oil or wine, however Ezekiel 4:11 is the only place in the Bible where it is used in reference to the measurement of water, therefore, there must be some association with oil, and or wine. Let's examine a few Scriptures, and glean the interpretation for a possible reason why Ezekiel was told by GOD to substitute a hin of oil or wine, with water; and why only 1/6th of a hin.

Isaiah 61:1-3 will be our starting point: *The Spirit of the Lord GOD is upon Me; because the LORD hath anointed Me to preach good tidings unto the meek; He hath sent Me to bind up the brokenhearted, to proclaim liberty to the captives, and the opening of the prison to them that are bound; to proclaim the acceptable year of the LORD, and the day of vengeance of our God; to comfort all that mourn; to appoint unto them that mourn in Zion, to give unto them beauty for ashes, the oil of joy for mourning, the garment of praise for the spirit of heaviness; that they might be called trees of righteousness, the planting of the LORD, that He might be glorified.* Here we see the bondage breaking power of Yeshua Jesus on display; this was a time of mourning, repentance and seeking the mercies of the LORD GOD for Israel. Being in exile was no laughing matter because such domination comes with autocratic laws and commandments of their captors as Nebuchadnezzar was a king who served strange gods. Ezekiel had to intercede for the whole house of Israel because the years ahead would be filled with marked depression, sorrows, and woes. Israel and Judah had found themselves in a predicament that only an intervention of GOD could resolve. They had lost their expression off happiness because they rejected the source of their pleasure which is found in none other than the LORD their GOD. The prophet Jeremiah said: *Therefore they shall come and sing in the height of Zion, and shall flow together the goodness of the LORD, for wheat, and for wine, and for oil, and for the young flock and for the heard: and their soul shall be as a watered garden; and they shall not sorrow any more at all* (31:12).

Oil and wine spoke of healing, but now the LORD GOD, compassionate and full of mercy uses a sixth of a hin of water as a substitute, because these precious offerings were taken from them by their captors. The LORD however gave them the perfect substitution which is water. Israel had to be cleansed before she could be healed. GOD had a plan for His people, it was never His intention that they should suffer; this was their own doing. Like a good Father, the Lord would avenge their captors after their period of punishment had run its course. Isaiah 10:20-27 is a message of hope, never forget, the righteous do suffer at times with the wicked, but GOD always saves for Himself a remnant: *And it shall come to pass in that day, that the remnant of Israel, and such as are escaped of the house of Jacob, shall no more again stay upon him that smote them; but shall stay upon the LORD, in truth. The remnant shall return, even the remnant of Jacob, unto the mighty GOD. For though Thy people Israel be as the sand of the sea, yet a remnant of them shall return: the consumption decreed shall overflow with righteousness. For the Lord GOD of hosts shall make a consumption, even determined, in the midst of all the land. Therefore thus saith the Lord GOD of hosts, O My people that dwellest in Zion, be not afraid of the Assyrian: he shall smite thee with a rod, and shall lift up his staff against thee, after the manner of Egypt. For yet a very little while, and the indignation shall cease, and mine anger in their destruction. And the LORD of hosts shall stir up a scourge for him according to the slaughter of Midian at the rock of Oreb: and as his rod was upon the sea, so shall he lift it up after the manner of Egypt. And it shall come to pass in that day, that his burden shall be taken away from off thy shoulder, and his yoke from off thy neck, and the yoke shall be destroyed because of the anointing.* A remnant would return to Jerusalem after Israel's punishment had run its course and a sixth part of a hin of water would quench the parched lips of Ezekiel every now and then as he intercedes for his brethrens. The hin measurement was never before associated with water and never again would it be repeated. But why did the LORD commanded Ezekiel to consume only one-sixth of a hin of water periodically?

Any part of six is symbolic of man, but the revelation is much deeper that this fact. First of all; man can survive without food but not without water. Secondly; water was recommended by the LORD as oil and wine are symbolic of the anointing; peace; tranquility; and favor. These were not a favorable time for Israel, therefore, water the sustainer of life became the substitute. Ezekiel was instructed to have one sixth of a hin of water every now and then. This takes us to the most important aspect of one-sixth of a hin of water. Remember one-sixth, is one part of six, therefore there are five parts left.

Ezekiel the prophet is here commanded by GOD to be an intercessor at this point in Israel's history, but he was not the only person whom GOD was using instrumentally for the ultimate freedom of Israel and the rebuilding of the temple in Jerusalem. In fact the LORD called a total of six men as intercessors; each with an appointed task, a spiritual mandate, a cohesive network to bring about His divine plan for His people. The sixth part of a hin of water was a source of cleansing, purification, and reassurance that the LORD was still with them and cared much about their future as a nation. In those days of gloom and despair, the LORD GOD had a plan to preserve a remnant for Himself. The oil and wine of the good times was but a memory and the water of cleansing was needed for repentance and purification. A sixth part therefore is: Ezekiel interceding among his brethren by the river Chebar; Daniel, Shadrach, Meshach, Abed-Nego doing their part at the King's palace; and lastly, King Cyrus; who would be the new super power in Persia. This was a total of six men to make up the whole; the LORD'S instrument for Israel's freedom and restoration of Jerusalem, the city of GOD. Let's read Daniel 2:47-49; 2 Chronicles 36:22, 23 and Ezra 1:5-8 NKJV: *The king answered Daniel, and said, "Truly your GOD is the GOD of gods, the LORD of kings, and a revealer of secrets, since you could reveal this secret." Then the king promoted Daniel and gave him many great gifts; and he mane him ruler over the whole province of Babylon, and chief administrator over all the wise men of Babylon. Also Daniel petitioned the king, and he set Shadrach, Meshach, and Abed-Nego over the affairs of the province of Babylon; but Daniel sat in the gate of the King. . . . Now in the first year of Cyrus King of Persia, that the word of the LORD by the mouth of Jeremiah might be fulfilled, the LORD stirred up the spirit of Cyrus the king of Persia, so that he made a proclamation throughout all his kingdom, and also put it in writing, saying, Thus says Cyrus king of Persia: All the kingdoms of the earth the LORD GOD of heaven has given me. And He has commanded me to build Him a house at Jerusalem which is in Judah. Who is among you of all His people? May the LORD his GOD be with him, and let him go up . . . . Then the heads of the fathers' houses of Judah and Benjamin, and the priests and the Levites, with all whose spirits God had moved, arose to go up and build the house of the LORD which is in Jerusalem. And all those who were around them encouraged them with articles of silver and gold, with goods and livestock, and with precious things, besides all that was willing offered. King Cyrus also brought out the articles of the house of the LORD, which Nebuchadnezzar had taken from Jerusalem and put in the temple of his gods; and Cyrus king of Persia brought them out by the hand of Mithredath the treasurer, and counted them out to Sheshbazzar the prince of Judah.* The records of these books are only a snap shot of the mighty acts of GOD towards His people during dark times. GOD's selected team; Ezekiel and Daniel, Shadrach and Meshach, Abed-Nego and King Cyrus, were a network of six men over a period of seventy years; each used by the LORD to prepare Israel for their homecoming, as a demonstration of His infinite love and mercy, grace and redemption.

The LORD continued to explain to the prophet his dietary restrictions. An observation was noted here, that He called the bread barley cakes. Remember, barley was only one of the ingredients used for the making of this bread, yet Abba Father named the bread barley cakes. The prophet was also taken by surprise by the LORD's direction to bake this special bread using human excrement as fuel. What could have been the reason for calling the bread barley cakes and why such a detestable order to use human feces as fuel? The answer lies in the fact that the LORD's vigilant zeal for His people was abused and barley which is symbolic of His jealousy was chosen for the name of the cakes. The second observation noted, was that barley was the number two ingredient and this number is symbolic of either agreement or disagreement. In this case it is used in converse because the LORD had a case against the whole house of Israel. Lastly, feces are symbolic of sin. Ezekiel successfully pleaded with the LORD and He granted the prophet's desire; instead of using human waste for fuel, Ezekiel was told to use cow's dung instead. The exchange of the source of fuel was by no means to lessen the punishment but a display of GOD'S mercy.

As part of the temple offerings, dung was used as the sin offering; Exodus 29:14 states: *But the flesh of the bullock, and his skin, and his dung, shalt thou burn with fire without the camp: it is a sin offering.* The scepter of righteousness was broken; a dark cloud of disease and death loomed over the settlers of Chebar because of their rebellion. In Deuteronomy 31:16-18 the LORD predicts the disobedience of Israel: *The LORD said to Moses, "Behold you are about to lie down with your fathers;, and these people will rise and play the harlot with the strange gods of the land, into the midst of which they are going, and will forsake Me and break My covenant which I have made with them. Then My anger will be kindled against them in that day, and I will forsake them and hide My face from them, and they will be consumed, and many evils and troubles will come upon them; so that they will say in that day, 'Is it not because our God is not among us that these evils have come upon us?' But I will surely hide My face in that day because of all the evils which they will do, for they will turn to other gods,* NASB. Israel in the eyes of their captors was considered abandoned by their GOD. Unbeknown to them, they were however not forgotten; Jeremiah 25:12-13 applying the NLT states: *'Then, after the seventy years of captivity are over, I will punish the king of Babylon and his people for their sins," says the LORD. "I will make the country of the Babylonians a waste land forever. I will bring upon them all the terrors I have promised in this book – all the penalties announced by Jeremiah against the nation.* The Lord would however avenge the oppressors of His people Israel in due time.

Chapter 5

Verses 1-4

And thou, son of man, take thee a sharp knife, take thee a barber's razor, and cause it to pass upon thy beard: then take thee balances to weigh, and divide the hair. Thou shalt burn with fire a third part in the midst of the city, when the days of the siege are fulfilled: and thou shalt take a third part, and smite about it with a knife: and a third part thou shalt scatter in the wind; and I will draw out a sword after them. Thou shalt also take thereof a few in number, and bind them in thy skirts. Then take of them again, and cast them in the midst of the fire, and burn them in the fire; for thereof shall a fire come forth in all the house of Israel.

Being a priest and prophet, Ezekiel's obedience, integrity and humility, was once again put to the test. Leviticus 21:5 quoting the NIV states: *Priests must not shave their heads or shave off the edges of their beards or cut their bodies. They must be holy to their God and must not profane the name of their God. Because they present the food offerings to the LORD, the food of their God, they are to be holy.* The LORD was not breaking His own teachings which governed the religious affairs of His people, He was simply making a point that the house of Israel would realize He was not pleased with them therefore the marring of the hair or beard was a demonstration of their revolt against Him.

As an intercessor to the house of Israel, Ezekiel faithfully accepted his orders. The people were rebellious and Ezekiel's actions would be an outward expression of the

LORD'S displeasure. The book of Ezekiel is filled with many symbolisms and once again the LORD speaks to the nation by employing a series of these arbitrary signs. Sampson's hair was shaven from his head, and the source of his strength waned (see Judges 16:5; 16-19). Israel, like Samson, had no inherent strength; their strength was divinely given. Israel rejected GOD, who was their strength and He departed (Psalm 18; 22:19; 27; 28:7; 37:39; 62:7). Ezekiel's shaved head and beard was a sign to Israel that they had polluted themselves, thereby becoming a reproach unto GOD. A very important point worth highlighting is the fact that man has no power to grow his hair; the hair and beard will re-grow naturally because of its life sustaining follicles, which symbolically points to the future re-establishment and spiritual renewal of God's people, as a remnant will be saved thereby continuing the legacy of the Jewish people.

Ezekiel's was ordered to weigh and divide the hair. Weighing the hair is symbolic of justice and truth. Proverbs 11:1 states: *A false balance is abomination to the LORD: but a just weight is His delight.* The LORD delights Himself in justice; His justice is perfect and His sentence fair. The prophet now weighs the hair to demonstrate that the strength of Israel was cut off and they were now being judged for their unrighteousness. The LORD'S scale never lies; it will expose deceit and sin and reveal truth and righteousness. A good example and reference would be metal; it may appear to be of value at a glance; but its authenticity and true value is revealed when it is weighed. The heart of Israel was being revealed by the one who knows all its secrets. The house of Israel was placed in Abba Father's just scale, and came up lacking.

Ezekiel was instructed to burn a third of the hair in the center of the city, which was symbolic of the coming judgment and the severity of their punishment at the hands of the Babylonians upon those who remained in Jerusalem. The second and third portion of hair would be inflicted with the heavy blows of a sword which meant that they would be persecuted and killed, and those who survived the onslaught, would be scattered throughout the earth. These were three woes of judgment against the whole house of Israel, each carrying an equally unpleasant punishment. There is however hope because a remnant would return to Jerusalem, some with great festivity and jubilation, while others with tears of joy.

Verses 5-10

Thus saith the Lord GOD; This is Jerusalem: I have set it in the midst of the nations and countries that are round about her. And she hath changed My judgments into wickedness more that the nations, and My statutes more than the countries that are round about her: for they have refused My judgments and My statutes, they have not walked in them. Therefore thus saith the Lord GOD; Because ye multiplied more than the nations that are round about you, and have not walked in My statutes, neither have kept My judgments, neither have done according to the judgments of the nations that are round about you; therefore thus saith the Lord GOD; Behold, I, even I, am against thee, and will execute judgments in the midst of thee in the sight of the nations, and I will do in thee that which I have not done, and whereunto I will not do any more the like, because of all thine abominations. Therefore the fathers shall eat the sons in the midst of thee, and the sons shall eat their fathers; and I will execute judgments in thee, and the whole remnant of thee will I scatter into all the winds.

We see the plurality of the Godhead in their consensual agreement by positioning Jerusalem at the center above all nations and countries thereby establishing this city as their own. The state of Israel and the city of Jerusalem is a spiritual time clock that ultimately points to the return of Yeshua Messiah the Anointed One of God. Jerusalem is called the city of GOD yet corruption and defilement consumed it, thereby setting in motion the judgment of GOD. The whole earth would hear of Israel's punishment and bemoan them. If God's judgment and punishment was so severe against Israel; what will be His ruling against the nations that have turned away and publically rejected Him? Dearth fell upon the land and the people resorted to cannibalism. Abba Father will never endorse such acts of human degradation but people will resort to detestable and unimaginable practices to preserve their own life even to the detriment of others.

Being acutely aware of human propensities, the Lord GOD verbalized what was already in the heart of the people. 2 Kings 6:25-29 applying the NIV gives an example of what people will do, when faced with starvation and death: *There was a great famine in the city; the siege lasted so long that a donkey's head sold for eighty shekels of silver, and a quarter of a cab of seed pods for five shekels. As the king of Israel was passing by on the wall, a woman cried to him, "Help me, my lord the king!" The king replied, "If the LORD does not help you, where can I get help for you? From the threshing floor? From the winepress? Then he asked her, "What's the matter?" She answered, "This woman said to me, 'Give up your son so we may eat him today, and tomorrow we'll eat my son.' So we cooked my son and ate him. The next day I said to her, 'Give up your son so we may eat him,' but she had hidden him."* This was a real famine in Israel, which showed the lowest of human degradation; the people actually resorted to cannibalism. In Jeremiah 17:9-10 we read: "*The human heart is most deceitful of all things, and desperately wicked. Who really knows how bad it is? But I, the LORD, search all hearts and examine secret motives. I give all people their due rewards, according to what their actions deserve,*" NLT. The Lord GOD was not promoting cannibalism; He simply exposed what was already in their hearts. The edict for such an atrocity would be the dismantling and fragmenting of the house of Israel. Psalm 103:8-14 states: *The LORD is merciful and gracious, slow to anger, and plenteous in mercy. He will not always chide: neither will He keep His anger forever. He hath not dealt with us after our sins; nor rewarded us according to our iniquities. For as the heaven is high above the earth, so great is His mercy toward them that fear Him. As far as the east is from the west, so far hath He removed our transgressions from us. Like as a father pitieth his children, so the LORD pitieth them that fear Him. For He knoweth our frame; He remembereth that we are dust.* We reap what we have sown. How can anyone accuse Abba Father of being unjust? Nothing goes un-noticed; the pleasure of sin is temporary, it will be judged and rewarded when least expected.

Verses 11-17

Wherefore, as I live, saith the Lord GOD; Surely, because thou hast defiled My sanctuary with all the detestable things, and with all thine abominations, therefore will I also diminish thee; neither shall mine eye spare, neither will I have any pity. A third part of thee shall die with the pestilence, and with famine shall they be consumed in the midst of thee: and a third part shall fall by the sword round about thee; and I will scatter a third part into all the winds, and I will draw out a sword after them. Thus shall mine anger be accomplished, and I will cause My fury to rest upon them, and I will be comforted: and they shall know that I the LORD have spoken it in My zeal, when I have accomplished My fury in them. Moreover I will make thee waste, and a reproach among the nations that are round about thee, in the sight of all that pass by. So it shall be a reproach and a taunt, an instruction and an astonishment unto the nations that are round about thee, when I shall execute judgments in thee in anger and in fury and in furious rebukes. I the LORD have spoken it. When I shall send upon them the evil arrows of famine, which shall be for their destruction, and which I will send to destroy you: and I will increase the famine upon you, and will break your staff of bread: so will I send upon you famine and evil beasts, and they shall bereave thee; and pestilence and blood shall pass through thee; and I will bring the sword upon thee. I the LORD have spoken it.

These verses are closely related to Ezekiel 5:1-4; the LORD repeats His judgment, which means He would not relent or repent, He had spoken and His rulings were final. The Supreme Judge of Israel is GOD Himself and His determination was impartial needing no further debate. Israel was culpable; plea bargains were useless and the punishment for their crimes handed down. Psalm 9:7-11 states: *The law of the LORD is perfect, converting the soul: the testimony of the LORD is sure, making wise the simple. The statutes of the LORD are right, rejoicing the heart: the commandment of the LORD is pure, enlightening the eyes. The fear of the LORD is clean, enduring for ever: the judgments of the LORD are true and righteous altogether. More to be desired are they than gold, yea, than much gold: sweeter also than honey and the honeycomb. Moreover by them is thy servant warned: and in keeping of them there is great reward.* The LORD GOD and His Word are immutable. He lays down the foundation for righteous and peaceable living; therefore, He must judge sin. Plagues or pestilence, unrest or famine, which comes upon a land, is the direct result of continued and unrepentant rebellion against GOD. Israel could have enjoyed His favor, but they choose a rebellious and profane lifestyle instead; one for which they would regret.

Despite all of this Israel remains under the protective radar of GOD and in spite of their thorns of persecution and threats of complete annihilation; the GOD of Israel is their righteous Judge and it is at His ruling that the people are punished. For those who are parents, what would be your reaction if someone takes it upon themselves to arbitrarily and severely punish your child or children without your approval? Isn't Abba Father a Parent also? Hebrews 12:6-11 applying the NKJV states: *"For whom the LORD loves He chastens, and scourges every son whom He receives." If you endure chastening, God deals with you as with sons; for what son is there whom a father does not chasten? But if you are without chastening, of which all become partakers, then you are illegitimate and not sons. Furthermore, we have had human fathers who corrected us, and we paid them respect. Shall we not much more readily be in subjection to the Father of spirits and live? For they indeed for a few days chastened us as seemed best to them, but He for our profit, that we may be partakers of His holiness. Now no chastening seems to be joyful for the present, but painful; nevertheless, afterward it yields the peaceable fruit of righteousness to those who have been trained by it.* Justice was served and the wise in heart remained upright, as the whole nation experienced great adversities.

Chapter 6

Verses 1-4

And the word of the LORD came unto me, saying, Son of man, set thy face toward the mountains of Israel, and prophesy against them, and say, Ye mountains of Israel, hear the word of the Lord GOD; Thus saith the Lord GOD to the mountains, and to the hills, and to the rivers, and to the valleys; Behold, I, even I, will bring a sword upon you, and I will destroy your high places. And your altars shall be desolate, and your images shall be broken: and I will cast down your slain men before your idols.

Ezekiel states: "*And the word of the LORD came unto me saying,*" what a marvelous and humbling experience. This servant of GOD had found both favor and pleasure with Abba Father and was granted the privilege of both hearing and seeing the Word of God, the pre-incarnate Son once again. The prophet instantly knew he was about to be given prophetic instructions for his brethrens. This however was only the beginning, because the LORD would visit and speak with Ezekiel on many other occasions. Once again the LORD employs symbolic language to instruct Ezekiel to prophesy to the mountains, hills, rivers, and valleys, but in fact He was describing places where the heathen nations would set up their shrines to worship their visible pagan idols as well as the host of heaven. Israel is monotheistic; they serve the Eternal Existing One, Creator of the visible and the invisible. This knowledge however did not stop them from following the ways of the heathens. The LORD now exclaimed that He was bringing a sword to these places and the sword is in reference to His judgment and not His protection. Israel had been repeatedly warned not to follow after the gods of the heathen; they responded affirmatively, but not long thereafter, broke their vows and adopted the religious culture of their neighbors. No one practicing pagan worship would be spared. The people forgot that the eyes of the LORD were keeping watch over Israel at all times.

Verses 5-10

And I will lay the dead carcasses of the children of Israel before their idols; and I will scatter your bones round about your altars. In all your dwelling places the cities shall be laid waste, and the high places shall be desolate; that your altars may be laid waste and made desolate, and your idols may be broken and cease, and your images may be cut down, and your works may be abolished. And the slain shall fall in the midst of you, and ye shall know that I am the LORD. Yet will I leave a remnant, that ye may have some that shall escape the sword among the nations, when ye shall be scattered through the countries. And they that escape of you shall remember Me among the nations whither they shall be carried captives, because I am broken with their whorish heart, which hath departed from Me, and with their eyes, which go a whoring after their idols: and they shall loathe themselves for the evils which they have committed in all their abominations. And they shall know that I am the LORD, and that I have not said in vain that I would do this evil unto them.

Israel's repeated warnings by the prophets were to no avail, judgment was eminent and closer than they thought. This land and people were called by GOD to be an example to the world but failed. Only a small surviving group of Hebrews would be left as the rest were scattered abroad. There would be no Torah among them. The descendants of the remnant would have to rely solely on oral tradition to explain the cause of their sufferings. The Babylonians trashed Jerusalem and razed it by fire; all temple treasures were carted off by them and items once used in the service and worship of the LORD, was placed in the temple of the Babylonian gods or stored among the treasures of the King (see Ezra 1:7; 5:14; 6:5; 2 Kings 24:13; 2 Chronicles 36:7). Cities were left desolate except for a handful of peasants. Temple worship and sacrifices would come to an abrupt cessation that would last for seventy years. Images that were a mark of Israel's idolatrous behavior were smashed to smithereens; thereby proving that they were indeed worthless, being the workings of man's imagination and evil heart. There is only one GOD and the worship whether of images, idols, or individuals would end in the judgment of the LORD upon a people.

Israel repeatedly broke the heart of GOD as they lusted after the gods of the heathens. Ezekiel knew in his soul that the predicament of Israel was by their doing. He also knew that they were his brethren and as a priest and prophet he had to intercede in their behalf as the LORD had instructed. GOD has always had compassion for His people. He would send deliverers when they repented; although soon thereafter, they would forget His goodness towards them. Psalm 78:32-42 states: *In spite of all this they still sinned and did not believe in His wonderful works. So He brought their days to an end in futility and their years in sudden terror. When He killed them, then they sought Him, and returned and searched diligently for God; and they remembered that God was their rock, and the Most High God their Redeemer. But they deceived Him with their mouth and lied to Him with their tongue. For their heart was not steadfast toward Him, nor were they faithful in His covenant. But He, being compassionate, forgave their iniquity and did not destroy them; and often He restrained His anger and did not arouse all His wrath. Thus He remembered that they were but flesh, a wind that passes and does not return. How often they rebelled against Him in the wilderness and grieved Him in the desert! Again and again they tempted God, and pained the Holy One of Israel. They did not remember His power, the day when He redeemed them from the adversary,* NASB. The Word of GOD speaks for itself; recurrent blatant sin will be judged; God is patient, but never must we forget, that He has a low tolerance for un-repentant sin. The LORD God created us especially for His glory; but He forces no one to either serve Him or worship Him; that choice is ours. Time is about over, we are surviving in this wicked world only by the grace of the Almighty.

Verses 11-14

Thus saith the Lord GOD; Smite with thine hand, and stamp with thy foot, and say, Alas for all the evil abominations of the house of Israel! for they shall fall by the sword, by the famine, and by the pestilence. He that is far off shall die of the pestilence; and he that is near shall fall by the sword; and he that remaineth and is besieged shall die by the famine: thus will I accomplish My fury upon them. Then shall ye know that I am the LORD, when their slain men shall be among their idols round about their altars, upon every high hill, in all the tops of the mountains, and under every green tree, and under every thick oak, the place where they did offer sweet savor to all their idols. So will I stretch out My hand upon them, and make the land desolate, yea, more desolate that the wilderness toward Diblath [Riblah], in all heir habitations: and they shall know that I am the LORD.

Ezekiel embarked on a prophetic role-play, of clapping his hands and stomping his feet frantically to portray the displeasure and disgust of the LORD against the house of Israel. Israel had stepped from under the safety of their GOD into the domain of the king of Babylon who would afflict and kill them. Those not killed would die from starvation or diseases and those living among the ruins of the once glorious city of Jerusalem would not escape death either. 2 Chronicles 36:15-21 quoting the NASB states: *The LORD, the God of their fathers, sent word to them again, and again by His messengers, because He had compassion on His people and on His dwelling place; but they continually mocked the messengers of God, despised His words and scoffed at His prophets, until the wrath of the LORD arose against His people, until there was no remedy. Therefore He brought up against them the king of the Chaldeans who slew their young men with the sword in the house of their sanctuary, and had no compassion on young man or virgin, old man or infirm, He gave them all into his hand. All the articles of the house of God, great and small, and the treasures of the house of the LORD, and the treasures of the king and of his officers, he brought them all to Babylon. Then they burned the house of God and broke down the wall of Jerusalem, and burned all its fortified buildings with fire and destroyed all its valuable articles. Those who had escaped from the sword he carried away to Babylon; and they were servants to him and to his sons until the rule of the kingdom of Persia, to fulfill the word of the LORD by the mouth of Jeremiah, until the land had enjoyed its Sabbaths. All the days of its desolation it kept Sabbaths until seventy years were complete.* The LORD does not take pleasure in the death of evil people (Ezekiel 18:23; 33:11). Let us recap Israel's fall from grace from Jeremiah 2:19-30: *Thine own wickedness shall correct thee, and thy backslidings shall reprove thee: know therefore and see that it is an evil thing and bitter, that thou hast forsaken the LORD thy God, and that My fear is not in thee, saith the Lord GOD of host. For of old time I have broken thy yoke, and burst thy bands; and thou saidst, I will not transgress; when upon every high hill and under every green tree thou wanderest, playing the harlot. Yet I had planted thee a noble vine, wholly a right seed: how then art thou turned into the degenerate plant of a strange vine unto Me? For though thou wash thee with nitre [lye], and take thee much soap, yet thine iniquity is marked before Me, saith the LORD GOD. How canst thou say, I am not polluted, I have not gone after Baalim? See thy way in the valley, know what thou hast done: thou art a swift dromedary traversing her ways; a wild ass used to the wilderness, that snuffeth up the wind at her pleasure; in her occasion who can turn her away? All they that seek her will not weary themselves; in her month they shall find her. Withhold thy foot from being unshod, and thy throat from thirst: but thou saidest, There is no hope: no; for I have loved strangers, and after them will I go. As the thief is ashamed when he is found, so is the house of Israel ashamed; they; their kings, their princes, and their priests, and their prophets, saying to a stock, Thou art my father; and to a stone, Thou hast brought me forth: for they have turned their back unto Me, and not their face: but in the time of their trouble they will say, Arise, and save us. But where are thy gods that thou hast made thee? Let them arise, if they can save thee in the time of thy trouble: for according to the number of thy cities are thy gods, O Judah. Wherefore will ye plead with Me? Ye all have transgressed against Me, saith the LORD. In vain have I smitten your children; they received no correction: your own sword hath devoured your prophets, like a destroying lion,* (see also 2 Kings 17:7-23 for further readings).

Total ruin was pronounced by the LORD upon His people for their idolatrous lifestyle, for rejecting the Word of the LORD, and for slaying His messengers. The LORD declared to stretch out His hand upon Israel, which meant the indignation of His judgment in retribution for their sins was stirred. The stretched out hand of the LORD is definitely not a good sign; it speaks of a last resort, and a judgment that would not be delayed. Horrific days were ahead as the insolence of Israel's towards the only true GOD was about to be rewarded. A nation whose foundation is built upon the LORD reigns in peace but a nation that frowns upon His righteousness has sealed their own fate.

Chapter 7

Verses 1-4

Moreover the word of the Lord came unto me, saying, Also, thou son of man, thus saith the Lord GOD unto the land of Israel; An end, the end is come upon the four corners of the land. Now is the end come upon thee, and will judge thee according to thy ways, and will recompense upon thee all thine abominations. And Mine eye shall not spare thee, neither will I have pity: but I will recompense thy ways upon thee, and thine abominations shall be in the midst of thee: and ye shall know that I am the LORD.

We see verse one opening with the word, "moreover," which meant in addition to the judgments previously pronounced there were still more to come as the bad news had gotten even worse. All would be affected one way or the other, from the greatest to the least. The verdict was final, the ruling upheld. Glorious Israel called to be an example to the earth is judged and her punishment would be felt both far and near. The list of Israel's crimes was exceedingly lengthy, spanning several hundred years and justice was finally being served upon reckless Israel. Abba Father came with a guilty verdict, seventy years of Babylonian oppression. After this period of time, the LORD would re-convene for a clemency hearing under the reign of a new monarchy governed by the prophesied king Cyrus. Isaiah 44:24-28 states: *Thus saith the LORD, thy Redeemer, and He that formed thee from the womb, I am the LORD that maketh all things; that stretched forth the heavens alone; that spreadeth abroad the earth by Myself; that frustrateth the tokens of the liars, and maketh diviners mad; that turneth wise men backward, and maketh their knowledge foolish; that confirmeth the word of His servant, and performeth the counsel of His messengers; that saith to Jerusalem, Thou shalt be inhabited; and to the cities of Judah, Ye shall be built, and I will raise up the decayed places thereof: that saith to the deep, Be dry, and I will dry up thy rivers: that saith of Cyrus, he is my shepherd, and shall perform all My pleasure: even saying to Jerusalem, Thou shalt be built; and to the temple, Thy foundation shall be laid.*

The name Cyrus means "Son," which takes on a dual interpretation because it also points to the coming of Yeshua Messiah; the Anointed One; the only begotten of Abba Father, who would set His people free for the final time in the history of man, never again to suffer indignation, persecution or estrangement. Yeshua Messiah, being the Root and Offspring of David, from the tribe of Judah, will reclaim Jerusalem and the whole house of Israel. The Apostle Paul states in Romans 1:18-21 quoting the NIV: *The wrath of God is being revealed from heaven against all the godlessness and wickedness of men who suppress the truth by their wickedness, since what may be known about God is plain to them, because God has made it plain to them. For since the creation of the world God's invisible qualities His eternal power and divine nature have been clearly seen, being understood from what has been made, so that men are without excuse.* The ten northern tribes of Israel were already exiled in Assyria (see 2 Kings 17:7-24). Foreigners occupied Samaria and Jerusalem a well fortified city, which gave the residence of the south a false sense of security, but now it lies in ruins.

The army of King Nebuchadnezzar laid siege on Jerusalem for several years resulting in a severe psychological breakdown of its residents. Finally through desperation, hunger and poor advice from leadership, the city fell. Some dwellers were killed and others thrown into prison; it was the settlers of Jerusalem's turn to be humbled by the LORD. They saw the plight of their brethren who once lived in the northern kingdom but believed in their own strength to survive. The fortified city walls of Jerusalem accompanied by specialized security strategies were no match for psychological warfare. It broke the spirit of the people causing internal frictions between leaders and subjects, which lead to distrust, mayhem, and an unwilling surrender to the Babylonians. The hands of the LORD were lifted and it was far too late for repentance. Like the northern kingdom, the end had come for Judah as well.

Verses 5-16

Thus saith the LORD GOD: An evil, behold, is come. An end is come, the end is come: it watcheth for thee; behold, it is come. The morning is come unto thee, O thou that dwellest in the land: the time is come, the day of trouble is near, and not the sounding again of the mountains. Now will I shortly pour out My fury upon thee, and accomplish Mine anger upon thee: and I will judge thee according to thy ways, and will recompense thee for all thine abominations. And Mine eye shall not spare, neither will I have pity: I will recompense thee according to thy ways and thine abominations that are in the midst of thee; and ye shall know that I am the LORD that smiteth. Behold the day, behold, it is come: the morning is gone forth; the rod hath blossomed, pride hath budded. Violence is risen up into a rod of wickedness: none of them shall remain, nor of their multitude, nor of any of theirs: neither shall there be wailing for them. The time is come, the day draweth near: let not the buyer rejoice, nor the seller mourn: for wrath is upon all the multitude thereof. For the seller shall not return to that which is sold, although they were yet alive: for the vision is touching the whole multitude thereof, which shall not return; neither shall any strengthen himself in the iniquity of his life. They have blown the trumpet, even to make all ready; but none goeth to the battle: for My wrath is upon all the multitude thereof. The sword is without, and the pestilence and the famine within: he that is in the field shall die with the sword; and he that is in the city, famine and pestilence shall devour him. But they that escape of them shall escape, and shall be on the mountains like doves of the valley, all of them mourning, every one for his iniquity.

There were many prophets sent by GOD in the past; warning the house of Israel to repent but their words fell on mostly deaf ears. The prophet Zephaniah declared an oracle of the coming destruction of Jerusalem a little over fifty years prior to the reign of king Zedekiah, for it was during his reign that the prophetic utterance was fulfilled (see Zephaniah 1:1-18). The LORD GOD, who spoke these words through Zephaniah, now informs Ezekiel of His pending judgment. We must remember that Ezekiel was already in captivity when he saw visions of GOD and received his prophetic mantle. The LORD GOD explained to Ezekiel both the reason and remedy for Judah's punishment, so with great boldness, the prophet sets out to be GOD's mouthpiece to them. The old would recall their past sins and that of their fathers, while the young would bemoan their lawlessness and unwillingness to change.

Violence had stirred up the breeding ground for all sort of evil, Judah did what seemed right in their eyes as their leaders and elders refrained to openly rebuke them; in fact, they were not role models for the young and impressionable ones who followed their poor examples. Judgment had come and all would be affected. Jeremiah 16:9-13 states: *For thus saith the LORD of hosts, the God of Israel; Behold, I will cause to cease out of this place in your eyes, and in your days, the voice of mirth, and the voice of gladness, the voice of the bridegroom, and the voice of the bride. And it shall come to pass, when thou shalt show this people all these words, and they shall say unto thee, Wherefore hath the LORD pronounced all this great evil against us? Or what is our iniquity? Or what is our sin that we have committed against the LORD our God? Then shalt thou say unto them, Because your fathers have forsaken Me, saith the LORD, and have walked after other gods, and have served them, and have worshiped them, and have forsaken Me, and have not kept My law: and ye have done worse than your fathers; for, behold, ye walk every one after the imagination of his evil heart, that they may not hearken unto Me: therefore will I cast you out of this land into a land that ye know not, neither ye nor your fathers; and there shall ye serve other gods day and night; where I will not show you favor,* (see also Isaiah 24:1-13). These are all prophecies of double reference: that which has happened before, will undoubtedly happen again in the course of history. Israel is the olive tree while Gentile Believers are engrafted into its vine (see Romans 11:16-27).

There was now total debacle, anarchy, and riotous outburst; everyone looking out for himself. Mass confusion was spreading like wildfire as fear gripped the city of Jerusalem. The alarm was sounded for all soldiers to prepare for battle, but those enlisted to serve, were ill-prepared and knew they were outnumbered; fighting would be mere suicide. The army of Nebuchadnezzar was closing in, the people had rejected sound advice, and the LORD GOD was left without any alternative, but to stop His ears to their plea for mercy. Can you see what is happening here? Those who escaped the sword also died a horrible death. Disease and starvation was rampant, yet there was no remedy. The remnant that escaped to the mountains would spend their days and nights in fear; fleeing when no one was in pursuit.

Verses 17-22

They shall also gird themselves with sackcloth, and horror shall cover them; and shame shall be upon all faces, and baldness upon all their heads. They shall cast their silver in the streets, and their gold shall be removed: their silver and their gold shall not be able to deliver them in the day of the wrath of the LORD: they shall not satisfy their souls, neither fill their bowels: because it is a stumbling block of their iniquity. As for the beauty of his ornament, he set it in majesty: but they made the images of their abominations and of their detestable things therein: therefore have I set it far from them. And I will give it into the hands of the strangers for a prey, and to the wicked of the earth for a spoil; and they shall pollute it. My face will I turn also from them, and they shall pollute My secret place: for the robbers shall enter into it, and defile it.

It is said that a nation is as strong as its defense system but is this factual? Mankind has always forgotten that his ways are known by the LORD and victory would only be truly attained by those who trusted in His name (Psalm 20:7, 8; Jeremiah 6:10-26). The citizens of Jerusalem were caught off guard; they were ill-prepared to handle the vast Babylonian army as the siege continued without an end in sight. As the people reached their breaking point, without warning, Nebuchadnezzar's army launched a surprise attack upon Jerusalem; killing, burning, scattering and also seizing that which was of value. They had no mercy upon the rich or poor, small or great; all felt the devastating effect of this ruthless army who did not know the GOD of the Hebrews. The people of Jerusalem were in mourning, being overtaken by horror and grief as calamity struck. Their loved ones lay dead or dying and those left in the city were taken as slaves, while those who fled to the mountains were in constant fear for their lives. The few left in the ruins of Jerusalem were now tenant farmers of the Babylonians: tilling the soil of the land they once owned.

Those who had great wealth could purchase neither favor nor freedom. Their riches that was once the source of their pride, power and contentment was now worthless. The LORD GOD remembered their golden calf; now, they were bound in chains of iron and their worthless idols were not able to save them from the cruel treatment of Nebuchadnezzar. For the next seventy years, Judah would long for freedom and the days when the Sabbaths and high holy days were celebrated. They would long for the spring and fall festivals and earnestly desire to see Jerusalem that great city once again. After seventy years of exile, would Israel continue to trifle with God with detestable images in His Holy Place?

Verses 23-27

Make a chain: for the land is full of bloody crimes, and the city is full of violence. Wherefore I will bring the worst of the heathen, and they shall possess their houses: I will also make the pomp of the strong to cease; and their holy places shall be defiled. Destruction cometh; and they shall seek peace, and there shall be none. Mischief shall come upon mischief, and rumor shall be upon rumor; then they shall seek a vision of the prophet; but the law shall perish from the priest, and counsel from the ancients. The king shall mourn, and the prince shall be clothed with desolation, and the hands of the people of the land shall be troubled: I will do unto them after their way, and according to their deserts will I judge them; and they shall know that I am the LORD.

A city which is rifled, ransacked, or plundered by acts of violence, inevitably becomes desolate. Ezekiel was next told by the LORD to make a chain, which spoke of the bondage of sin as well as the bondage of slavery. The city of Jerusalem was filled with idolatrous practices which were the gravest of all their crimes against the LORD. Jeremiah repeatedly warned the leaders and people: "*Thus says the LORD, 'Just so will I destroy the pride of Judah and the great pride of Jerusalem. This wicked people, who refuse to listen to My words, who walk in the stubbornness of their hearts and have gone after other gods to serve them and to bow down to them, let them be just like this waistband which is totally worthless. For as the waistband clings to the waist of a man, so I made the whole household of Israel and the whole household of Judah cling to Me,' declares the LORD, 'that they might be for Me a people, for renown, for praise and for glory; but they did not listen,'* " 13:9-11 NASB. Here lies the downfall of the northern and southern kingdom; they rejected truth, and for being bullheaded; landed in the evil clutches of the Babylonian king. This was certainly an indictment against them; for the least desirable of nations now possessed their homes and real estate.

Jeremiah who lived in Jerusalem during this dark period laments: *Who is he who speaks and it comes to pass, when the Lord has not commanded it? Is it not from the mouth of the Most High that woe and wellbeing proceed? Why should a living man complain, a man for the punishment of his sins? Let us search out and examine our ways, and turn back to the LORD; let us lift our hearts and hands to God in heaven. We have transgressed and rebelled; You have not pardoned. You have covered Yourself with anger and pursued us; You have slain and not pitied. You have covered Yourself with a cloud, that prayer should not pass through. You have made us an offscouring and refuse in the midst of the peoples. All our enemies have opened their mouths against us. Fear and snare have come upon us, desolation and destruction,* Lamentations 3:37-47 NKJV. The whole house of Israel made for themselves a bed of thorns; now they had to lay in it. Mischief was multiplied against Judah and the story of their enslavement was repeatedly changed by those who attempted to explain it. In utter desperation they sought for a prophet to inquire of the LORD; but there was no vision. Next they begged the priest to rehearse the Law, but there was no Torah. They searched out the camp for the aged men, surly they can help; but they uttered not a wise advice; even the king and his sons were in mourning, facing the same peril as they. Fear and confusion, weeping and hopelessness were the order of the day. They sought for help and insight but they themselves had no hindsight.

Chapter 8

Verses 1-5

And it came to pass in the sixth year, in the sixth month, in the fifth day of the month, as I sat in mine house, and the elders of Judah sat before me, that the hand of the LORD GOD fell upon me. Then I beheld, and lo a likeness as the appearance of fire: from the appearance of His loins even downward, fire; and from His loins even upward, as the appearance of brightness, as the color of amber. And He put forth the form of an hand, and took me by a lock of mine head; and the spirit lifted me up between the earth and the heaven, and brought me in the visions of God to Jerusalem, to the door of the inner gate that looketh toward the north; where was the seat of the image of jealousy. And, behold, the glory of the God of Israel was there, according to the vision that I saw in the plain. Then said He unto me, Son of man, lift up thine eyes now the way toward the north. So I lifted up mine eyes the way toward the north, and behold northward at the gate of the altar this image of jealousy in the entry.

Ezekiel gives precise timelines and locations for these visions. The exiles were now settled in their new surroundings where they had homes. It is said that the elders were seated before Ezekiel the prophet; indicating that they were seeking to hear a word from the LORD. Their request was granted but these leaders were in for a wakeup call as the LORD was about to expose their evil and secret deeds. As they sat, the weightiness of the presence of the LORD was perceived by Ezekiel and immediately the prophet saw a vision. Faster than the speed of thought, Ezekiel finds himself standing before the LORD, similar to the first vision by Chebar (Ezekiel 1:27). Whenever Ezekiel is taken away in these higher forms of visionary experiences, he is lost for words and this time is no different from the rest. He describes that from the waist of the LORD to His feet was a pulsating glow of light and heat; and from His waist upward, a beautiful orange transparency far more breathtaking than a sparkling bonfire.

As Ezekiel gazed in awe and wonder at the glory of the LORD, the Spirit of GOD lifts him by a portion of his hair above the earth and in an instant he found himself standing before the entrance of the doorway which leads to the inner court on the north side of the temple in the city of Jerusalem. There to his horror he saw still standing, the platform of the image that provoked the wrath of GOD; the final straw that brought judgment upon the people. Psalm 135:13-18 applying the NASB states: *Your name, O LORD, is everlasting, Your remembrance, O LORD, throughout all generations. For the LORD will judge His people and will have compassion on His servants. The idols of the nations are but silver and gold, the work of man's hands. they have mouths, but they do not speak; they have eyes, but they do not see; they have ears, but they do not hear, nor is there any breath at all in their mouths. Those who make them will be like them, yes, everyone who trusts in them.* What really was this image of jealousy that provoked the LORD God of Israel?

Once again the familiar sight of the glory of the LORD consumed the prophet's attention. Six years in captivity seemed like only a second, as Ezekiel recollects his first experience of being caught up in the presence of the LORD by the river Chebar (Ezekiel1:2-28). Being overwhelmed by GOD's glory and realizing that in spite of the fact that the people shared the holy temple of the LORD GOD with idols; the LORD never left because of His unbroken promise to be a Father unto them. The prophet could only see the platform of the image from the vantage point where he stood, but as he got closer to the entrance where the altar was located, to his utter bewilderment, there stood the image of jealousy.

Verses 6-10

He said furthermore unto me, Son of man, seest thou what they do? Even the great abominations that the house of Israel committeth here, that I should go far off from My sanctuary? But turn thee yet again, and thou shalt see greater abominations. And He brought me to the door of the court; and when I looked, behold a hole in the wall. Then said He unto me, Son of man dig now in the wall: and when I had digged in the wall, behold a door. And He said unto me, Go in, and behold the wicked abominations that they do here. So I went in and saw; and behold every form of creeping things, and abominable beasts, and all the idols of the house of Israel, portrayed upon the wall round about.

What sorrow the children of Israel caused the LORD; they were driven from their homeland and the truth is now being revealed. Grave idolatry was being practiced in secret and those who truly followed the commands of the LORD, were now suffering as well. In the construction of the tabernacle in the wilderness; the LORD gave Moses specific instructions for the fashioning of every aspect of it. To identify the exact location of this altar of jealousy lets revisit the layout of the first temple and its furnishings. Exodus 40:22-35 quoting the NIV states: *Moses placed the table in the Tent of Meeting on the north side of the tabernacle outside the curtain and set out the bread on it before the LORD, as the LORD commanded him. He placed the lampstand in the Tent of Meeting opposite the table on the south side of the tabernacle and set up the lamps before the LORD, as the LORD commanded him. Moses placed the gold altar in the Tent of Meeting in front of the curtain and burned fragrant incense on it, as the LORD commanded him. Then he put up the curtain at the entrance to the tabernacle. He set the altar of burnt offering near the entrance to the tabernacle, the Tent of Meeting, and offered on it burnt offerings and grain offerings, as the LORD commanded him. He placed the basin between the Tent of Meeting and the altar and put water in it for washing, and Moses and Aaron and his sons used it to wash their hands and feet. They washed whenever they entered the Tent of Meeting or approached the altar, as the LORD commanded Moses. Then Moses set up the courtyard around the tabernacle and altar and put up the curtain at the entrance of the courtyard. And so Moses finished the work. Then the cloud covered the Tent of Meeting, and the glory of the LORD filled the tabernacle. Moses could not enter the Tent of Meeting because the cloud had settled upon it, and the glory of the LORD filled the tabernacle.* The tent of meeting on the north side was the location where the LORD GOD met with the children of Israel. This was indeed the Holy Place and the table of showbread was located there. The showbread is also known as: bread of display; shewbread; bread of faces, Bread of the Presence and Lechem Hapanim. On this table were twelve loaves divided into two equal rows (Exodus 25:23-3; Leviticus 24:5-9; Numbers 4:7). These loaves were replaced every Sabbath, and those removed were usually eaten by the priest because the bread was holy unto the LORD, therefore fit to be eaten by the Levites who ministered in the temple (1 Samuel 21:1-6; Matthew 12:3-4). The LORD was stirred to jealousy and the reason for this lies in the imbedded truth about the Holy Place.

As the symbolic reference to the Outer Court speaks of the flesh or body; the place where sin rules (Romans 7:18), the Holy Place points symbolically to the soul which is the seat of the emotions, thoughts and actions; this is the area of man in need of salvation and sanctification. The table of showbread was on the north side of the Tent of Meeting and the north is also symbolic of man in authority. Abba Father sent His Son who poured out His soul for ours (Isaiah 53:12). The table of showbread therefore speaks of none other than Yeshua Jesus Himself our Bread of Life (John 6:48-51). He is the one who came to seek and save the lost; He is the one that we feast upon. It was in the Holy Place; the realm of the soul; the place where the Bread of Life redeems man where this idol was located. Judah followed after the ways of the heathens, who offered bread unto their gods. They were foolish to set such an abominable object in the Holy Place, which indicated that this was a voluntary decision: an act of the freewill and therefore blatant rebellion because they knew the teachings that governed the life of every Hebrew. The table of showbread and its displays were:

- A symbol of GOD's presence among His people

- Yeshua Jesus the Bread of life and redeemer of the soul

- The surrender of the soul to the King of all king as represented by frankincense

- A memorial unto the LORD to restore His people unto Himself

- An everlasting covenant of God's government symbolic of the loaves being twelve in number

Ezekiel needed to see these things, because it cleared up all pre-conceived notions regarding the fall of Jerusalem and the exile of its people. The LORD GOD had not forsaken the house of Israel; His people had forsaken Him!

In this vision, the prophet stood at the threshold of the Holy Place where he noticed something quite unusual: there was a hole in the wall. Commanded by the LORD to dig at that site, Ezekiel realized that beyond this hole was a secret chamber. On opening the door to this chamber and to his horror; the elders of the children of Israel were engaged in loathsome evil rituals with detestable creatures. These citizens who were rulers over the people and who appeared to be God-fearing on the outside were a part of a heinous secret society unbeknown to those they vowed to serve. They were surrounded by portrayals on the walls which depicted hideous idolatrous symbols. Only a veil separated the Holy Place from the Holiest of all, yet just a step backwards these abominable practices were being performed as the leaders of the house of Israel departed from the truth. They swore to serve the LORD God, but in secret, pledged their allegiance to the underworld; forgetting that the LORD of heaven and earth was all-knowing and aware of their secrets and acts of idolatry.

The whole house of Israel had transgressed, instead of serving GOD; they turned to wicked and ungodly practices. The Apostle Paul wrote these inspiring words in Romans 1:18-25: *For the wrath of God is revealed from heaven against all ungodliness and unrighteousness of men, who hold the truth in unrighteousness; because that which may be known of God is manifest in them; for God hath shewed it unto them. For the invisible things of Him from the creation of the world are clearly seen, being understood by the things that are made, even His eternal power and Godhead; so that they are without excuse: because that, when they knew God, they glorified Him not as God, neither were thankful; but became vain in their imaginations, and their foolish hearts was darkened. Professing themselves to be wise, they became fools, and changed the glory of the uncorruptible God into an image made like to corruptible man, and to birds, and fourfooted beasts, and creeping things. Wherefore God also gave them up to uncleanness through the lust of their own hearts, to dishonor their own bodies between themselves: who changed the truth of God into a lie, and worshipped and serve the creature more that the Creator, who is blessed forever. Amen.* These heinous practices were occurring in the Holy Place; a designated area of the Tent of Meeting where only the priests were permitted to go. This was another reason why Ezekiel had to see these brazen sins against the LORD for himself, because the priests appeared holy on the outside but within they toyed with evil desires. The leaders of Israel had totally lost all reverence for Abba Father. This evil trickled down to the people who also did the same, thereby revealing the true intentions of their heart (Proverbs 21:2). Israel had missed the mark, they did not repent in brokenness; instead, their rebellion grew worse as they tested the integrity of GOD'S covenant with them. These were respected religious leaders and teachers of the law, but the LORD revealed to Ezekiel that both leaders and people had polluted themselves; some in secret and some openly.

Verses 11-12

And there stood before them seventy men of the ancients of the house of Israel, and in the midst of them stood Jaazaniah the son of Shaphan, with every man his censer in his hand; and a thick cloud of incense went up. Then said He unto me, Son of man, hast thou seen what the ancients of the house of Israel do in the dark, every man in the chambers of his imagery? For they say, The LORD seeth us not; the LORD hath forsaken the earth.

The elders, who should have been an example for the people, were the ring-leaders. Jaazaniah stood out because he was of a godly heritage; his father was a scribe named Shaphan who lived during the reign of King Josiah who restored the high moral and spiritual values of the worship of the God of Israel. This was the same King Josiah who upheld the strict adherence to the teachings of God during his reign (2 Kings 22:3-20; 23:1-25). Jaazaniah brothers were; Elasah (Jeremiah 29:3), Gemariah (Jeremiah 36:10), and Ahikam (Jeremiah 39:14; 2 Kings 25:22). Jaazaniah was singled out by name, because, as a leader of the people he should have known better, but choose the pathway of evil and provoked GOD to jealousy. As the LORD continued to reveal the vileness of the children of Israel to Ezekiel, the prophet observed that the crimes of the people were getting progressively worse.

Verses 13-15

He said also unto me, Turn thee yet again, and thou shalt see greater abominations that they do. Then He brought me to the door of the gate of the LORD's house which was toward the north; and, behold, there sat women weeping for Tammuz. Then said He unto me, Hast thou seen this, O son of man? Turn thee yet again, and thou shalt see greater abominations than these.

Why were women weeping for Tammuz when this idol was associated with fertility and rebirth? The possible reason lies in the fact that Israel was an agricultural society and the women believed that weeping before this idol, would cause this image to hear them, resurrect and produce a bumper crop the following harvesting season. This was indeed an abominable crime against the LORD GOD who never failed to supply all their needs. Tammuz was the image of jealousy seated in the Holy Place.

Verses 16-18

And He bought me into the inner court of the LORD's house, and, behold, at the door of the temple of the LORD, between the porch and the altar, were about five and twenty men, with their back toward the temple of the LORD, and their faces toward the east; and they worshipped the sun toward the east. Then He said unto me, Hast thou seen this, O son of man? Is it a light thing unto the house of Judah that they commit here? For they have filled the land with violence, and have returned to provoke Me to anger: and, lo, they put the branch to their nose. Therefore will I also deal in fury: Mine eye shall not spare, neither will I have pity: and though they cry in Mine ears with a loud voice, yet will I not hear them.

The Babylonians, Assyrians, and Egyptians were worshipers of the sun. Israel was warned by GOD not to participate in such idolatrous practices (see Deuteronomy 4:15-19; 17:2-

6), yet they adopted the ways of these nations. Genesis 1:14-15 states: *Then God said, "Let there be lights in the firmament of the heavens to divide the day from the night; and let them be for signs and seasons, and for days and years; and let them be for lights in the firmament of the heavens to give light on the earth"; and it was so,* NKJV. God created the sun, to give light, heat and life to the earth, yet His people, instead of thanking Him for all the works of His hands; bowed themselves towards the east to worship them.

Judah was assigned to the east side of the Tent (Numbers 2:3), this is also the place reserved for Yeshua Jesus. It was towards the east that the men were engaged in worshiping the sun, which was a crime punishable by death (Numbers 3:38; Deuteronomy 17:2-6). Judah was in total rebellion and their idolatrous worship of the sun was a grave indictment. To make matters worse; the people performed rituals, by placing the branch to their nose not knowing that they were humiliating Yeshua Jesus the Righteous BRANCH who was GOD's gift to humanity! These offenders had exceeded their limits of taunts and reprisal would be swift and without mercy. The religious leaders and teachers of the law would live without the presence of GOD, and to live without the protective covering of the LORD would be like living in hell itself. Until seventy years were fulfilled, the people would yearn for freedom, but there would be none.

Chapter 9

Verses 1-4

He cried also in mine ears with a loud voice, saying, Cause them that have charge over the city to draw near, even every man with his destroying weapon in his hand. And, behold, six men came from the way of the higher gate, which lieth toward the north, and every man a slaughter weapon in his hand; and one man among them was clothed with linen, with a writer's inkhorn by his side: and they went in, and stood beside the brazen altar. And the glory of the God of Israel was gone up from the cherub, whereupon He was, to the threshold of the house. And He called to the man clothed with linen, which had the writer's inkhorn by his side; and the LORD said unto him, Go through the midst of the city, through the midst of Jerusalem, and set a mark upon the foreheads of the men that sigh and that cry for all the abominations that be done in the midst thereof.

The vision continues and it grieved the LORD for what was about to take place among His people. The six men who appeared before Him for instructions were equipped with weapons to destroy and among them, was a very special person with a writer's inkhorn at his side to record the number of those who were slain as well as those whose life was spared. The decree was given to mark in the foreheads of those who mourn over the utter degradation and moral decay of the whole house of Israel, because they would be the only ones that would be spared. Before leaving to carry out their assignment, the six men convened at the brazen altar in the outer court because this altar was the designated place where burnt offerings and petitions were presented before the LORD (Exodus 29:10-14).

The outer court is symbolic of the flesh and sins, thereby marking the area where sin is judged. Two observations were also made here. First of all these were not angels because the Hebrew word used was **Ish** [376] indicating that they were men. In general, six is also the number assigned to man, therefore to say "six men," is employing double reference as two aspect of man is being revealed speaking volumes about our indecisiveness; an inherent weakness because of our fallen state. The second observation takes the form of a question. Was the man assigned to mark the righteous a typology of Yeshua or was He Yeshua Himself who suffered for us in the flesh thereby condemning sin in the flesh (1 Peter 4:1 Romans 8:3)?

Ezekiel will see this man once again and without any doubt his identity will be revealed. By Ezekiel's own account, the man wore a linen garment. The Hebrew word used here for linen is **Bad** [906]; it speaks of division or the act of dividing. These are the words of Yeshua Jesus recorded in Luke 12:51-57 applying the NKJV: *"Do you suppose that I came to give peace on earth? I tell you, not at all, but rather division. For from now on five in one house will be divided: three against two, and two against three. Father will be against son and son against father, mother against daughter and daughter against mother, mother-in-law against her daughter-in-law and daughter-in-law against mother-in-law."* Then He also said to the multitudes, *"Whenever you see a cloud rising out of the west, immediately you say, 'A shower is coming'; and so it is. And when you see the south wind blow, you say, 'There will be hot weather'; and there is. Hypocrites! You can discern the face of the sky and of the earth, but how is it you do not discern this time?* "*Yes, and why even of yourselves, do you not judge what is right?* This act of division was not one of favoritism, but points to the reality that many in a household will reject their own flesh and blood for having made up in their minds to follow Yeshua Jesus and His teachings and for this reason the home will be divided. Now the first of the six men; the only one identified by his clothing had a writer's inkhorn by his waist. It was his responsibility to separate the righteous from the unrighteous. These things will be repeated before the kingdom of God and His Son is revealed a second time upon the earth. After the marking of the people, the glory of the LORD prepares to exit and what great tribulations will follow His departure.

The lifting of the glory of GOD was an ominous sign that something catastrophic was about to overtake the land. As lawlessness and debauchery spread like an epidemic amongst the people; the presence of the LORD began departing from the Mercy Seat being borne by a mighty Cherub. Before leaving the Most Holy Place, which symbolically refers to the spirit of man, and the holy habitation of the Spirit of the Living God, the man with the writer's inkhorn on his side was summoned first and given orders to place a mark upon the foreheads of the people who abhorred the shameful, vile and detestable practices of those around them.

The LORD GOD judges sin and 2 Peter 2:4-10 states: *For if God spared not the angels that sinned, but cast them down to hell, and deliver them into chains of darkness, to be reserved unto judgment; and spared not the old world, but saved Noah the eighth person, a preacher of righteousness, bringing in the flood upon the world of the ungodly; and turning the cities of Sodom and Gomorrah into ashes condemned them with an overthrow, making them an example unto those that after should live ungodly; and delivered just Lot, vexed with the filthy conversation of the wicked: (for that righteous man dwelling among them, in seeing and hearing, vexed his righteous soul from day to day with their unlawful deeds); the Lord knoweth how to deliver the godly out of temptations, and to reserve the unjust unto the day of judgment to be punished: but chiefly them that walk after the flesh in the lust of uncleanness, and despise government. Presumptuous are they, self-willed, they are not afraid to speak evil of dignities.* One of the six men, who volunteered to carry out the will of the

LORD, was also given the task to spare the righteous by marking them in their foreheads. We see a similar sealing of the saints in Revelation 7:2-3: *And I saw another angel ascending from the east, having the seal of the living God: and he cried with a loud voice to the four angels, to whom it was given to hurt the earth and the sea, saying, Hurt not the earth, neither the sea, nor the trees, till we have sealed the servants of our God in their foreheads.*

Not only does the forehead describe the area above the eyebrows, its deeper meaning refers implicitly of the intellect, the faculty of the mind which has the capacity for making decisions; thereby concurring with the fact that only those who abhorred and grieved over the shameful offences being perpetrated by those they lived amongst, would survive the onslaught that was soon to follow. Evil begets evil and our deeds are actually seeds that will either bear fruitful things or refuge, worthy only to be discarded and be burnt (Mathew 24:24; Romans 12:9).

Verses 5-7

And to the others He said in mine hearing, Go ye after him through the city, and smite: let not your eye spare, neither have ye pity: slay utterly old and young, both maids and little children, and women: but come not near any man upon whom is the mark; and begin at My sanctuary. Then they began at the ancient men which were before the house. And He said unto them, Defile the house, and fill the courts with the slain: go ye forth. And they went forth, and slew in the city.

What devastation, the man clothed in linen first marked the righteous in their foreheads before destruction reigned all around them; beginning first in no other place, but the house of God (1 Peter 4:17-19). The house of GOD became defiled with all the dead bodies within and without, thus making it ceremonially unclean; Numbers 19:11-16 states: *He that toucheth the dead of any man shall be unclean seven days. He shall purify himself with it on the third day, and on the seventh day he shall be clean: but if he purify not himself on the third day, then the seventh day he shall not be clean. Whosoever toucheth the dead body of any man that is dead, and purifieth not himself, defileth the tabernacle of the LORD; and that soul shall be cut off from Israel: because the water of separation was not sprinkled upon him, he shall be unclean; his uncleanness is yet upon him. This is the law, when a man dieth in a tent: all that come into the tent, and all that is in the tent, shall be unclean seven days. And every open vessel, which hath no covering bound upon it, is unclean. And whosoever toucheth one that is slain with a sword in the open fields, or a dead body, or a bone of a man, or a grave, shall be unclean seven days.* Here the cleansing or purification period was seven days, but in this last act of separating the righteous from the wicked, the temple would lay waste for seventy years. After the fulfillment of these ten seasons of seven years of punishment, the temple would once more be cleansed, broken walls mended and the glory of the LORD restored. This will be fulfilled because the number ten symbolically points to the restoration of divine order!

Many important facts have been revealed so far in Ezekiel chapter nine which will have a profound effect on world history, the fulfillment of Bible prophecy and the return of Yeshua Jesus. The righteous must now pray for the spirit of Issachar to rest upon them; that they, too, like the sons of Issachar, may gain understanding into the time and season we live in. The next few years will be one of unrest, turmoil, and tremendous woes for all. Those who have hidden the Word of God in their hearts will never deny Yeshua Jesus, but the fate of the weak and carnal is uncertain. As it were in the days of Noah, so shall it be in these last days. Many will blaspheme the name of the LORD GOD and even the righteous will question their belief in One true God, His Son Yeshua whom Gentiles call Jesus and the ever present Holy Spirit abiding in us. Ponder these things:

6 = man; on the sixth day man was formed from the dust of the earth by the LORD God (Genesis 1:26-31)

66 = the number of books in the Holy Bible; 39 in the Old Covenant and 27 in the New Covenant

666 = the number assigned to anti-Christ; it is not a physical mark, but a religious system, a type of brain washing that will sweep across the entire earth, and many Believers in Yeshua Jesus will be forced to denounce their faith or be martyred. What then will be our choice?

There is hope; between man (6) and anti-Christ (666), is the Word of God (66). Anti-Christ dogma is spreading and will soon govern the earth. We will only overcome by the blood of the Lamb and by the word of our testimony, holding fast to the truth as we face death; knowing that to be absent from the body is to be present with the Lord (Revelation 12:11; 2 Corinthians 5:8). To recap, the righteous were first sealed in their foreheads indicating that their hearts were in right-standing with God. The man who sealed them wore linen which speaks of separating or dividing. Notice also that the man in linen had a weapon too, but his mission was not to slaughter but to save. Lastly and with great grief of spirit, the dividing began among God's very own elect.

Verses 8-11

And it came to pass, while they were slaying them, and I was left, that I fell upon my face, and cried, and said, Ah Lord GOD! Wilt Thou destroy all the residue of Israel in thy pouring out of thy fury upon Jerusalem? Then said He unto me, the iniquity of the house of Israel and Judah is exceeding great, and the land is full of blood, and the city full of perverseness: for they say, The LORD hath forsaken the earth, and the LORD seeth not. And as for Me also, Mine eye shall not spare, neither will I have pity, but I will recompense their way upon their head. And, behold, the man clothed with linen, which had the inkhorn by his side, reported the matter, saying, I have done as Thou hast commanded me.

This was one of the most horrific visions Ezekiel had ever experienced and the prophet was overwhelmed by the utter devastation that came upon all of Jerusalem. Ezekiel falls to the ground and remained bowed in reverence to the Most High God, pleading and interceding for mercy on behalf of his brethren, but judgment had already been served. The sins of the people had come up for final ruling and intercession by this just man was a little too late. Time was now over as the patience of the LORD had run its course and The LORD was left with no other choice, but to weed out the infection which was among them. The man clothed in linen was the only one who returned to the LORD with the report that his assignment was completed. Ecclesiastes 9:1-6 quoting the NLT sums up the matter: *This, too, I carefully explored: Even though the actions of godly and wise people are in God's hands, no one knows whether God will show them favor. The same destiny ultimately awaits everyone, whether righteous or wicked, good or bad, ceremonially clean or unclean, religious or irreligious. Good people receive the same treatment as sinners, and people who make promises to God are treated like people who don't. It seems so tragic that everyone under the sun suffers the same fate. That is why people are not more careful to be good. Instead, they choose their own mad course, for they have no hope. There is nothing ahead but death anyway. There is hope only for the living. As they say, "It's better to be a live dog than a dead lion!" The living at least know they will die, but the dead know nothing. They have no further reward, nor are they remembered. Whatever they did in their lifetime loving, hating, envying is all long gone. They no longer play a part in anything here on earth.* Righteousness is pleasing to the Lord; may the righteous continue in his or her righteousness.

Chapter 10

Verses 1-7

Then I looked, and, behold, in the firmament that was above the head of the cherubim there appeared over them as it were a sapphire stone, as the appearance of the likeness of a throne. And He spake unto the man clothed with linen, and said, Go in between the wheels, even under the cherub, and fill thine hand with coals of fire from between the cherubim, and scatter them over the city. And he went in, in my sight. Now the cherubim stood on the right side of the house, when the man went in: and the cloud filled the inner court. Then the glory of the LORD went up from the cherub, and stood over the threshold of the house; and the house was filled with the cloud, and the court was full of brightness of the LORD's glory. And the sound of the cherubim's wings was heard even to the outer court, as the voice of the Almighty God when He speaketh. And it came to pass, that when He had commanded the man clothed with linen, saying, Take fire from between the wheels, from between the cherubim; then he went in, and stood beside the wheels. And one cherub stretched forth his hand from between the cherubim unto the fire that was between the cherubim, and took thereof, and put it into the hands of him that was clothed with linen: who took it, and went out.

Ezekiel vision gathers momentum; he is in the third heaven once again as he did being a fresh exile by the river Chebar. In Ezekiel chapter one, the prophet reluctantly left the third heaven not knowing that to stay there, he would cease to exist on earth. This dimension is more real than that of ours, being outside the confines of time; nothing grows old or dies. Ezekiel finds himself once again in the very presence of the Almighty. All around him was the rapturous melody of worship unto Abba Father saturating the heavens like the sound of a million waterfalls rolled into one. This is the assurance of all Believers that one day; we will both live and worship the LORD GOD face to face eternally. Hebrews 12:22-24 states: *But you have come to Mount Zion, to the city of the living God, the heavenly Jerusalem. You have come to thousands upon thousands of angels in joyful assembly, to the church of the firstborn, whose names are written in heaven. You have come to God, the judge of all, to the spirits of the righteous made perfect, to Jesus the mediator of a new covenant, and to the sprinkled blood that speaks a better word than the blood of Abel,* NIV. What a welcome the prophet must have received; granted the privilege yet again of being the special guest of Abba Father.

The prophet was about to meet someone in the city of the Living God, someone whom he had met before and this would be a mighty surprise and consolation to Ezekiel, because his first encounter was bitter sweet. What will be Ezekiel's reaction this time? The prophet mustered all the strength that he could gather knowing this was not a pleasure trip; he was on an important assignment as the watchman for the exiled Jews living in Babylon. As Ezekiel surveyed the grandeur of this magnificent city, once again he gaze in wonder as he did the first time on what appeared to be a throne over the expanse where the Cherubim decree the glory, power and authority of the LORD in worship. Revelation 4:5-13 gives a clear picture of what the prophet saw: *And from the throne proceeded lightening, thunderings, and voices. Seven lamps of fire was burning before the throne, which are the seven Spirits of God. Before the throne there was a sea of glass, like crystal. And in the midst of the throne, and around the throne, were four living creatures full of eyes in front and in back. The first living creature was like a lion, the second living creature like a calf, the third living creature had a face like a man, and the fourth living creature was like a flying eagle. The four living creatures, each having six wings, were full of eyes around and within. And they do not rest day and night, saying: "Holy, holy, holy, Lord God Almighty, who was and is and is to come!" whenever the living creatures give glory and honor and thanks to Him who sits on the throne, who lives forever and ever, the twenty-four elders fall down before Him who sits on the throne and worship Him who lives forever and ever, and cast their crowns before the throne, saying: "You are worthy, O Lord, to receive glory and honor and power; for you created all things, and by Your will they exist and were created," NKJV.*

The intensity of the glory and radiance of Abba Father made it almost impossible for the prophet to see clearly as he barely catches a glimpse of the throne of GOD and recollects the breathtaking iridescence of the structure having seen it in a previous vision. Ezekiel describes its appearance as being like that of a sapphire stone suspended over the heads of the Cherubim. The prophet was indeed in the throne room of Abba Father, where the radiance of His glory shone forth more brilliantly than the sun. Just then, He heard the voice of the Almighty giving instructions to a man clothed in line, the same man who had the writers ink horn by his side, the one assigned to place a mark in the foreheads of the righteous. Who really is he, and what was he doing in the throne room?

In Ezekiel chapter nine this man was given authority by Abba Father to seal in the foreheads, those who were grieved over the absolute depravity of mankind in their midst. Ezekiel is now face to face with the one who placed the seal upon the foreheads of the just (Ezekiel 9:8). The prophet hears the voice of the LORD instructing the man who was dressed in linen to position himself between the wheels and fill his hand with coals of fire to scatter over the city. This man must be very important to have been given such authority in both heaven and earth by Abba Father. Ezekiel observed that this same man, who sealed the righteous, was now told to scatter fire over the city. Why was such great authority given to him in heaven to scatter coals of fire over the city? Was he going to scatter the coals of fire in the City of the Living God, the New Jerusalem or was he going to scatter them over the broken down ruins of the city of Jerusalem on earth? These questions are about to be answered but first let's identify the man clothed in linen.

Daniel 10:4-6 explains: *On the twenty-forth day of the first month, as I was standing on the bank of the great river, the Tigris, I looked up and there before me was a man dressed in linen, with a belt of fine gold from Uphaz around his waist. His body was like topaz, his face like lightening, his eyes like flaming torches, his arms and legs like the gleam of burnish bronze, and his voice like the sound of a multitude,* NIV. The description of this person does not require a lot of detective work, but let's put the pieces together by looking at another Scriptural documentation. Revelation 1:9-15 states: *I, John both your brother and companion in the tribulation and kingdom and patience of Jesus Christ, was on the island that is called Patmos for the word of God and for the testimony of Jesus Christ. I was in the Spirit on the Lord's Day, and I heard behind me a loud voice, as of a trumpet, saying, "I am the Alpha and the Omega, the First and the Last," and, "What you see, write in a book and send it to the seven churches which are in Asia: to Ephesus, to Smyrna, to Pergamos, to Thyatira, to Sardis, to Philadelphia, and to Laodicea." Then I turned to see the voice that spoke with me. And having turned I saw seven golden lampstands, and in the midst of the seven lampstands One like the Son of Man, clothed with a garment down to the feet and girded about the chest with a golden band. His head and hair were white like wool, as white as snow, and His eyes like a flame of fire; His feet were like fine brass, as if refined in a furnace, and His voice as the sound of many waters; He had in His right hand seven stars, out of His mouth went a sharp two-edged sword, and His countenance was like the sun shining in its strength,* NKJV. These accounts bear some similarities.

Now in Ezekiel's visions the man was only dressed in linen and the reason for this was not to conceal His identity. In Ezekiel 10:2, He was told by the LORD to take coals of fire from among the Cherubim, and scatter them over the city; a job that only one with authority could do. He was no ordinary man; He was the Son of the Living GOD, Yeshua Jesus the Messiah and Savior of the world. He alone can such authority be given in heaven and in the earth:

- Mathew 28:18 – *And Jesus came and spake unto them, saying, All power is given unto Me in heaven and in earth.*

- John 1:1-3 – *In the beginning was the Word, and the Word was with God and the Word was God. The same was in the beginning with God. All things were made by Him; and without Him was not any thing made that was made* (see Genesis chapter one)

- 1 John 1:1-3 – *That which was from the beginning, which we have heard, which we have seen with our eyes, which we have looked upon, and our hands have handled, of the Word of life; (for the life was manifested, and we have seen it, and bear witness, and shew unto you that eternal life, which was with the Father, and was manifested unto us;) that which we have seen and heard declare we unto you that ye also may have fellowship with us: and truly our fellowship is with the Father, and with His Son Jesus Christ.*

- John 3:35 – *The Father loveth the Son, and hath given all things into His hand.*

- Mathew 11:27 – *All things are delivered unto Me of My Father: and no man knoweth the Son, but the Father; neither knoweth any man the Father, save the Son, and He to whomsoever the Son will reveal Him*

- John 17:1-5 – *These words spake Jesus, and lifted up His eyes to heaven, and said, Father, the hour is come; glorify thy Son, that thy Son also may glorify Thee: as Thou hast given Me power over all flesh, that He should give eternal life to as many as thou hast given Him. And this life eternal, that they might know Thee the only true God, and Jesus Christ, whom Thou hast sent. I have glorified Thee on the earth: I have finished the work which Thou gavest Me to do. And now, O Father, glorify Thou Me with Thine own self with the glory which I had with Thee before the world was.*

These are but a few Scriptures in the Holy Bible that authenticates the preeminence of Yeshua Jesus above all others. Ezekiel saw the pre-incarnate Son of the Living God whom he, as well as others, simply described as the man clothed in linen. He was given the authority to go between the wheels, which was previously explained in Ezekiel chapter one, as metaphorically and symbolically referring to the Word of God, perpetually revolving on its circuit to accomplish that which it was sent forth to do (Isaiah 55:11). Now that we know the identity of the man dressed in linen as being the pre-incarnate Son of GOD; Ezekiel watches as He reaches under the Cherub, takes a handful of burning coal then proceeds to scatter them over the city. Why did He scatter the coals of fire over the city? What point was He conveying to the prophet?

First of all coals of fire is a symbol of purification, it cleanses the mind, as well as the mouth. James 3:8-11 applying the NASB states: *But no one can tame the tongue; it is a restless evil and full of deadly poison. With it we bless our Lord and Father, and with it we curse men, who have been made in the likeness of God; from the same mouth come both blessing and cursing. My brethren, these things ought not to be this way. Does a fountain send out from the same opening both fresh and bitter water?* The prophet Isaiah also had an encounter with God in the year his beloved, but sickly Uzziah also known as Azariah, king of Judah died (2 Kings 15:1-5; Chronicles 26:1-21). This prophet of God had a mighty vision, which would forever change his life: *In the year of King Uzziah's death I saw the Lord sitting on a throne, lofty and exalted, with the train of His robe filling the temple. Seraphim stood above Him, each having six wings: with two he covered his face, and with two he covered his feet, and with two he flew. And one called out to another and said, "Holy, Holy, Holy, is the LORD of hosts, the whole earth is full of His glory." And the foundations of the threshold trembled at the voice of him who called out, while the temple was filling with smoke. Then I said, "Woe is me, for I am ruined! Because I am a man of unclean lips, and I live among a people of unclean lips; for my eyes have seen the King, the LORD of hosts." Then one of the seraphim flew to me with a burning coal in his hand, which he had taken from the altar with tongs. He touched my mouth with it and said, "Behold, this has touched your lips; and your iniquity is taken away and your sin forgiven,"* Isaiah 6:1-7 NASB. Instantly Isaiah became aware of his foul mouth, because the holiness of GOD revealed it. Isaiah wasted no time rationalizing, but pleaded for mercy; GOD graciously forgave him and he later became a mighty prophet of the LORD of hosts.

Coals of fire serve the purpose of purging iniquities and sin thereby cleansing both the mind (intellect and emotions), as well as the mouth. Proverbs 4:23-24 advises: *Above all else, guard your heart for everything you do flows from it. Keep your mouth free of perversity; keep corrupt talk from your lips,* NIV. The act of scattering the coals over the city was a demonstration of the love of God, the One who is full of mercy and grace; to remove the iniquities and sins of the people. The only person found worthy was Yeshua HaMashiach Himself! Isaiah 53:6 speaks prophetically of Yeshua Jesus, our sin bearer: *All we like sheep have gone astray; we have turned every one to his own way; and the LORD hath laid on Him the iniquity of us all.* We are but rebels when we trample on His goodness. The earthly city of Jerusalem needed cleansing, because the heavenly

Jerusalem; the City of GOD in heaven, was already pure. The coals of fire was scattered upon the earth, as a perfect gesture of GOD'S redemptive plan for all those who call upon His name, therefore it was the Redeemer Yeshua Jesus; the Living Word who was deemed qualified to accomplish this task.

Ezekiel 10:3 drives the point home that this was in fact Yeshua Jesus our Messiah. The prophet stated that the man went in while the Cherubim stood on the right side of the temple and a cloud enveloped the inner court. The inner court is also known as the Holy Place, which symbolically speaks of the human soul. Separating the inner court (soul), from the Most Holy Place (spirit), was a veil that only the high priest was permitted to enter once a year on Yom-Kippur also known as "Day of Atonement" the Jews holiest day of the year (Leviticus 23:26; 16:29-30). This holiday is marked with fasting, repentance and purification. Because the Cherubim are associated with the Mercy Seat, Ezekiel 10:3 is actually telling us that indeed it was Yeshua Jesus who entered the Most Holy Place as the cloud filled the inner court. He became the perfect atonement for all whereby our sins are forgiven that we may be reconciled to God through His redemptive work.

The Hebrew word transliterated "cloud," is **Anan** [6051]; it speaks of the eternal state of existence or presence of God over the tabernacle. Throughout the Old and New Covenant; we see clouds associated with the presence of God declaring that truly He is: I AM that I AM. It is also stated in Ezekiel 10:4 that *the house was filled with the cloud, and the court was full of the brightness of the LORD'S glory*. The word "filled," is the Hebrew **Male** [4390], which points to completion or finality. Here we see the unfolding of the purification of the soul of man (inner court) to be a perfect, holy and habitable sanctuary. The handful of coal was retrieved from the Most Holy Place (the spirit), by Yeshua Jesus the true High Priest, and scattered abroad as a symbol of His final purifying work in man. Because

Ezekiel saw these things in a vision; they were being done in the perfect Tabernacle of Abba Father's kingdom.

In the construction of the earthly tabernacle, the LORD told Moses: "*See that you make them according to the pattern shown you on the mountain*" Exodus 25:40 NIV. The tabernacle in the wilderness was a pattern of its prototype already existing in heaven, the City of GOD; the New Jerusalem where Yeshua Jesus is the High Priest. Hebrews 8:1-10 confirms this: *Now this is the main point of the things we are saying: we have such a High Priest, who is seated at the right hand of the throne of the Majesty in the heavens, a Minister of the sanctuary and of the true tabernacle which the Lord erected, and not man. For every high priest is appointed to offer both gifts and sacrifices. Therefore it is necessary that this One also have something to offer. For if He were on earth, He would not be a priest, since there are priests who offer the gifts according to the law; who serve the copy and shadow of the heavenly things, as Moses was divinely instructed when he was about to make the tabernacle. For He said, "See that you make all things according to the pattern shown you on the mountain." But now He has obtained a more excellent ministry, inasmuch as He is also Mediator of a better covenant, which was established on better promises. For if that first covenant had been faultless, then no place would have been sought for a second. Because finding fault with them, He says: "Behold, the days are coming, says the LORD, when I will make a new covenant with the house of Israel and with the house of Judah not according to the covenant that I made with their fathers in the day when I took them by the hand to lead them out of the land of Egypt; because they did not continue in My covenant, and I disregarded them, says the LORD. For this is the covenant that I will make with the house of Israel after those days, says the LORD: I will put My laws in their mind and write them on their hearts; and I will be their God, and they shall be My people,* NKJV.

What a mighty revelation, Ezekiel saw the true High Priest and the heavenly Tabernacle. He saw the finished work of Yeshua Jesus on the Cross. And he saw the living Cherubim, and not one made of beaten gold. Ezekiel witnessed transference of the teachings of GOD from tablets of stone to the minds or hearts of His people. Yeshua Jesus entered once into the inner court (the soul of man) to be a Merciful Mediator and High Priest for our unrighteousness Hebrews 9:11-22. The Apostle Paul states in Romans 1:18-22: *For the wrath of God is revealed from heaven against all ungodliness and unrighteousness of men, who hold the truth in unrighteousness; because that which may be known of God is manifest in them; for God hath shewed it unto them. For the invisible things of Him from creation of the world are clearly seen, being understood by the things that are made, even His eternal power and Godhead; so that they are without excuse: because that, when they knew God, neither were thankful; but became vain in their imaginations, and their foolish heart was darkened. Professing themselves to be wise, they became fools.* Yeshua Jesus became Abba Father's Mediator for the soul of mankind; He was the Man dressed in linen, our everlasting High Priest.

It was now a little over twenty-four years into Ezekiel's captivity. The prophet had to think about what he had seen in these visions to encourage his brethren in bondage that although life seemed dismal there was hope. The manifested presence of the GOD of Israel ascended above the Cherubim and hovered at the entrance of the temple accompanied by a cloud that was like none other, because its Hebrew root describes one that was large and fearsome to look at. This cloud was charged with tremendous electrical power, which not only produced a mighty, thunderous, menacing, and near deafening sound, but also exploded with flashes of lightening leaving the prophet transfixed in awe of its spectacular display, as it illuminates the temple as well as the court-yard. Accompanying this awesome display of the cloud, and of equal intensity, was the sound of the wings of the Cherubim. No human ears can endure such volumes as it far surpasses that of an airplane whether landing of taking off. The prophet describes the sound of the Cherubim's wings in Ezekiel 1:24 as:

- The noise of great waters
- The voice of the Almighty
- The voice of speech
- The noise of a host

The Apostle John in Revelation 5:12 wrote: *Then I looked, and I heard the voice of many angels around the throne, the living creatures, and the elders; and the number of them was ten thousand times ten thousand, and thousands of thousands, saying with a loud voice: "Worthy is the Lamb who was slain to receive power and riches and wisdom, and strength and honor and glory and blessing,"* NKJV. In mathematics "of" means to multiply, therefore the total number of worshipers around the throne was one hundred one million (101,000,000). To arrive at this number: 10,000 x 10,000 = 100,000,000 and 1,000 x 1,000 =1,000,000; when these numbers are added the total number of worshipers were 101,000,000. This is a tremendously large number. Now think of this number as voices in a chorus; the world's largest choir is nothing to compare with that of heaven. One hundred one million voices declaring the glory of GOD! Now equate this to the description of the sound of the wings of the Cherubim in Ezekiel 10:5, which the prophet describes as being the sound of the voice of the Almighty when He speaks. These are tremendously enormous living creatures if their wings are able to produce sounds that are near equal to the voice of the Almighty. These volumes far exceed frequencies of twenty thousand hertz; the capacity detected by the human ear. Can you see why we will need a new spiritual body to live in heaven? Earth's current population is estimated to be seven thousand million or seven billion (7,000,000,000). One hundred one million (101,000,000), represents the heavenly chorus which is approximately 0.693% of earths' population, what a glorious reunion it will be when the redeemed of the Lord meets the Living Word and join with the hosts of heaven in worship.

Yeshua stands between the wheels, which is the infinite commission of the revolving Word of God to the ends of the earth. The wheel; much like a wedding ring a symbol of unity and an everlasting covenant that the Lord will be with us even until the end of the age (Matthew 28:20). A deeper meaning of the wheel; the revolving Word of God, also tells the story that Yeshua Jesus is the Bridegroom and His chosen people are His Bride. In volume three of *Ezekiel Unmasked* we will see the Gentiles also sharing in Israel's glorious inheritance. The Word of God is the foundation of our belief; because the Word is the Son of Abba Father who became flesh and lived on this earth over two thousand years ago (John 1:14; 1 John 1:1-2). Remember the Lord has promised to write His Word on our hearts, and it is the Word of God, the ever present revolving wheel, which is our covenant of blessings that will prepare us to meet our Redeemer: hold on to this promise.

Yeshua Jesus is the Word that became flesh; the Son of GOD and man who defeated Satan, and since it was man that lost to him, Yeshua Jesus was the chosen Son sent by Abba Father to redeem us. Yeshua Jesus came as the second Adam; He defeated the deceiver thereby reclaiming us for the Father. We must never forget that it was Yeshua's shed blood on a tree that became His Cross whereby we are saved; there is no other way! The wheel is the Word of God that will accomplish all that the Father intended and when all is said and done and the final prophecy is fulfilled, time will be no more. Isaiah 55:11 states: *So will My word be which goes forth from My mouth; it will not return to Me empty, without accomplishing what I desire, and without succeeding in the matter for which it was sent,* NASB. The Word of GOD is a double edged sword that purifies and also punishes and the fire given to Yeshua by the cherub speaks of the vengeance of God upon those who rejects the Word (Deuteronomy 32:41; Romans 12:19).

Verses 8-17

And there appeared in the cherubim the form of a man's hand under their wings. And when I looked, behold, the four wheels by the cherubim, one wheel by one cherub, and another wheel by another cherub: and the appearance of the wheels was the colour of a beryl stone. And as for their appearances, they four had one likeness as if a wheel had been in the midst of a wheel. When they went, they went upon their four sides; they turned not as they went, but to the place whither the head looked they followed it; they turned not as they went. And their whole body, and their backs, and their hands, and their wings, and their wheels, were full of eyes round about, even the wheels that they four had. As for the wheels, it was cried unto them in my hearing, O wheel. And every one had four faces: the first face was the face of a cherub, and the second face was the face of a man, and the third the face of a lion, and the fourth the face of an eagle. And the cherubim were lifted up. This is the living creature that I saw by the river Chebar. And when the cherubim went, the wheels went by them: and when the cherubim lifted up their wings to mount up from the earth, the same wheels also turned not from beside them. When they stood, these stood; and when they were lifted up, these lifted up themselves also: for the spirit of the living creature was in them.

Ezekiel observed what appeared to be the hand of a man under the wings of the Cherubim just as he did in the first vision. The appearance of a man's hand under the wings of the cherubim is symbolic of the Lord's protection over us. Psalm 34:7 states: *The angel of the LORD encampeth round about them that fear Him, and delivereth them.* Psalm 91:1 concurs: *He that dwelleth in the secret place of the Most High shall abide under the shadow of the Almighty.* The current position of the Cherubim is under the shadow of the Almighty exalting the LORD GOD. Now the appearance of a man's hand under the wings of the Cherubim is a message to the saints in Yeshua Jesus that not only will He always protect them, but the hands of a man under the Cherubim's wings points to man's restored position of power and authority in God.

This second vision bears many similarities to Ezekiel's first in chapter one. All of God's creation has a story to tell that debunks the evolutionist. As King David peers into the depth of space and marvel at the wonders of the creation of God Almighty, he pens these words: *The heavens are telling of the glory of God; and their expanse is declaring the work of His hands. Day to day pours forth speech, and night to night reveals knowledge. There is no speech, nor are there words; their voice is not heard,* Psalm 19:1-3 NASB. Ezekiel expresses that the wheels were identical. If the wheel represents the Word of God, then its revolution and revelation is the same within man. There is no other Word that is the breath of God; 2 Timothy 3:16-17 puts it this way: *All Scripture is God breathed and is useful for teaching, rebuking, correcting and training in righteousness, so that the man of God may be thoroughly equipped for every good work,* NIV. And the Word of God is settled in heaven, Psalm 119:89. The very appearance of the Cherubim tells a wonderful story that we have already gone over in chapter one. We see them glorifying GOD in heaven night and day without rest because the nature of GOD is woven into their being.

The wheel revolving within the larger wheel is an act of Holy Spirit imbibing the Word of God within us. The Spirit of God is a thirst quencher for the soul of those who believe (John 7:38). In John 16:13-14 Yeshua Jesus: *"But when the Spirit of truth, comes, He will guide you into all the truth; for He will not speak on His own initiative, but whatever He hears, He will speak; and He will disclose to you what is to come. He will glorify Me, for He will take of Mine and will disclose it to you,* NASB. Holy Spirit utilizes the Logos within us, by turning it over and over again just like a revolving wheel and with each turn, the revelation of God is deepened and our sanctification heightened to achieve Abba Father's ultimate goal to make us pure and spotless.

He first shows us the Word macroscopically and as we continue to feed upon it, Holy Spirit turns the Word yet again and microscopic revelatory truths are given; first in small doses, which increases with each level of spiritual maturity. This is made possible through our fellowship with Holy Spirit who delights in seeing us grow in the Lord.

Like the Cherubim, man will one day reach his full potential in GOD, being perfected by Yeshua Jesus. Sanctification is therefore the never ending pilgrim of the Believer until he meets his Creator. This is an ongoing process; we must remain full and begin to overflow with the evidence that the Word of God on the inside is changing us on the outside. The actions of these Cherubim demonstrated cohesiveness, which shows unity in purpose. There was never scuffling for preeminence; they looked out for the best interest of each other and the same goes for the people of God. team work must be a lesson we all learn, that God's perfect will may be done for us here on earth as it is in heaven (Mathew 6:10). Ezekiel looks in wander at the exceeding number of eyes all over the bodies of these living creatures; being eternally conscious of all that goes on around them. Their backs and hands, their wings and even their wheels within the larger wheels were full of eyes.

The splendor and majesty of our LORD portrays a message here concerning His Son Yeshua Jesus. In the Hebrew text "eyes," is **Ayin** [5869], which speaks of affliction. **Ayin** points to an outside force as the source of inflicting great suffering, pain and distress upon another, both physically and mentally. Isaiah prophetically spoke of Yeshua's suffering: *He is despised and rejected of men; a Man of sorrows, and acquainted with grief: and we hid as it were our faces from Him; He was despised and we esteemed Him not. Surely He hath borne our griefs, and carried our sorrows: yet we did esteem Him stricken, smitten of God, and afflicted. But He was wounded for our transgressions, He was bruised for our iniquities: the chastisement of our peace was upon Him; and with His stripes we are healed. All we like sheep have gone astray; we have turned every one to his own* *way; and the LORD hath laid on Him the iniquity of us all. He was oppressed, and He was afflicted, yet He opened not His mouth: He is brought as a Lamb to the slaughter, and as a sheep before her shearers is dumb, so He opened not His mouth. He was taken from prison and from judgment: and who shall declare His generation? For He was cut off from the land of the living: for the transgression of My people was He stricken. And He made His grave with the wicked, and with the rich in His death; because He had done no violence, neither was any deceit in His mouth. Yet it pleased the LORD to bruise Him; He hath put Him to grief: when thou shalt make His soul an offering for sin, He shall see His seed, He shall prolong His days, and the pleasure of the Lord shall prosper in His hand. He shall see of the travail of His soul, and shall be satisfied: by His knowledge shall My righteous servant justify many; for He shall bear their iniquities. Therefore will I divide Him a portion with the great, and He shall divide the spoil with the strong; because He hath poured out His soul unto death: and He was numbered with the transgressors; and He bare the sin of many, and made intercession for the transgressors,* 53:3-12. The Cherubim were created to portray the suffering of Yeshua Jesus on the Cross. Those responsible for Yeshua's death were offended by His teaching and preaching, and for this His body, back, and extremities were severely marred for our transgressions. Is it any wonder that these beings rest on the Mercy seat in the tabernacle? Is it any wonder that they are before the LORD GOD day and night in eternal worship to Him who sits on the throne and to the Lamb slain from the foundation of the world?

The Cherubim are an everlasting reminder to Abba Father of the sacrifice of His Son; the Bridegroom, who will one day present the elect of GOD to Him. Note also that the eyes were in both wheels; a portrayal of the affliction of the saints also because of the Word of God. Yeshua Jesus said to His followers: *"Then shall they deliver you up to be afflicted, and shall kill you: and ye shall be hated of all nations for My name's sake. And then many shall be offended, and shall betray one another, and shall hate one another. And many false prophets shall rise, and shall deceive many. And because iniquity shall abound, the love of many shall wax cold. But he that shall endure unto the end, the same shall be saved,"* Matthew 24:9-13. Saints of God; our time on this earth is quite short, even if we live to be a hundred and twenty years old; our days are but a vapor in the eyes of our Lord. Let nothing separate us from the love of God. These are the words of our Savior: *"He who loves his life will lose it, and he who hates his life in this world will keep it for eternal life,"* John 12:25 NKJV. There is so much we can learn from these living creatures because the Lord created them to be an everlasting witness and reminder to all mankind of all that Yeshua Jesus suffered for our redemption. There was so much for Ezekiel to assimilate, as his attention was drawn to the sound of a voice which called out, *"O wheel!"* The prophet turns, eager to learn more, he noticed something quite different about the appearance of these living creatures. Although bearing many similarities to the ones in the first vision, the order, absence or replacement of faces of the Cherubim in this vision tells in most part a different story.

Cherubim of first vision Ezekiel 1:10	Cherubim of second vision Ezekiel 10:14
First face – Man	First face – Cherub
Second face – Lion	Second Face – Man
Third face – Ox (oxen)	Third face – Lion
Fourth face – Eagle	Fourth face – Eagle

In the first vision the faces of the Cherubim featured four attributes of man: the first was man as ruler. The second attribute was man in Yeshua Jesus, represented by the young lion. The third was man as a bondservant; represented by the ox/oxen and the fourth; man as a watchman or prophet, represented by the eagle. In the second vision that we are about to examine the symbolic interpretation is different because something changed about the features of these living creatures, the only face that retained its position and symbolic meaning is the eagle. With this in mind, let's examine the symbolic references of the faces of these Cherubim in Ezekiel chapter ten.

Man was the principal figure in the first vision, whereas in the second, the Cherub took the lead role, this is the first and most important change that will impact the interpretation of this second vision. The ox is eliminated and man takes its place. Next, the position of the lion also changes from being second in the first vision to third in the second vision. The only position that remained unchanged was that of the eagle (see chart). The following is the interpretation of the faces of the Cherubim in Ezekiel's second visit to the throne room of GOD, revealed by their transliterated Hebrew equivalent.

The Hebrew transliteration for Cherub is **Keruv** [3742], it means an act of worship whereby one is blessed, praised and adored. The next face was of a man and here the Hebrew word **Adham** [120] is used in a collective sense to describe both male and female. The third face was that of a lion and its Hebrew transliteration is **Ariy** [738], describing the piercing of a lion. **Ariy** is also a derivative of **Arah** [717], which means to pluck. Finally is **Nesher** [5404], the Hebrew word for eagle which means to lacerate. The faces of the Cherub in Ezekiel 10:14 is revealing to us a story about Yeshua Jesus' suffering for all mankind that takes us to a familiar book in the Old Covenant, packed with Messianic prophesies.

In reference to Yeshua Jesus the Messiah, Isaiah 53:3-10 states: *He is despised and rejected of men; a man of sorrows, and acquainted with grief: and we hid as it were our faces from him; he was despised, and we esteemed him not. Surely he hath borne our griefs, and carried our sorrows: yet we did esteem him stricken, smitten of God, and afflicted. But he was wounded for our transgressions, he was bruised for our iniquities: the chastisement of our peace was upon him; and with his stripes we are healed. All we like sheep have gone astray; we have turned every one to his own way; and the LORD hath laid on him the iniquity of us all. He was oppressed, and he was afflicted, yet he opened not his mouth: he was brought as a lamb to the slaughter, and as a sheep before is shearers is dumb, so he opened not his mouth. He was taken from prison and from judgment: and who shall declare his generation? For he was cut off out of the land of the living: for the transgression of my people was he stricken. And he made his grave with the wicked, and with the rich in his death; because he had done no violence, neither was any deceit in his mouth. Yet it pleased the LORD to bruise him; he hath put him to grief: when thou shalt make his soul an offering for sin, he shall see his seed, he shall prolong his days, and the pleasure of the LORD shall prosper in his hand.* Yeshua's suffering for mankind gave Him the authority to stand in the gap for all humanity. He is our intercessor as well as our Redeemer. The face of an ox was eliminated from the second vision, because Yeshua Jesus freely laid down His perfect life for us all. He did so as a bondservant as well as a Son. He is the Lion from the tribe of Judah who was pierced, plucked and lacerated for the sins of us all. This is the story behind the Ezekiel 10:14 faces of the Cherub. Sinful man needed a Redeemer and Abba Father was pleased to sacrifice His only Son with the knowledge that He would be raised from the dead. Yeshua Jesus stripped Hades of its power and defeated death, hell and the grave to the pleasure and celebration of Abba Father and all the host of heaven.

Verses 18-22

Then the glory of the LORD departed from off the threshold of the house, and stood over the cherubim. And the cherubim lifted up their wings, and mounted up from the earth in my sight: when they went out, the wheels also were beside them, and every one stood at the door of the east gate of the LORD's house; and the glory of the God of Israel was over them above. This is the living creature that I saw under the God of Israel by the river of Chebar; and I knew that they were the cherubim. Every one had four faces apiece, and every one four wings; and the likeness of the hands of a man was under their wings. And the likeness of their faces was the same faces which I saw by the river of Chebar, their appearances and themselves: they went every one straight forward.

This was the last straw, the people had dishonored God and His presence was about to depart temporarily from its physical abode. The glory of GOD would however return on the feast of Shavuot (Pentecost), hundreds of years later on the memorial day, when Torah was given to Moses by God. The great rejoicing we must have is in knowing that on this second occasion the LORD returned to the temple within man. Acts 2:1-4 states: *On the day of Pentecost all the believers were meeting together in one place. Suddenly there was a sound from heaven like the roaring of a mighty windstorm, and it filled the house where they were sitting. Then, what looked like flames or tongues of fire appeared and settled on each of them. And everyone present was filled with the Holy Spirit and began speaking in other tongues, as the Holy Spirit gave them this ability,* NTL. The temple of God; His holy presence now resides in man, (see 1 Corinthians 3:16; 6:19). In Exodus 19:6, the God of Israel declares unto His people: "*And you shall be to Me a kingdom of priests and a holy nation,*" NASB (see also 1 Peter 2:9). When the presence of God departs from a people, lawlessness eventually controls them; but for the righteous He promises never to leave or forsake.

The house of Israel practiced every form of abominable wickedness, but the final act that stretched Abba Father's patience to its limit, was placing an image in His temple, thus making it equal with God, thereby breaking the first commandment: you shall have no other god besides Me, Exodus 20:3. In Jeremiah 27:6, the LORD called Nebuchadnezzar "*My servant*" because he was used by GOD as His rod of chastisement and all of Judah; good and evil, small and great felt the sting of His judgment to some degree.

The righteous are strategically placed where the LORD can use them the most. Even though the godly experience great hardship at times, it must never be viewed as punishment; but the grace of the Almighty to perfect us, while using us to save others; therefore we must count it all joy. What might seem like an injustice at first glance; is God's way of getting the most out of His people for their spiritual growth and for His glory. He sees our strengths and will use every bit of it to save others. Remember Amos 8:11-12 for the hour of God's wrath is upon us: *Behold, the days come, saith the Lord GOD, that I will send a famine in the land, not a famine of bread, nor a thirst for water, but of hearing the words of the LORD. And they shall wonder from sea to sea, and from the north even unto the east, they shall run to and fro to seek the word of the LORD, and shall not find it.* Saints don't give up and never give in, if we lose our life in this world, we will preserve it in the next (Matthew 16:25; Mark 8:35; Luke 9:24; 17:33). The presence of God, lifted from the physical temple yet found its way in a better sanctuary, which is the heart of man. Keep looking upward, our time of redemption is nearer than we think.

Chapter 11

Verses 1-3

Moreover the Spirit lifted me up, and brought me unto the east gate of the LORD's house, which looketh eastward: and behold at the door of the gate five and twenty men; among whom I saw Jaazaniah the son of Azur, and Pelatiah the son of Benaiah, princes of the people. Then said He unto me, Son of man, these are the men that devise mischief, and give wicked counsel in this city: which say, It is not near; let us build houses: this city is the caldron, and we be the flesh.

In this vision Ezekiel was once again taken in the spirit to Jerusalem towards the eastern gate of the temple. The prophet had to be shown the past secrets of the leaders that no one was aware of. These were men who were entrusted with the task of being decision makers for the people, but instead, they were planning great mischief by offering evil and unwise counsel. A search in the family tree of Jaazaniah the son of Azur yielded a difference between both him and the Jaazaniah son of Shaphan mentioned in Ezekiel 8:11. The Jaazaniah of Ezekiel 11:1, had a brother who was a false prophet named Hananiah (Jeremiah 28); both men simply shared the same name.

The Spirit of the LORD showed Ezekiel the cunning and mischievous plans of those who were leaders in Jerusalem before the exile. Ezekiel looks on as if watching a close caption television; his heart must have been very heavy with grief, as once again he is shown the depth of depravity of those chosen to be both the spiritual and democratic leaders of the people. These men were devising sinister plans to oppress their fellow brethren through trickery, while they themselves would become wealthy as a direct result of the oppression of others. Proverbs 10:23-25 states: *To do evil is like sport to a fool, but a man of understanding has wisdom. The fear of the wicked will come upon him, and the desire of the righteous will be granted. When the whirlwind passes by, the wicked is no more, but the righteous has an everlasting foundation,* NKJV. The Lord knew the hearts and plans of those in leadership; they were but wolves in sheep's clothing and although their words dripped with honey, their hidden agenda would soon be revealed as something bitter to endure. The people had great admiration and respect for their leaders, not knowing their true motivations. They jokingly referred to the city as a boiler vessel and themselves as the meat to be cooked in it; meaning: chaos would consume the land and as the people flee the mayhem, they would remain in the city to seize possessions of value that were left behind. This plan was being set in motion under the guise of national security measures when in fact the leaders created the chaos to subvert the nation without protest; a deceptive, yet effective smoke screen.

Verses 4-7

Therefore prophesy against them, prophesy, O son of man. And the Spirit of the LORD fell upon me, and said unto me, Speak; Thus have ye said, O house of Israel: for I know the things that come into your mind, every one of them. Ye have multiplied your slain in this city, and ye have filled the streets thereof with the slain. Therefore thus saith the LORD GOD; Your slain whom ye have laid in the midst of it, they are the flesh, and this city is the caldron: but I will bring you forth out of the midst of it.

The group of twenty-five men led by Jaazaniah whose name means *"the Lord hears"* and Pelatiah whose name means *"the Lord delivers;"* received an oracle pronounced upon them as the Spirit of the Lord uses Ezekiel to declares His message of displeasure to them. Their plans to destroy their own people would not go unpunished by the LORD. The word came forth as the Spirit of the Living God moved upon Ezekiel; there would be no construction of homes but the scattered bodies of the dead would be the flesh indeed, unable to heed any command and the city of Jerusalem would be the boiling vessel as the judgment of the LORD would commence there. The city of Jerusalem that Jaazaniah and his cohorts Pelatiah and their evil friends had great plans to purchase, would have all its prime real estate razed by fire, plundered, and survivors of this great onslaught would be exiled. Proverbs 19:21 fittingly states: *There are many devices in a man's heart; nevertheless the counsel of the LORD, that shall stand.* Evil plans of men are known by the LORD God of the whole earth; He will make these plans worthless which inevitably causes ruin.

Verses 8-13

Ye have feared the sword; and I will bring a sword upon you, saith the Lord GOD. And I will bring you out of the midst thereof, and deliver you into the hands of strangers, and will execute judgments among you. Ye shall fall by the sword; I will judge you in the border of Israel; and ye shall know that I am the LORD. This city shall not be your caldron, neither shall ye be the flesh in the midst thereof; but I will judge you in the border of Israel: and ye shall know that I am the LORD: for ye have not walked in My statutes, neither executed My judgments, but have done after the manners of the heathen that are round about you. And it came to pass, when I prophesied, that Pelatiah the son of Benaiah died. Then fell I down upon my face, and cried with a loud voice, and said, Ah Lord GOD! Wilt thou make a full end of the remnant of Israel?

The ensuing oppression was very familiar to the children of Israel. They repented as much as they reverted to doing evil, and the thing which they greatly feared: the lifting of the hand of the LORD was followed by severe hardship as a direct consequence of their rebellion. No sooner had Ezekiel prophesied against this unscrupulous group of men Pelatiah died. Why was Jaazaniah spared? The likely answer lies in the fact that Pelatiah is from the priestly tribe of Levites who were servants of the LORD. The Levites inheritance was in the GOD of Israel; they belonged to Him and considered ceremonially clean (see Numbers 8:13-20). Pelatiah surely knew that as a Levite, he belonged to God, yet he was the vice counsel of Jaazaniah in this illegal land deal.

It is also important to note that Pelatiah's grandfather was Jehoiada the father of Benaiah who was a man of valor and a high ranking officer who served King David (1 Chronicles 11:22-25). Jehoiada was called an Aaronite; which is officially a Levite the priestly class selected by the LORD to be His ministers. Pelatiah, whose name means "*the Lord delivers,*" bore the iniquity of his confederates because he was a Levite. Pelatiah broke the Levitical covenant thereby dishonoring the LORD. Being a Levite, Pelatiah should have advised the men not to carry out such a devious act against their own flesh and blood, but instead, he was one of the ringleaders. Because of this foolish error, and taking his dedication to the LORD for granted, he paid a very high cost in that he died.

Verses 14-21

Again the word of LORD came unto me, saying, Son of man, thy brethren, even thy brethren, the men of thy kindred, and all the house of Israel wholly, are they unto whom the inhabitants of Jerusalem have said, Get you far from the LORD: unto us is this land given in possession. Therefore say, Thus saith the Lord GOD; Although I have cast them far off among the heathen, and although I have scattered them among the countries, yet will I be to them as a little sanctuary in the countries where they shall come. Therefore say, Thus saith the Lord GOD; I will gather you from people, and assemble you out of the countries where ye have been scattered, and I will give you the land of Israel. And they shall come thither, and they shall take away all the detestable things thereof and all the abominations thereof from thence. And I will give them one heart, and I will put a new spirit within you; and I will take the stony heart out of their flesh, and will give them a heart of flesh: that they may walk in My statutes, and keep My ordinances, and do them: and they shall be My people, and I will be their God. But as for them whose heart walketh after the heart of their detestable things and their abominations, I will recompense their way upon their own heads, saith the Lord GOD.

Ezekiel was distraught; Pelatiah was a close kin of the prophet being both descendants from the tribe of Levi. The LORD however had a comforting word for the prophet. He promised him that a remnant from among his brethren would be saved although He had given them over to the hands of their oppressors. Jerusalem was but a ruinous heap, but the prophets and holy men who were among the exiles in Babylon would be God's visible presence (little sanctuary) among the people. The scattered house of Israel would one day however, as promised by Abba Father, return to the land.

Israel is the most valuable piece of real estate on the face of the earth because it was chosen by Abba Father not only to be the home of His very own people, but as the name implies: God prevails. The returning exiles were promised a different heart, they would have the presence of Holy Spirit within to instruct and guide them. It would no longer be by works, but by faith that they would keep the teachings of God, as Holy Spirit would be their constant companion and guide. The children of Israel were instructed to remove every abominable and detestable think from the land to make it ceremonially clean. Until this day the children of Israel have not done so, and for this reason they continue to pay the price through wars and oppression.

Verses 22-25

Then did the cherubim lift up their wings, and the wheels beside them; and the glory of the God of Israel was over them above. And the glory of the LORD went up from the midst of the city, and stood upon the mountain which is on the east side of the city. Afterwards the Spirit took me up, and brought me in a vision by the Spirit of God into Chaldea, to them of the captivity. So the vision that I had seen went up from me. Then I spake unto them of the captivity all the things that the LORD had shewed me.

The abiding place of the Cherubim was over the Mercy Seat as the LORD instructed His servant Moses. These living creatures are always identified with the presence, glory and worship of the LORD. They are the armor bearers and rockets boosters of His glory. They are also the trust or force required to lift His glory, from the Mercy Seat; much like a space shuttle from its launching pad. The wheel which is the Word of God and the wings of the Cherubim are like the three main engines located in their bodies which provided the added thrust to lift the glory from the Mercy Seat. The near deafening sound ushered in a time of mourning as the glory departed. Many times over the house of Israel were warned; they stoned the prophets, placed some in jail, and others lost their lives for making known the plans of the LORD, but Israel did not repent, and the LORD honored His Word spoken by the mouth of His anointed ones.

Laughter now ceases as anguish ensues. The presence of the LORD by His sheer lovingkindness and tender mercies would only be like a little sanctuary among the Jews because of His prophets and righteous ones among the rebellious. This was a day like none other as Israel's only hope; the GOD of Abraham, Isaac, and Jacob was about to take a long leave of absence. The glory of Abba Father departed like a shuttle lifting from its launching pad and hovered over the Mount of Olives also known as Har Ha-Zeitim; a very important place in Bible prophecy. It is recorded In

2 Samuel chapter 15 that King David fled to this Mount where he wept bitterly, after his own son and some of his trusted friends betrayed him, and that was exactly what Israel had done to the LORD their GOD.

Facts concerning the Mount of Olives/Har Ha-Zeitim:

- Yeshua's triumphant entry into the city of Jerusalem – Matthew 23:1-11; Mark 11:1-11; Luke 19:28-38; John 12:12-19
- Yeshua wept over Jerusalem from there – Luke 19:37-41
- Yeshua taught there – Mathew 24 and 25
- Yeshua prayed there – Mathew 26:30
- Yeshua ascended into heaven from there – Acts 1:9-12
- Yeshua's will one day descend there – Zachariah chapter 14.

The grief stricken prophet was shown the departure of the glory of the LORD and the vision of his visit to Jerusalem ended. Holy Spirit now takes Ezekiel back to Babylon, where his fellow brethren were in exile and he rehearsed to them all the things which the GOD of Israel had showed him; from the reason for their punishment, to the departing of His glory. The people however were not left without hope because the days were ahead when the LORD'S favor would be poured out once again upon His people. Fast forwarding to Ezekiel 37:12-14, the prophet is instructed by the LORD to declare unto the house of Israel the following oracle: *Therefore prophesy and say unto them, Thus saith the Lord GOD; Behold, O My people, I will open your graves, and cause you to come up out of your graves, and bring you into the land of Israel. And ye shall know that I am the LORD, when I have opened your graves, O My people, and brought you up out of your graves, and shall put My Spirit in you, and ye shall live, and I shall place you in your own land: then shall ye know that I the LORD have spoken it, and performed it, saith the LORD.* Joy is on the horizon for the chosen people of God.

Chapter 12

Verses 1-16

The word of the LORD also came unto me, saying, Son of man, thou dwellest in the midst of a rebellious house, which have eyes to see, and see not; they have ears to hear, and hear not: for they are a rebellious house. Therefore, thou son of man, prepare thee stuff for removing, and remove by day in their sight; and thou shalt remove from thy place to another place in their sight: it may be they will consider, though they be a rebellious house. Then shalt thou bring forth thy stuff by day in their sight, as stuff for removing: and thou shalt go forth at even in their sight, as they that go forth into captivity. Dig thou through the wall in their sight, and carry out thereby. In their sight shalt thou bear it upon thy shoulders, and carry it forth in the twilight: thou shalt cover thy face, that thou see not the ground: for I have set thee for a sign unto the house of Israel. and I did so as I was commanded: I brought forth my stuff by day, as stuff for captivity, and in the even I digged through the wall with mine hand; I brought it forth in the twilight, and I bare it upon my shoulder in their sight. And in the morning came the word of the LORD unto me, saying, Son of man, hath not the house of Israel, the rebellious house, said unto thee, What doest thou? Say thou unto them, Thus saith the Lord GOD; This burden concerneth the prince in Jerusalem, and all the house of Israel that are among them. Say, I am your sign: like as I have done, so shall it be done unto them: they shall remove and go into captivity. And the prince that is among them shall bear

> upon his shoulder in the twilight, and shall go forth: they shall dig through the wall to carry out thereby: he shall cover his face, that he see not the ground with his eyes. My net also will I spread upon him, and he shall be taken in My snare: and I will bring him to Babylon to the land of the Chaldeans; yet shall he not see it, though he shall die there. And I will scatter toward every wind all that are about him to help him, and all his bands; and I will draw out the sword after them. And they shall know that I am the LORD, when I shall scatter them among the nations, and disperse them in the countries. But I will leave a few men of them from the sword, and from the famine, and from the pestilence; that they may declare all their abominations among the heathen whither they come; and they shall know that I am the LORD.

The people consciously chose the path of least resistance; everyone practiced varying degrees of lawlessness. Forgetting that sin pays wages, they stubbornly rejected the teachings of the LORD, the prophets and also their prophetic warnings; turning their backs on holiness, they ran with arms wide open to the riotous heathens. Ezekiel does as he is told and with prophetic role-play, acted out in clear viewing of the exiles, the attempted escape of their leaders under the cover of darkness. The captives looked on in curiosity at Ezekiel's shenanigans, not quite understanding what he was doing, but Ezekiel was simply following the orders of the LORD. Now they had to decipher his performance, however, this was not intended to be a riddle, but a rebuke. The leaders contemplated to elude the punishment of the LORD by escaping through several breaches in the city wall, but their plans clearly end in futility being no match for the Babylonian guards who surrounded the entire city of Jerusalem, keeping vigilant watch to capture anyone who would attempt to escape.

Ezekiel dug in the wall for all Israel to see and by the time he was finished it was already getting dark. What made his job even more tedious, was the fact that his face was covered as a demonstration of the disguise and deception that Israel's leaders stooped to in their hour of desperation. This was also an omen as well, of the uncertainty of Judah's future, as many who watched Ezekiel's prophetic role-play would die in Babylon before the allotted seventy years of Babylonian captivity expired. They would be bound by the laws of a strange and idolatrous culture and mingle with a diverse ethnic group as perverse as many of them were. As Ezekiel continued his prophetic dramatization; Judah saw right before their very eyes the unfolding of a hard life in Babylon; the house of Israel would continue to pay bitter dividends for many years to come; being forced to do things they knew were wrong or otherwise face the death penalty.

Exile and foreign domination was therefore a sign to the people that it was the LORD that was punishing them. The leaders of the house of Judah had many horrific secrets which the common people were not aware of. The LORD had abandoned them for a cause; if this was not so, He would not have showed Ezekiel the detestable practices of their leaders. That which was done in secret was now being revealed, and all Israel would know that their spiritual and tribal leaders were all corrupt.

Jeremiah who was one of the prophets that warned the people of Judah and frequently lamented over her downward spiral, was living in Jerusalem at the time of the siege; he documented the fall of their leaders and the destruction of Jerusalem: *In the ninth year of Zedekiah king of Judah, in the tenth month, came Nebuchadnezzar king of Babylon and all his army against Jerusalem, and they besieged it. And in the eleventh year of Zedekiah, in the fourth month, the ninth day of the month, the city was broken up. And all the princes of the king of Babylon came in, and sat in the middle gate, even Nergal-sharezer, Samgar-nebo, Sarsechim, Rabsaris, Nergal-sharezer, Rabmag, with all the residue of the princes of the king of Babylon. And it came to pass, that when Zedekiah the king of Judah saw them, and all the men of war, then they fled and went forth out of the city by night, by the way of the king's garden, by the gate betwixt the two walls: and he went out the way of the plain. But the Chaldeans' army pursued after them, and overtook Zedekiah in the plains of Jericho: and when they had taken him, they brought him up to Nebuchadnezzar king of Babylon to Riblah in the land of Hamath, where he gave judgment upon him. Then the king of Babylon slew the sons of Zedekiah in Riblah before his eyes: also the king of Babylon slew all the nobles of Judah. Moreover he put out Zedekiah's eyes, and bound him with chains, to carry him to Babylon. And the Chaldeans burned the king's house, and the houses of the people, with fire, and brake down the walls of Jerusalem. Then Nebuzar–adan the captain of the guard carried away captive into Babylon the remnant of the people that remained in the city, and those that fell away, that fell to him, with the rest of the people that remained. But Nebuzar– adan the captain of the guard left of the poor of the people, who had nothing, in the land of Judah, and gave those vineyards and fields at the same time,* Jeremiah 39:1-10. It was fulfilled as prophesied; the king of Judah, his sons and other leaders and advisors were put to death at the decree of the king of Babylon. Notice in verse three of the above quotation that the name Nergal-sharezer appeared twice with all the royal chiefs and leaders of the Babylonian army. The second occurrence of the name is preceded by the name Rabmag; this however is not an error. As a point of clarity, the mentioning of Nergal-sharezer twice followed by Rabmag was referring to the title or rank of a royal officer who was head of all the royal chief leaders. The same goes for Rabsaris: this was also a title used in reference to the chief of the eunuchs; indicating that Sarsechim was the chief eunuch. Nebuzar-adan, the captain of the Babylonian guard now decides who should stay in Jerusalem and who should be taken off to the Babylonian Empire as either slaves or servants.

Here we see transference of wealth, as Nebuzar-adan left the poorer class of Israelites in the ruins of Jerusalem and gave them vineyards and fields, while those who fled and later surrendered, along with those who were taken captive from the city, were on their way to Babylon. Psalm 49:1-13 states: *Listen to this, all you people! Pay attention, everyone in the world! High and low, rich and poor listen! For my words are wise, and my thoughts are filled with insight. I listen carefully to many proverbs and solve riddles with inspiration from a harp. Why should I fear when trouble comes, when enemies surround me? They trust in their wealth and boast of great riches. Yet they cannot redeem themselves from death by paying a ransom to God. Redemption does not come so easily, for no one can ever pay enough to live forever and never see the grave. Those who are wise must finally die, just like the foolish and senseless, leaving all their wealth behind. The grave is their eternal home, where they will stay forever. They may name their estates after themselves, but their fame will not last. They will die just like animals. This is the fate of fools, though they are remembered as being wise,* NLT. The oppression of the poor does not go unnoticed; neither does the cry of the destitute goes unheard. When the LORD sends destruction upon the wicked, who can stop it, or who can avert or change its course? Only true repentance would stay His judgment.

The LORD kept His promise as He always does and a remnant people returned to Jerusalem after their seventy years of Babylonian exile, to help Nehemiah and Ezra in the rebuilding of the broken down walls of the city and the rebuilding of the temple that was also in ruins. The returning exiles also restored the worship of Abba Father and reestablished the required temple sacrifices. Several hundred years later in 70 A.D. there was yet another Diaspora; but as we have already highlighted; the Hebrews begun returning to Israel in May 1948, and continues to do so as the LORD had spoken, never to be dispersed again. Anti-Semitism ravaged the middle ages. Diseases of epic proportion, which raged in Europe in the mid-nineteenth century, killed more than half of the Jewish population living there. There was also the holocaust of the twentieth century and the constant threat of annihilation by the many nations who wish to see Israel extinct. The sword has continued to follow the

Hebrews throughout time and geographical regions; yet the LORD has always left for Himself a remnant, never totally abandoning His people.

Verses 17-20

Moreover the word of the LORD came to me, saying, Son of man, eat thy bread with quaking, and drink thy water with trembling and with carefulness; and say unto the people of the land, Thus saith the Lord GOD of the inhabitants of Jerusalem, and of the land of Israel; they shall eat their bread with carefulness, and drink their water with astonishment, that her land may be desolate from all that is therein, because of the violence of all them that dwell therein. And the cities that are inhabited shall be laid waste, and the land shall be desolate; and ye shall know that I am the LORD.

Something dreadful and unexpected was about to break loose upon the land. Everyone, including the prophet, was told to eat and drink with trepidation, for looming over their heads were horrific uncertainties for the future; a sharp yet constant feeling of emotional distress, desolation and separation of families, dispersal, and the fear and anguish of not knowing what lies ahead. Sin had ran its course to the over-flowing; but soon the Lord GOD would show up and show off as the GOD of Israel. The presence of the few precious righteous was not enough to stop the mayhem that was about to strike the land. All that was held as valuable was either burned to the ground or taken away and given to others. The people chose a taskmaster and by doing so, they must now pledge allegiance to a dictator and an ideology against their moral and spiritual values.

Verses 21-28

And the word of the LORD came unto me, saying, Son of man, what is that proverb that ye have in the land of Israel, saying, the days are prolonged, and every vision faileth? Tell them therefore, Thus saith the Lord GOD; I will make this proverb to cease, and they shall no more use it as a proverb in Israel; but say unto them, The days are at hand, and the effect of every vision. For there shall be no more any vision nor flattering divination within the house of Israel. for I am the LORD: I will speak, and the word that I shall speak shall come to pass; it shall be no more prolonged: for in your days, O rebellious house, will I say the word, and will perform it, saith the Lord GOD. Again the word of the LORD came to me, saying, Son of man, behold, they of the house of Israel say, The vision that he seeth is for many days to come, and he prophesieth of times that are far off. Therefore say unto them, Thus saith the Lord GOD; There shall none of My words be prolonged any more, but the word which I have spoken shall be done, saith the Lord GOD.

All warnings of the coming judgment upon the land went unheeded and an unsettling cloud of doom slowly but unwaveringly moved in. False prophets who herald peace were all proven to be liars as the people observe the fulfillment of the spoken Word of God by His servants whom He had sent. The prophet Jeremiah expressed his grief because of these diviners: *Thy prophets have seen vain and foolish things for thee: and they have not discovered thine iniquity, to turn away thy captivity; but have seen for thee false burdens and causes of banishment,* Lamentations 2:14. It is never in the heart of God to abandon His children or cause them grief or pain, but He must address unrepentant sin. Very few heeded the warnings of the prophets when they had a chance to do so; now hopelessness, doom and despair lie ahead. If the people had lived in righteousness they would have enjoyed peace and prosperity, but instead, they choose lawlessness. The Word of God states: *"If My people who are called by My name will humble themselves, and pray and seek My face, and turn from their wicked ways, then I will hear from heaven, and will forgive their sin and heal their land. . . Righteousness exalts a nation, but sin is a reproach to any people,* 2 Chronicles 7:14 and Proverbs 14:34 NKJV. The LORD was about to sweep the land by the prophetic tongue of His servants, and nothing in earth or heaven could delay its coming. The labor pains would not relent, the delivery was eminent as the LORD GOD poured out His indignation upon Judah.

Chapter 13

Verses 1-10

And the word of the LORD came unto me, saying, Son of man, prophesy against the prophets of Israel that prophesy, and say thou unto them that prophecy out of their own hearts, Hear ye the word of the LORD; thus saith the Lord GOD; Woe unto the foolish prophets, that follow their own spirit, and have seen nothing! O Israel, thy prophets are like the foxes in the deserts. Ye have not gone up into the gaps, neither made up the hedge for the house of Israel to stand in the battle in the day of the LORD. They have seen vanity and lying divination, saying, The LORD saith: and the LORD hath not sent them: and they made others to hope that they would confirm the word. Have ye not seen a vain vision, and have ye not spoken a lying divination, whereas ye say, The LORD saith it; albeit I have not spoken? Therefore thus saith the Lord GOD; Because ye have spoken vanity, and seen lies, therefore, behold, I am against you, saith the Lord GOD. And Mine hand shall be upon the prophets that see vanity, and that divine lies: they shall not be in the assembly of My people, neither shall they be written in the writing of the house of Israel, neither shall they enter into the land of Israel; and ye shall know that I am the Lord GOD. Because, even because they have seduced My people, saying, Peace; and there was no peace; and one built up a wall, and lo, others daubed it with untempered morter.

This admonition transcends time and therefore a warning to all who claim they speak by the mouth of the Lord. He will not have pity on false prophets who are unrepentant as their words are like poison to an already gangrenous wound. False prophets are:

- Men pleasers
- They speak ill against true prophets of God
- They are controlled by evil spirits
- Their words are without judgment and reproof
- They are men pleasers and draws attention to themselves
- They seduce men and seek favors of all kind
- They tell the people what they want to hear instead of the truth
- If their prophecies are fulfilled their sayings are accomplished through demonic influence (see Exodus 7:8 to 8:19)

These are a few identifying marks of a false prophet. As a note of caution: false prophets also operate in the demonic counterfeit parallel of the word of knowledge and wisdom, they do not know the most important facts about the future! If evil spirits including their prince knew the future; Yeshua Jesus our Lord would not have been our Redeemer! Demons can perform that which false prophets have spoken concerning the past, present and some futuristic events, but only the LORD knows all the deepest secrets and truths of the future. In 1 John 4:1-3 quoting the NIV it is stated: *Dear friends, do not believe every spirit, but test the spirits to see whether they are from God, because many false prophets have gone out into the world. This is how you can recognize the Spirit of God: Every spirit that acknowledges that Jesus Christ has come in the flesh is from God, but every spirit that does not acknowledge Jesus is not from*

God. This is the spirit of the antichrist, which you have heard is coming and even now is already in the world. God is totally against false prophets (see Deuteronomy 18:20-22).

Check out the prophet's spiritual credentials. These are our Lord's own words, *"Beware of the false prophets, who come to you in sheep's clothing, but inwardly are ravenous wolves. You will know them by their fruits. Grapes are not gathered from thorn bushes nor figs from thistles, are they? So every good tree bears good fruit, but the bad tree bears bad fruit. A good tree cannot produce bad fruit, nor can a bad tree produce good fruit. Every tree that does not bear good fruit is cut down and thrown into the fire. So then, you will know them by their fruits. Not everyone who says to Me, 'Lord, Lord,' will enter the kingdom of heaven, but he who does the will of My Father who is in heaven will enter. Many will say to Me on that day, 'Lord, Lord, did we not prophecy in Your name, and in Your name cast out demons, and in Your name perform many miracles?' And then I will declare to them, 'I never knew you; DEPART FROM ME, YOU WHO PRACTICE LAWLESSNESS"* Mathew 7:15-23 NASB.

A true prophet never draws attention to himself but lead others to Yeshua Jesus. The life of a true prophet is abased and he cannot be bought. He is broken and carries the burden that God gives him with great humility. He fears not repercussions that his words may cause; because he fears not man but GOD alone. Only the words of a true prophet will stand; while those of the false prophets will be their condemnation (Revelation 14:13). The words of the false prophet were described as being like untempered mortar because they were tried by the LORD and found to be lies; failing the ultimate test of truth which is GOD Himself.

Verses 11-16

Say unto them which daub with untempered morter, that it shall fall: there shall be an overflowing shower; and ye, O great hailstones, shall fall; and a stormy wind shall rend it. Lo, when the wall is fallen, shall it not be said unto you, Where is the daubing wherewith ye have daubed it? Therefore thus saith the Lord GOD; I will even rend it with a stormy wind in My fury; and there shall be an overflowing shower in Mine anger, and great hailstones in My fury to consume it. So will I break down the wall that ye have daubed with untempered morter, and bring it down to the ground, so that the foundation thereof shall be discovered, and it shall fall, and ye shall be consumed in the midst thereof: and ye shall know that I am the LORD. Thus will I accomplish My wrath upon the wall, and upon them that have daubed it with untempered morter, and will say unto you, The wall is no more, neither they that daubed it; to wit, the prophets of Israel which prophesy concerning Jerusalem, and which see visions of peace for her, and there is no peace, saith the Lord GOD.

The people were persuaded and led astray by false prophets who told them literally to relax, take it easy and enjoy a peaceful life. The prophetic allegory of building a temporary wall means to pacify the people for a season. Their words were neither tested for authenticity or integrity nor did they meet the ultimate revelatory standards as being truly spoken by God. Untempered morter therefore speaks of falsehood. Time is our litmus test of truth that will validate the words of the false prophets as indeed not from God; proving them to be liars. Remember the words of our Savior in Mathew 7:19, 22-23 *"Every tree that bringeth not forth good fruit is hewn down, and cast into the fire . . . . Many will say to Me in that day, Lord, Lord, have we not prophesied in thy name? And in Thy name have cast out devils? And in Thy name done many wonderful works? And then will I profess unto them, I never knew you: depart from Me, ye that work iniquity.* This indeed is an act of transgression and the unrepentant false prophets will be cut off forever from the body of Yeshua Jesus because they were imposters. A righteous God will judge unrighteousness; He has no favorites; His judgment is blind. Prophecies from God are spoken by true prophets to bring about repentance. They were never intended to make one happy; but for the hearers to look inwardly, bowing themselves before the mercies of a Holy God and cry out in agony and a feeling of abject remorse, regret and sorrow for their sins. If contrition is absent, it leads to hardened hearts and the judgment of God on a people or land.

Verses 17-23

Likewise, thou son of man, set thy face against the daughters of thy people, which prophecy out of their own heart; and prophecy thou against them, and say, Thus saith the Lord GOD; Woe to the women that sew pillows to all armholes, and make kerchiefs upon the head of every stature to hunt souls! Will ye hunt the souls of My people, and will ye save the souls alive that come unto you? And will ye pollute Me among My people for handfuls of barley and for pieces of bread, to slay the souls that should not die, and to save the souls alive that should not live, by your lying to My people that hear your lies? Wherefore thus saith the Lord GOD; Behold, I am against your pillows, wherewith ye there hunt the souls to make them fly, and I will tear them from your arms, and will let the souls go, even the souls that ye hunt to make them fly. Your kerchiefs also will I tear, and deliver My people out of your hand, and they shall no more be in your hand to be hunted; and ye shall know that I am the LORD. Because with lies ye have made the heart of the righteous sad; and strengthened the hands of the wicked, that he should not return from his wicked way, by promising him life: therefore ye shall see no more vanity, nor divine divinations: for I will deliver My people out of your hand: and ye shall know that I am the LORD.

Again the Lord uses allegory to describe the false prophetesses in the nation who prophesy for gain. These women were said to have sewn pillows to every armholes and also making handkerchiefs to be placed upon the head. The symbolic interpretation refers to the practices of these women who manufactured amulets and lucky charms that were worn by their recipients. These objects were to be placed on certain parts of the body as directed, but there was nothing charming about these objects, in fact they were believed to be a source of curses or spells, which would bring harm to the godly. The people who bought the amulets were deceived into believing that the LORD was in agreement with their usage, but in fact, they were curses. These people used the name of the LORD as a deceptive religious advertisement to sell their wares and obscure their true motives. Unknown to the buyers, demonic incantations were woven into these lucky charms for the sole purpose of causing bad omens to plague the righteous. But the eyes of the LORD were watching. 2 Peter 2:9 is a warning to all: *The Lord knoweth how to deliver the godly out of temptations, and to reserve the unjust unto the Day of Judgment to be punished,* NKJV. The day is coming when our Lord will separate the wheat from the weed. It will be a time of great mourning when the false prophets, both male and female are exposed for all the evil they have done.

Chapter 14

Verses 1-11

Then came certain of the elders of Israel unto me, and sat before me. And the word of the LORD came unto me, saying, Son of man, these men have set up their idols in their heart, and put the stumbling block of heir iniquity before their face: should I be inquired of at all by them? Therefore speak unto them, and say unto them, Thus saith the Lord GOD; Every man of the house of Israel that setteth up his idol in his heart, and putteth the stumblingblock of his iniquity before his face, and cometh to the prophet, I the LORD will answer him that cometh according to the multitude of his idols; that I may take the house of Israel in their own heart, because they are all estranged from Me through their idols. Therefore say unto the house of Israel, Thus saith the Lord GOD; Repent, and turn yourselves from your idols; and turn away your faces from all your abominations. For every one of the house of Israel, or of the stranger that sojourneth in Israel, which separateth himself from Me, and setteth up his idols in his heart, and putteth the stumblingblock of his iniquity before his face, and cometh to a prophet to enquire of him concerning Me; I the LORD will answer him Myself: and I will set My face against that man, and will make him a sign and a proverb, and I will cut him off from the midst of My people; and ye shall know that I am the LORD. And if the prophet be deceived when he hath spoken a thing, I the LORD have deceived that prophet, and I will stretch out My hand upon him, and will destroy him from the midst of My people Israel. and they shall bear the punishment of their iniquity: the punishment of the prophet shall be even as the punishment of him that seeketh unto him; that the house of Israel may go no more astray from Me, neither be polluted any more with all their transgressions; but that they may be My people, and I may be their God, saith the Lord GOD.

The leaders of Israel came to Ezekiel to inquire of the LORD, knowing well they were evil and corrupt with devious intentions. Their hearts deceived them into believing they lacked nothing, yet they were blind. They came into this world physically naked and would indeed leave this world spiritually naked as well. They served their gods of pagan images in secret, but nothing in heaven or earth can conceal itself from God's searching eyes. Seeking out Ezekiel was for show and false pretence; appearing godly, they sat before the prophet and the LORD responded. Even after Judah was exiled in Babylon they were still prideful; Babylonian tyranny had not bereft them from being arrogant.

The Lord now calls for repentance before it was too late. Those who separated themselves from Abba Father were sealing their own fate. Idolatry is a grave sin against the LORD, and for such practices Israel suffered. The LORD also warned the false prophets that they would not escape His ruling. These deceivers would bear the punishment of the people who inquired of them; as it was by their advice that they sinned. Here is yet another warning to the children of God: remove from your dwelling places all forms of charms, amulets, figurines, carvings and three dimensional forms of any idols, whether sculpted or modeled, molten, carved or casts from any material whether stone, clay, wood, copper, silver or gold; these may be spiritual gateways or portals for demonic activity, which may cause a variety of curses and misfortune to be upon yourself and also your family. The LORD calls these things an abomination, even if they are used as an act of worship unto Him. Indeed it would not be Almighty GOD that worship is being offered, but unto Satan himself.

Verses 12-23

The word of the LORD came again to me, saying, Son of man, when the land sinneth against Me, by trespassing grievously, then will I stretch out Mine hand upon it, and will break the staff of the bread thereof, and will send famine upon it, and will cut off man and beast from it: though these three men, Noah, Daniel, and Job, were in it, they should deliver but their own souls by their righteousness, saith the Lord GOD. If I cause noisome beasts to pass through the land, and they spoil it, so that it be desolate, that no man may pass through because of the beasts: though these three men were in it, as I live, saith the Lord GOD, they shall deliver neither sons nor daughters; they only shall be delivered, but the land shall be desolate. Or if I bring a sword upon that land, and say, Sword, go through the land; so that I cut off man and beast from it: though these three men were in it, as I live, saith the Lord GOD, they shall deliver neither sons nor daughters, but they only shall be delivered themselves. Or if I send a pestilence into that land, and pour out My fury upon it in blood, to cut off from it man and beast: though Noah, Daniel, and Job, were in it, as I live, saith the Lord GOD, they shall deliver neither son nor daughter; they shall but deliver their own souls by their righteousness. For thus saith the Lord GOD; how much more when I send My four sore judgments upon Jerusalem, the word, and famine, and the noisome beast, and the pestilence, to cut off from it man and beast? Yet, behold, therein shall be left a remnant that shall be brought forth, both sons and daughters: behold, they shall come forth unto you, and ye shall see their way and their doings: and ye shall be comforted concerning the evil that I have brought upon Jerusalem, even concerning all that I have brought upon it. And they shall comfort you, when ye see their ways and doings: and ye shall know that I have not done without cause all that I have done in it, saith the Lord GOD.

The Lord does nothing without a reason: Psalm 32:5-7 applying the NKJV states: *I acknowledged my sin to You, and my iniquity I have not hidden. I said, "I will confess my transgressions to the LORD," and You forgave the iniquity of my sin. For this cause everyone who is godly shall pray to You in a time when You may be found; surely in a flood of great waters they shall not come near him. You are my hiding place; You shall preserve me from trouble; You shall surround me with songs of deliverance.* David was called a man after God's own heart (1 Samuel 13:14; 16:1; Acts 13:22). As seen in several of his pleas, David would always repent whenever he missed the mark. When sin wrapped its condemning armor around him, he would cry out to God in true repentance. God will withhold His planned punishment when we repent, but here in our study of Ezekiel, we see that most of the leaders and people were corrupt and walked in defiance. The few righteous among them who feared God and stood in the gap would stir the compassion of the LORD, because He never forgets the cries of the righteous. We see here in the opening verses of this study (14:12-23): there is no covering; each person is judged based on his or her own righteousness or lack thereof.

In these twelve verses the Lord mentioned Noah, Daniel, and Job as being righteous men, and so they were. All three bore a very significant and similar quality in that they were all intercessors or mediators between God and man. Next we observe the LORD saying to Ezekiel three times, *"Though these three men were in it;"* tells yet another story which is: God will not change His mind, nor cancel His plans, but He will remember the righteous and will save them on account of their righteousness.

Priest and people alike were living a compromised life and because judgment was not immediate; their lawlessness escalated to a greater height until Abba Father had to do something about it. This is the propensity of human nature: when calamity strikes we come together; forgetting our difference, but after a few weeks the impact of the disaster gradually fades away for most, if not all. God is truly merciful, when a nation or people commit iniquity; they step from under the protective covering of the Lord, thereby becoming an easy target for the enemy. Calamity is therefore justified; not that God caused it, but because the people brought it upon themselves. The Lord GOD knows that safety is found only in Him. The enemy comes to steal, kill and to destroy (John 10:10). Calamity comes when the people opens the door for it. The prayers of the righteous are seen here as being a safe haven for themselves it does not cover family or friends.

The house of Israel faced many challenges: famine, diseases, death and destruction, persecutions and wars, because they refused to retreat to the safety of God's presence. Destruction now follows the people as well as the land, stripping it of the living. The evil beasts that were let loose were referring to the Babylonians and other nations that would be the source of their calamities. No matter what form persecution took; wherever the Jews went oppression followed them like an avenging wild animal. The LORD however promised to leave a remnant to preserve His people. The Hebrew word used in Ezekiel 14:22 for "remnant" is **Peletah** [6413], it simply means that a group would escape death to preserve their lineage. Isaiah 37:31-32 states: *And the remnant that is escaped of the house of Judah shall again take root downward, and bear fruit upward: for out of Jerusalem shall go forth a remnant, and they that escape out of Mount Zion: the zeal of the LORD of hosts shall do this.* The Jewish bloodline will be preserved throughout eternity and the modern detective called DNA will reveal the true Jew to the surprise of many.

The next word we will examine is "noisome;" it is mentioned four times in the Bible, Psalm 91:3; Ezekiel 14:15, 21 and Revelation 16:2. This word is used to describe the nature and character of the beasts and its goal was to bring dearth and death upon the city of Jerusalem. Ezekiel was already in Babylon when the LORD gave him this vision; therefore it was a depiction of the woes that would follow Judah. That which was started by the Babylonians will be finished by a nation influenced by the spirit of Babylon until Yeshua Messiah returns and put an end to Israel's sufferings. The Levite Asaph penned these words: *O God, the nations have come into Your inheritance; Your holy temple they have defiled; they have laid Jerusalem in heaps. The dead bodies of Your servants they have given as food for the birds of the heavens, the flesh of your saints to the beasts of the earth. Their blood they have shed like water all around Jerusalem, and there was no one to bury them. we have become a reproach to our neighbors, a scorn and derision to those who are around us. How long, LORD? Will You be angry forever? Will your jealousy burn like fire? Pour out Your wrath on the nations that do not know You, and on the kingdoms that do not call on Your name. for they have devoured Jacob, and laid waste his dwelling place. Oh, do not remember former iniquities against us! Let Your tender mercies come speedily to meet us, for we have been brought very low. Help us O God our salvation, for the glory of Your name; and deliver us, and provide atonement for our sins, for Your name's sake! Why should the nations say, "Were is their God?" Let there be known among the nations in our sight the avenging of the blood of your servants which has been shed. Let the groaning of the prisoner come before You; according to the greatness of your power preserve those who are appointed to die; and return to our neighbors sevenfold into their bosom their reproach with which they have reproached You, O Lord. So we, Your people and sheep of Your pasture, will give you thanks forever: we will show forth your praise to al generations;* Psalm 79 NKJV, (see also Lamentations 1:1-11). The repeated warnings to the people of Judah by the prophets of God went unheeded. Was the LORD to be blamed for the ill wind that blew upon Israel? The four punishments: the sword, famine, evil beasts, and plagues were all punishments of death, yet a merciful Father to Israel kept a remnant alive for Himself as His own eye witnesses who would rehearse the story of Israel's reward for sin and rebellion as well as their triumphant victories when they walked in righteousness and the fear of the LORD.

Chapter 15

Verses 1-8

And the word of the LORD came unto me, saying, Son of man, What is the vine tree more than any tree, or than a branch which is among the trees of the forest? Shall wood be taken thereof to do any work? Or will men take a pin of it to hang any vessel thereon? Behold, it is cast into the fire for fuel; the fire devoureth both the ends of it, and the midst of it is burned. Is it meet for any work? Behold, when it was whole, it was meet for no work: how much less shall it be meet yet for any work, when the fire hath devoured it, and it is burned? Therefore thus saith the Lord GOD; As the vine tree among the trees of the forest, which I have given to the fire for fuel, so will I give the inhabitants of Jerusalem. And I will set My face against them; they shall go out from one fire, and another fire shall devour them; and ye shall know that I am the LORD, when I set My face against them. And I will make the land desolate, because they have committed a trespass, saith the Lord GOD.

In questioning Ezekiel about the vine tree the LORD continues to use symbolic language to refer to the whole house of Israel. When the LORD spoke with Ezekiel it was not time for trivia neither was it to get an answer from the prophet. The LORD put forth a series of questions to Ezekiel in this short chapter to bring about his attention to the sins of the twelve tribes. Ezekiel became more aware of the reason for the deportation by the questions and sensed the betrayal and pain that the LORD felt for His people. Big sister Israel was no better that Judah in their crimes against God. What really is the vine tree or branches? Why did the LORD draw reference to a tree? He is the King of Israel, He betrothed them, He is married to them, and therefore Israel is closely and generationally connected to Yeshua Jesus who is the ultimate true vine. Jesus said in John 15:4-5: *Abide in Me, and I in you. As the branch cannot bear fruit of itself unless it abides in the vine, so neither can you unless you abide in Me. I am the vine, you are the branches; he who abides in Me and I in him, he bears much fruit, for apart from Me you can do nothing,* NASB. In Exodus 4:22 and Jeremiah 31:7-9 Israel is called His first born to which Gentiles are engrafted.

The LORD is here speaking of the whole house of Israel whom He has blessed to be a light to the world; a city on a hill that cannot be hid (Matthew 5:14). Israel is the chosen nation of God as seen throughout the entire cannon of Scriptures, yet many have low spiritual and moral values. Through them Gentiles would be blessed, but instead, the Gentiles oppressed them for a season until the tables were turned following the six day war of June 5th–10th 1967 when Israel regained the upper hand. This was a miracle from God and a turning point in their history as Abba Father's favor turns towards His people once again and allowed them to defeat their enemies; recapturing Jerusalem although greatly outnumbered. They are the legal residents of Israel, but this land truly belongs to the LORD (Psalm 24). Israel remains stiff-necked and because of their failure to acknowledge the LORD as their Supreme ruler, they will continue to suffer as they insist on doing things their way. Arrogance is a mark of pride and with it comes disastrous consequences leading to the unnecessary loss of lives. Israel's President, Prime Minister and leaders of the Knesset are no different from their forefathers. Israel must earnestly seek the face of the LORD their God for military direction or suffer greatly at the hands of their enemies. Military power without God's power is no power at all; yet Abba Father will retain the honor of His name, by giving this tiny democratic nation victory over greater nations against all odds.

The Word of God is the same, yesterday, today, and forevermore. The God of the Torah is also the God of the entire cannon of Scriptures. He sent His only Son Yeshua HaMashiach of the blood line of David, whom most Jews have rejected unto this day. It was this same Yeshua Jesus their brethren who was crucified, laid in a borrowed tomb of a rich follower, resurrected on the third day then ascended into heaven. One day Yeshua will return as prophesied, to reclaim His inheritance (Luke 24:46-52; Acts 1:9-11; John 6:32-33). He gave His life for all, and many eye witnesses of His ministry on earth have died for this testimony of Him. Would anyone risk being killed or volunteer to give up their life for someone if their existence was verified and proven to be a myth or exposed as being an imposter?

To reject Yeshua Jesus is also a rejection of Abba Father and His Holy Spirit. It is impossible to separate the Godhead, since they testify of each other. Yeshua Jesus said in John 15:26, *"But when the Comforter is come, whom I will send unto you from the Father, even the Spirit of truth, which proceedeth from the Father, He shall testify of Me.* We cannot separate Father, Son or Holy Spirit. To deny any part of their Divine preeminence is to deny them all. The house of Israel has suffered historically because of their rejection of truth although Yeshua the true vine never left them. They have allowed corruption to take over like a diseased branch and were cut off from the vine by their own disobedience. Persecution has followed them down throughout the centuries; no matter where they went they became the target of physical and verbal abuse and even death. A point to note here is that all nations or peoples or organizations that have persecuted the house of Israel to the point of near extinction, have experienced the same calamity they desired for Israel, yet the seed of Abraham has continued to flourish like the stars of heaven until this day.

The Lord allows Israel's sufferings, but woe to those who takes pleasure in seeking their pain. Check the Holy Scriptures; no descendants of heathens who came against the nation of Israel are alive today to gloat over their historical victories and this should be a warning. A parent punishes his child, but woe to those who takes it upon themselves to punish Israel. To Israel: be careful of complacency, arrogance, and pride. Honor, serve and celebrate the Lord GOD in the beauty of holiness. Worship the LORD and He will make all your enemies your footstool. A message to the secular and unbelieving Jew: if Abba Father sets His face against you; you will be cut off like a rejected vine and another will be engrafted in your place.

Chapter 16

Verses 1-10

Again the word of the LORD came unto me, saying, Son of man, cause Jerusalem to know her abominations, and say, Thus saith the Lord GOD unto Jerusalem; Thy birth and thy nativity is of the land of Canaan; thy father was an Amorite, and thy mother an Hittite. And as for thy nativity, in the day thou wast born thy navel was not cut, neither wast thou washed in water to supple thee; thou wast not salted at all, nor swaddled at all. None eye pitied thee, to do any of these unto thee, to have compassion upon thee; but thou wast cast out in the open field, to the loathing of thy person, in the day that thou wast born. And when I passed by thee, and saw thee polluted in thine own blood, I said unto thee when thou wast in thy blood, live; yea, I said unto thee when thou wast in thy blood, Live. I have caused thee to multiply as the bud of the field, and thou hast increased and waxen great, and thou art come to excellent ornaments: thy breasts are fashioned, and thine hair is grown, whereas thou wast naked and bare. Now when I passed by thee, and looked upon thee, behold, thy time was the time of love; and I spread My skirt over thee, and covered thy nakedness: yea; I sware unto thee, and entered into a covenant with thee, saith the Lord GOD, and thou becamest Mine. Then washed I thee with water; yea, I thoroughly washed away thy blood from thee, and I anointed thee with oil. I clothed thee also with broidered work, and shod thee with badgers' skin, and I girded thee about with fine linen, and I covered thee with silk.

The LORD continues His dialogue with Ezekiel in which He reveals His undying love for Israel: where He took her from and what He had done for her; yet her eyes were not totally on Him. Every time He drew her close to His heart, she would appease Him only for a season. There was however a spiritual force within her the wrestling of a rebel in defiance, to separate her from the Almighty God, her only true hope. The arch enemy was the very one who worked through men to both corrupt and destroy all traces of the Hebrew heritage from the time they became a nation to the time of the Pharaohs. Worming his evil web of hatred down through the ages, he sought to destroy the young child Yeshua and when that did not work he turned one of His disciples against Him in an endless effort to destroy the Holy seed because his sinister plans were to rule above the LORD God of heaven and earth. Every trap and every attempt to destroy the Son of God proved to be a triumphant victory not only for Yeshua Jesus, but for all mankind. Abba Father will continue to forgive the trespasses of His people, because the war that rages within is influenced by the diabolical plans of the fallen arch angel and his evil underdogs. This is the core reason for the continuous turbulent winds of war against Israel to be defiant and resist the supreme authority of the LORD, not knowing that their safety and victory is found in GOD alone. That which applies to Israel, also applies to all Believers in Yeshua Messiah; both Jews and Gentiles; remember Yeshua's words: We will be hated, persecuted and killed for His name (Matthew 24:9).

The LORD now likens His people unto the conditions and circumstances of one that were born in the land of Canaan. In ancient times these people did not worship the GOD of Abraham, Isaac and Jacob. They were pagans who worshiped idols and the host of heaven; it was to these same images that Israel unashamedly turned to. The Hebrews who were born among the heathens also followed the decadent religious practices of their forefathers and the judgment of the LORD would not spare these idolaters; all would feel the effect of His disapproval.

Because of these abominable acts of unrighteousness, the LORD viewed the dwellers of the city of Jerusalem as being a people sired by an Amorite, while their mother was a Hittite. Both nations mentioned here were idol worshipers whom the LORD warned Moses not to mingle with or adopt their ways. We see this plainly in Exodus 34:10-17: *And He said, Behold, I make a covenant: before all thy people I will do marvels, such as have not been done in all the earth, nor in any nation: and all the people among which thou art shall see the work of the LORD: for it is a terrible thing that I will do with thee. Observe thou that which I command thee this day: behold, I drive out before thee the Amorite, and the Canaanite, and the Hittite, and the Perizzite, and the Hivite, and the Jebusite. Take heed to thy self, lest thou make a covenant with the inhabitants of the land whither thou goest, lest it be for a snare in the midst of thee: but ye shall destroy the altars, break their images, and cut down their groves: for thou shalt worship no other god: for the LORD, whose name is Jealous, is a jealous God: lest thou make a covenant with the inhabitants of the land, and they go a whoring after their gods, and one call thee, and thou eat of his sacrifice; and thou take their daughters unto thy sons, and their daughters go a whoring after their gods, and make thy sons go a whoring after their gods. Thou shalt make thee no molten gods,* (for further reading see also Leviticus 26:1; Habakkuk 2:18-19; Deuteronomy 4:14-21; Acts 17:22-31). This was the command of the LORD, yet the children of Israel did the exact opposite.

The analogy the LORD made of equating Israel's progenitors to that of an Amorite and a Hittite, was basically saying that these nations were a stench unto Him, but Israel was much worse; taking idolatry to a new and more detestable level. The LORD continued His conversation with Ezekiel by describing the Israelites as behaving like unwanted children who had been abandoned and left without father or mother to care for them; rearing them righteously and in the fear of the LORD. When the LORD looked upon the polluted state of His people, He had great compassion upon them;

declaring life over them even in the midst of their darkness and absolute depravity. The LORD goes on to state how He blessed the house of Israel; causing the nations around them to greatly fear them, and if that was not enough; He lauded them with great victories and prosperities yet they were never satisfied. The more Abba Father blessed Israel, was the more careless and unaffectionate they became, rejecting His freewill offering of unconditional love, mercy, and grace.

The LORD covered their shame by spreading His garment over them, which is to say, "I have called you and have chosen you to be Mine," (see Jeremiah 3:11-14; Ruth 3:9-12; 4:1-11). Abba Father's heart was obviously broken, as He continues His dialogue with Ezekiel over His betrothed Israel. He first spoke of washing them, alluding to their cleansing and separation as the custom of a betrothed wife. The next step in this preparation was the complete washing away of their blood, which spoke of their old sin nature. The blood of bullocks and goats were only a temporary solution but Yeshua's sacrifice of His own body offered once, became the permanent intercessor in heaven before the throne of GOD (see Hebrews 9:11-15). The third step after the LORD had cleansed Israel; was to anoint them with oil which meant He dedicated them unto Himself. This was the same plan procured for the body of Yeshua Jesus, by our washing, regeneration, reconciliation and renewing (Titus 3:5; John 16:13-15). Ezekiel 16:9 also alludes to the salvation plan; as it speaks of a thorough cleansing and sanctification.

There is so much that the LORD wants to reveal to us in these times. As we continue to analyze the Word of the LORD to the prophet Ezekiel, a duality in the prophetic is unveiled. In Ezekiel 16:10 the LORD spoke of not one, but two temples. The first temple was that of Moses and the second; a typology of His final work in man. Verse ten also speaks of being adorned with embroidered work, badger's skin, linen and silk; these are four very important points concerning Israel and the salvation plan for all of humanity.

In the making of the priestly garment, Moses was told: *And thou shalt embroider the coat of fine linen, and thou shalt make the miter of fine linen, and thou shalt make the girdle of needlework;* Exodus 28:39. The art of embroidery entails the use of needles to create a beautiful tapestry. Many will be superficially enamored by the finished product, yet never stop to think of the labor of love, time, skill, and effort, necessary to produce such an appealing finished product. The stitching of the fabric allows a certain pattern to be visualized, and with the completion of such fine needle work; a gradual and systematic unfolding of what was in the mind of the Creator is revealed. The needle must first pierce holes into the fabric and with each piercing a gradual transformation unfolds, until the entire fabric becomes a beautiful work of art. This is also the working of Holy Spirit as we yield to His gentle tugging, urging and encouragement to be light in this dark world. Many will follow a lit pathway, while many more will stumble in darkness. 1 John 1:5-7 states: *This then is the message which we have heard of Him, and declare unto you, that God is light, and in Him is no darkness at all. If we say that we have fellowship with Him, and walk in darkness, we lie, and do not the truth: but if we walk in the light, as He is in the light, we have fellowship one with another, and the blood of Jesus Christ His Son cleanseth us from all sin.* We must be the light of the world and only Holy Spirit can commence and complete this work in us; recreating and reconstructing the temple of man beginning first with a covering of badger's skin.

Many debates have been purported that the animal hide mentioned in these verses could not have been that of a badger since it was considered to be unclean, but this however is not our focus. The badger's skin points to our filth and the act of Yeshua Jesus in making us clean from all defilement. He became a protective covering for our sins because we are of great value to Him. 2 Corinthians 5:17-21 speaks of this new creative work: *Therefore, if anyone is in Christ, he is a new creation; old things have passed away; behold, all things have become new. Now all things are of God, who has reconciled us to Himself through Jesus Christ, and has given us the ministry of reconciliation, that is, that God was in Christ reconciling the world to Himself, not imputing their trespasses to them, and has committed to us the word of reconciliation. Now then, we are ambassadors for Christ, as though God were pleading through us: we implore you on Christ's behalf, be reconciled to God. For He made Him who knew no sin to be sin for us, that we might become the righteousness of God in Him,* NKJV. The badgers' skin therefore, is symbolic of Yeshua Jesus becoming sin for us that in Him, we might become the righteousness of God. The LORD clothed Israel with this protective layer to explain Yeshua's finished work on the Cross of Calvary because He became our covering there. The sins of mankind were pardoned as Yeshua Jesus gave up His life for all sinners.

The LORD now speaks of encircling and fastening His people with the finest linen. There are more than thirty references in the book of Exodus to fine linen; from the priestly garment, the veil of the temple and the hangings of the court. The flax plant is the source of the silky fiber processed to make linen; it is first soaked then beaten to loosen and separate the fibers. As with the embroidered work the end result is one of beauty, and a picture of Yeshua's finished work. Isaiah 53:5 states: *But He was wounded for our transgressions, He was bruised for our iniquities; the chastisement for our peace was upon Him, and by His stripes we are healed,* NKJV. Healing for the body of Yeshua was made possible through the suffering of Yeshua. The symbolism of the embroidered work, the covering of badgers' skin, and the girding with fine linen all points to rebirth and a new creation afforded by Yeshua Messiah. Hebrews 6:4-6 states: *For it is impossible for those who were once enlightened, and have tasted the heavenly gift, and have become partakers of the Holy Spirit, and have tasted the good word of God and the powers of the age to come, if they fall away, to renew them again to repentance, since they crucify again for themselves the Son of God, and put Him to an open shame.*

The beaten flax releases the fiber that makes the fine linen and fine linen is symbolic of the righteousness of the saints. Revelation 19:8 states: *And to her was granted that she should be arrayed in fine linen, clean and white: for the fine linen is the righteousness of saints.* Israel is here seen as being encircled in righteousness, she is no ordinary woman, but a betrothed bride. The LORD continues His dialogue with Ezekiel concerning Israel, by employing more symbolic language, *"I covered thee with silk."* The LORD chooses the very best coverings for His people. Silk was the fabric that made the garments of royalties; it is the signature of wealth and also the veil of the wedding gown, which covers the bride's face until her marriage vows are completed. Silk is mentioned only four times in the Bible; Ezekiel 16:10, 13; Proverbs 31:22 and Revelation 18:12; however, in Proverbs 31 a better rendering is linen. If Israel is here viewed as a bride, the addition of silk, which is the fabric of the wealthy and a mark of royalty, could possibly mean the crowning glory upon His elect that is to come. Silk was never used in the tabernacle of Moses, but, instead, points typologically to Israel future and final preparation for marriage: as a rebirth, a new creation in righteousness and a new temple for the habitation of the LORD. The time is upon us, when Yeshua's bride will complete her purification to be presented unto the Father.

Verses 11-14

I decked thee also with ornaments, and I put bracelets upon thy hands, and a chain on thy neck. And I put a jewel on thy forehead, and earrings in thine ears, and a beautiful crown upon thine head. Thus was thou decked with gold and silver; and thy raiment was of fine linen, and silk, and broidered work; thou didst eat fine flour, and honey, and oil: and thou wast exceeding beautiful, and thou didst prosper into a kingdom. And thine renown went forth among the heathen for thy beauty: for it was perfect through My comeliness, which I had put upon thee, saith the Lord GOD.

The description of the betrothal of Israel unto the LORD and their preeminence above all nations continues to be revealed in these verses. The LORD described how He clothed and bestowed His beloved people with great wealth and riches as His down payment for her marriage unto Him. This is no ordinary wedding but a spiritual agreement; an open and binding declaration, that Israel belongs to Him and His honored guests: the Gentiles, will share in Israel's blessings as we will see in volume three of this work. A beautiful crown was then placed upon Israel's head as a symbol of the coming coronation when they will be honored, and the body of Christ established, as belonging to Abba Father. We are living in the time of her preparation; the marriage supper of the Lamb is about to take place and only the bride and her invited guests will partake in this wonderful celebration. R.S.V.P before it is too late. Revelation 19:7-9 states: *Let us be glad and rejoice, and give honor to Him: for the marriage of the Lamb is come, and His wife hath made herself ready. And to her was granted that she should be arrayed in fine linen, clean and white: for the fine linen is the righteousness of saints. And He saith unto me, Write, Blessed are they which are called unto the marriage supper of the Lamb. And He saith unto me, These are the true sayings of God.* Israel is the bride, and the invitees are the engrafted Gentiles who will also be established as sons of God.

The Lord our Redeemer gave this parable about the kingdom that is to come, Matthew 22:2-14 applying the NKJV states: *"The kingdom of heaven is like a certain king who arranged a marriage for his son, and sent out his servants to call those who were invited to the wedding; and they were not willing to come. Again, he sent out other servants, saying, 'Tell those who are invited, "See, I have prepared my dinner; my oxen and fatted cattle are killed, and all things are ready. Come to the wedding."' But they made light of it and went their ways, one to his own farm, another to his business. And the rest seized his servants treated them spitefully, and killed them. But when the king heard about it, he was furious. And he sent out his armies, destroyed those murderers, and burn up their city. Then he said to his servants, 'The wedding is ready, but those who were invited were not worthy. Therefore go into the highways, and as many as you find, invite to the wedding.' So those servants went out into the highways and gathered together all whom they found, both bad and good. And the wedding hall was filled with guests. "But when the king came in to see the guests, he saw a man there who did not have on a wedding garment. So he said to him, 'Friend, how did you come in here without a wedding garment?" And he was speechless. Then the king said to the servants, bind him hand and foot, take him away, and cast him into outer darkness; there will be weeping and gnashing of teeth.' "For many are called, but few are chosen."* What sorrow awaits those who procrastinate? What pain will be felt by unbelievers? What disappointments will the haters of Yeshua and His Father experience when they realize that they were dead wrong? There will be no more time to repent or report their findings. There will be no more forgiveness and there will be no more answer to prayers. All that will be left will be tears of sorrow and the constant and grim reminder of what could have been, if they had accepted Abba Father's freewill offering of grace.

The tabernacle of Moses or Tent of Meeting was God's very presence among the children of Israel. In fact, the tabernacle of Moses and later the temple built by King Solomon was GOD'S visible temple for the children of Israel until the completed work of Yeshua on the Cross. The tabernacle speaks of God's love for Israel; it provided them with the elements required for righteous living, and it gave them the avenue and release from sin. It spoke of God's presence as their protector, and the reassurance that He would never leave or forsake them. He is and always will be their God in righteousness, judgment, lovingkindness, and grace, mercy and faithfulness, (Hosea 2:19-20). Israel had it good yet they trusted not in Abba Father, but placed their confidence in their good fortune not knowing that their pride and arrogance was about to be deflated for being a harlot.

Verses 15-19

But thou didst trust in thine own beauty, and playedst the harlot because of thy renown, and pouredst out thy fornications on everyone that passed by; his it was. And of thy garments thou didst take, and deckedst thy high places with divers colours, and playedst the harlot thereupon: the like things shall not come, neither shall it be so. Thou hast also taken thy fair jewels of My gold and of My silver, which I had given thee, and madest to thyself images of men, and didst commit whoredom with them, and tookest thy broidered garments, and coveredst them: and thou has set Mine oil and Mine incense before them. My meat also which I gave thee, fine flour, and oil, and honey, wherewith I fed thee, thou hast even set it before them for a sweet savor: and thus it was, saith the Lord GOD.

Complacency gripped the hearts of God's people, arrogance and pride was about to be turned into grief and pain. How could such a rich heritage and blessing turn into a curse? Israel repeatedly abandoned their God; they conducted business their way and in doing so, broke off their engagement in unfaithfulness. The bride to be had already been fitted for her wedding gown, precious jewels had already been secured, but Israel forgot the true meaning of betrothal, which set forth the terms and conditions that the agreement for marriage had already been approved by the Father and received His final blessings. Betrayal was seething in Israel's heart, because they really didn't love their God, and was clueless of the redemptive work He had prepared for them through His Son! If Israel had remained undefiled, they would not have been accused of harlotry! Yet because of the LORD'S integrity and love, He remained betrothed unto them.

The LORD God drew references from the tabernacle of Moses, its furnishings and priesthood to describe His betrothed bride Israel. He sets them apart from all nations and called them His own; yet they remained unfaithful until the time of their repentance and purification as we will soon see. A remnant of people will cleave unto the LORD God and those who have joined with Remnant Israel, they, too, will rejoice as being joint-heirs in their inheritance. There is hope; Yeshua Jesus spoke these words as an exemplar and also an encouragement to the Gentiles: *"The Kingdom of Heaven can be illustrated by the story of a king who prepared a great wedding feast for his son. When the banquet was ready, he sent his servants to notify those who were invited. But they all refused to come! So he sent other servants to tell them, 'The feast has been prepared. The bulls and fatten cattle have been killed, and everything is ready. Come to the banquet!' But the guests he had invited ignored them and went their own way, one to his farm, another to his business. Others seized his messengers and insulted them and killed them. "The king was furious, and he sent out his army to destroy the murderers and burn their town. And he said to his servants, 'The wedding feast is ready, and the guest I invited aren't worthy of honor. Now go out to the street corners and invite everyone you see.' So the servants brought in everyone they could find, good and bad alike, and the banquet hall was filled with guests,* Matthew 22:2-10 NLT.

The invitation is open to all; it is a personal decision to choose whom we will serve not only in this world, but also in the world to come. The fame and victories of Israel ensnared them, and instead of separating themselves from the world, they joined with the haters of God, and the precious things obtained through battle became their ornaments of idolatry. Israel forgot the goodness of the LORD and the many battles He won for them. They bowed themselves before worthless objects fashioned and molded by the workings of man's hands and wild imagination. If that were not bad enough, they took the holy articles and offerings of the LORD and set them forth as oblations to idols. Israel became careless and reckless and their riotous behavior was about to become more appalling.

Verses 20-34

Moreover thou hast taken thy sons and thy daughters, whom thou hast borne unto Me, and these hast thou sacrificed unto them to be devoured. Is this of thy whoredoms a small matter, that thou hast slain My children, and delivered them to cause them to pass through the fire for them? And in all thy abominations and thy whoredoms thou hast not remembered the days of thy youth, when thou wast naked and bare, and wast polluted in thy blood. And it came to pass after all thy wickedness, (woe, woe unto thee! Saith the Lord GOD;) that thou hast also built unto thee an eminent place, and hast made thee an high place in every street. Thou hast built thy high place at every head of the way, and hast made thy beauty to be abhorred, and hast opened thy feet to every one that passed by, and multiplied thy whoredoms. Thou hast also committed fornication with the Egyptians thy neighbours, great of flesh; and hast increased thy whoredoms, to provoke Me to anger. Behold, therefore I have stretched out My hand over thee, and have diminished thine ordinary food, and delivered thee unto the will of them that hate thee, the daughters of the Philistines, which are ashamed of thy lewd way. Thou hast played the whore also with the Assyrians, because thou wast unsatiable; yea, thou hast played the harlot with them, and yet couldest not be satisfied. Thou hast moreover multiplied thy fornication in the land of Canaan unto Chaldea; and yet thou wast not satisfied herewith. How weak is thine heart, saith the Lord GOD, seeing thou doest all these things, the work of an imperious whorish woman; in that thou buildest thine eminent place in the head of every way, and makest thine high place in every street; and hast not been as an harlot, in that thou scornest hire; but as a wife that committeth adultery, which taketh strangers instead of husband! They give gifts to all whores: but thou givest thy gifts to all thy lovers, and hirest them, that they may come unto thee on every side for thy whoredom. And the contrary is in thee from other women in thy whoredoms, whereas none followeth thee to commit whoredoms: and in that thou givest a reward, and no reward is given unto thee, therefore thou art contrary.

Ezekiel 16:20-22 has a dual interpretation, to prove this point let us look at what was happening in Israel at the time when the word of the LORD came to the prophet, next we will examine another revelation that was also unfolding. The people were being judged for taking their sons and daughters to be offered as sacrifice. To sacrifice children was an abominable practice of the heathens that the LORD abhorred and repeatedly warned Israel of the consequences of such practices. The chief reason for this was the fact that humans are sinful by nature and could not be a perfect sacrifice. Sin was a contaminant to our blood line, and for this reason, the LORD God instructed both priests and people alike to present certain unblemished animals as He had instructed for the sin and trespass offerings. This practice continued until Yeshua offered Himself; the perfect and most suitable offering for the sins of all mankind. From the death of Yeshua, the Hebrew people have ceased all temple sacrifices but continue to commemorate other Jewish traditions such as the observance of the Sabbaths, feasts, and festivals. In the coming reign of Yeshua Jesus on earth, these special events will take on a much deeper and reverential meaning.

The LORD God gave this strict order: *"And thou shalt not let any of thy seed pass through the fire to Molech, neither shall thou profane the name of thy God: I am the LORD,"* Leviticus 18:21 (see also 20:1-5). The LORD knew His plans of sending a Redeemer who would be sacrificed hundreds of years later; therefore, He prohibited the slaughter of imperfect sin tainted humans. The next reason for not offering humans as a sacrifice lies in the fact that such practices are tied to the occult. Leviticus 17:10-12 warns us: *And whatsoever man there be of the house of Israel, or of the strangers that sojourn among you, that eateth any manner of blood; I will even set My face against that soul that eateth blood, and will cut him off from among his people. For the life of the flesh is in the blood: and I have given it to you upon the altar to make an atonement for your souls: for it is the blood that maketh an atonement for the soul. Therefore I said unto the children of Israel, No soul of you shall eat blood, neither shall any stranger that sojourneth among you eat blood.* The life is in the blood and for this reason the Blood of Yeshua drives fear in the spiritual realm because it is perfect! Yeshua Jesus' DNA is sacred and pure, therefore, by its very essence of purity, the power of victorious life flows from it and this Satan and his host cannot bear for they too knows of the wonder working power of His blood!

The children of Israel knew the requirements of the teachings of God, yet they broke them by offering their children as sacrifices unto Molech, who is Satan himself. The name Molech means *"the reigning one,"* the prince and power of the air. Human sacrifice is the worst crime that anyone can commit, therefore an abominable stench to a Holy God and in these last days this practice has taken on a more sinister and diabolical undertone. The word of God stands firm forever; Psalm 33:11; 119:89; Isaiah 40:8; 1 Peter 1:25 and nothing will ever change this. These are Yeshua's own words: *"Heaven and earth shall pass away, but My words shall not pass away,"* Matthew 24:35; Mark 13:31; Luke 21:33. There is nothing new under the sun. The same God who judged Israel for offering their children unto Molech: *"the reigning one;"* will judge the earth in this present millennium for these same types of sin.

The sins of Israel progressed because punishment was not immediate. They conceptualize that God was unaware of the evil they perpetuated, but as they thought all was well; when they drank and made merry, judgment came. The silence of God is a warning period of His grace, He wants His people to repent, but even grace has limitations. Israel now raised the bar of insolence by building more elaborate places to perform idolatrous rituals and worship that were more grandeur than those constructed by their heathen neighbors. Sexual immoralities and orgies were vomited upon the earth and beguiled Israel sought after its pleasures.

In Ezekiel 16:25, the LORD referred to Israel as opening their feet to everyone that passed by; multiplying their promiscuity. Four hundred and thirty years living in Egypt, had diluted the beliefs and customs of many Hebrews thereby inflicting a great damage to their cultural and spiritual heritage. Although the LORD had chosen Jacob for Himself and Israel for His special treasure, they repeatedly rebelled against Him, Psalm 135:4. Israel left Egypt, but Egypt was still in them. They made a golden calf shortly after leaving that land; and at times begged to return to enjoy its delicacies. Four hundred plus years of being acclimated to the Egyptian culture would become a stumbling block between them and the LORD their God. Israel grew to be a vast nation, yet the presence of God grew lesser among them because they rebelled and stubbornly rejected their Spiritual Rock.

The Apostle Paul said: *"For I do not want you to be unaware, brethren, that our fathers were all under the cloud and all passed through the sea; and all were baptized into Moses in the cloud and in the sea; and all ate the same spiritual food; and all drank the same spiritual drink, for they were drinking from a spiritual rock which followed them; and the rock was Christ. Nevertheless, with most of them God was not well-pleased; for they were laid low in the wilderness. Now these things happened as examples for us, so that we would not crave evil things as they also craved. Do not be idolaters, as some of them were; as it is written, "THE PEOPLE SAT DOWN TO EAT AND DRINK, AND STOOD UP TO PLAY." Nor let us act immorally, as some of them did, and twenty-three thousand fell in one day. Nor let us try the Lord, as some of them did, and were destroyed by the serpents. Nor grumble as some of them did, and were destroyed by the destroyer. Now these things happened to them as an example, and they were written for our instruction, upon whom the ends of the ages have come. Therefore let him who thinks he stands take heed that he does not fall,"* 1 Corinthians 10:1-12 NASB. God is so compassionate; He gives His beloved children a chance and also a choice to repent. Psalm 30:5 states: *For His anger endureth but a moment; in His favor is life: weeping may endure for a night, but joy cometh in the morning.* The Lord never punishes without a cause. The rebellion of the people of God has continued to this day in one form or another. Those who will stand for godliness and holiness will be the remnant that will rise from these polluted ashes of human decadence.

By the mighty hand of God, the Israelites left Egypt at the end of the tenth plague, but instead of trusting in the Lord their GOD, they lusted after the visible gods of Egypt. Israel also followed the customs of the Philistines and Assyrians; worshiping the God of Israel, yet clinging to a host of idols. 2 kings 17:5-20 narrates: *Now the king of Assyria went throughout all the land, and went up to Samaria and besieged it for three years. In the ninth year of Hoshea, the king of Assyria took Samaria and carried Israel away to Assyria, and placed them in Halah and by the Harbor, the river of Gozan, and in the cities of the Medes. For so it was that the children of Israel had sinned against the LORD their God, who had brought them up out of the land of Egypt, from under the hand of Pharaoh king of Egypt; and they had feared other gods, and had walked in the statutes of the nations whom the LORD had cast out from before the children of Israel, which they had made. Also the children of Israel secretly did against the LORD their God things that were not right, and they built for themselves high places in all their cities, from watchtower to fortified city. They set up for themselves sacred pillars and wooden images on every high hill and under every green tree. There they burned incense on all the high places, like the nations whom the LORD had carried away before them; and they did wicked things to provoke the LORD to anger, for they served idols, of which the LORD had said to them, "You shall not do this thing," Yet the LORD testified against Israel and against Judah, by all of His prophets, every seer, saying, "Turn from your evil ways, and keep My commandments and My statutes, according to all the law which I commanded your fathers, and which I sent to you by My servants the prophets." Nevertheless they would not hear, but stiffened their necks, like the necks of their fathers, who did not believe in the LORD their God. And they rejected His statutes and His covenant that He had made with their fathers, and His testimonies which He had testified against them; they followed idols, became idolaters, and went after the nations who were all around them, concerning whom the LORD had charged them that they should not do like them. So they left all the commandments of the LORD their God, made for themselves a molded image and two calves, made a wooden image and worshiped all the host of heaven, and served Baal. And they caused their sons and daughters to pass through the fire, practiced witchcraft and soothsaying, and sold themselves to do evil in the sight of the LORD, to provoke Him to anger. Therefore the Lord was very angry with Israel, and removed them from His sight; there was none left but the tribe of Judah alone. Also Judah did not keep the commandments of the LORD their God, but walked in the statutes of Israel which they made. And the LORD rejected all the descendants of Israel, afflicted them, and delivered them into the hand of plunderers, until He had cast them from His sight,* NKJV. These verses plainly document the sins of Israel and their subsequent fall from grace. They were a called out people much like the body of Yeshua, but they lived a life of complacency, whoredom and idolatry, thereby rearing offspring who did not follow the LORD their God wholeheartedly. Israel preferred bondage rather than freedom, oppression more than the perfect will of God. They repeatedly cried out for help; but when help came and they were at rest; they subtly slipped into idolatry once again.

The LORD pours out His heart for His betrothed like a faithful husband would to an unfaithful wife. If only His unfaithful wife would realize that she is truly loved. If only she could free herself from the mixture of lie and truth that she tasted and found pleasurable. If only she would wake up from her drunken stupor, and realize that she was fed a mixture that was like oil and water. She is so taken in by darkness that very little light remain to show her the way. The eyes of the Lord kept watching; hoping that she would follow the leading of Holy Spirit to guide her back to the safe haven of His arms. She is so conformed to the ways of the world, and now must depend on the smallest grain of truth, still precariously holding on in her conscience and still resonating in her soul to recognize that she had been fed with lies all the days of her life. Her forerunners served her the delicates of sin and the twisting of the Word of God and it was now a difficult task for her to separate the smallest grains of truth from the near insurmountable sands of lies that she had unwittingly accepted from her birth.

Israel as well as the body of Christ have bought into the harlot system and are enjoying its favors not knowing that we have been deceived. We are being lured away from the righteous path set before us to be the light of the world. Our numbers are rapidly diminishing and our voices are systematically being weakened because we fear man and not the LORD our GOD.

Verses 35-43

Wherefore, O harlot, hear the word of the LORD: Thus saith the Lord GOD; Because thy filthiness was poured out, and thy nakedness discovered through thy whoredoms with thy lovers, and with all the idols of thy abominations, and by the blood of thy children, which thou didst give unto them; Behold, therefore I will gather all thy lovers, with whom thou hast taken pleasure, and all them that thou hast loved, with all them that thou hast hated; I will even gather them round about against thee, and will discover thy nakedness unto them, that they may see all thy nakedness. And I will judge thee, as women that break wedlock and shed blood in fury and jealousy. And I will also give thee into their hand, and they shall throw down thine eminent place, and shall break down thy high places: they shall strip thee also of thy clothes, and shall take thy fair jewels, and leave thee naked and bare. They shall also bring up company against thee, and they shall stone thee with stones, and thrust thee through with their swords. And they shall burn thy houses with fire, and execute judgments upon thee in the sight of many women: and I will cause thee to cease from playing the harlot, and thou also shalt give no hire any more. So will I make My fury toward thee to rest, and My jealousy shall depart from thee, and I will be quiet, and will be no more angry. Because thou hast not remembered the days of thy youth, but hast fretted Me in all these things; behold, therefore I also will recompense thy way upon thine head, saith the Lord GOD: and thou shalt not commit this lewdness above all thine abominations.

The Lord pronounced judgment upon His people. Israel was now the laughing stock of the nations who saw them as being worst than they were. The sons of God failed; instead of separating themselves from all that grieved Abba Father; they participated in the folly and whoredoms of the ungodly to the lowest point of child sacrifice. Because of these great sins, the nation was left without the support of their allies, and those who hated them would be the LORD'S instrument of judgment against them. Their noteworthy assets and places of worship would be destroyed. They would be deprived of that which was considered precious to them; their clothing as well as their jewels would be taken; leaving them impoverished, no better than a pauper. Persecution and death would follow, and all that their enemies couldn't transport would be razed by fire. They would cry out in despair but a holy God who hears would keep silent for a season.

Israel forgot Abba Father, now they must pay the price for all their evil ways until a holy, loving and righteous God looks upon their plight and sends them a deliverer. The prophet Jeremiah previously warned the people, but to no avail, 13:15-27 applying the NASB states: *Listen and give heed, do not be haughty, for the LORD has spoken. Give glory to the LORD your God, before He brings darkness and before your feet stumble on the dusky mountains, and while you are hoping for light He makes it into deep darkness, and turns it into gloom. But if you will not listen to it, my soul will sob in secret for such pride; and my eyes will bitterly weep and flow down with tears, because the flock of the LORD has been taken captive. Say to the king and queen mother, "Take a lowly seat, for your beautiful crown has come down from your head." The cities of the Negev have been locked up, and there is no one to open them; all Judah has been carried into exile, wholly carried into exile. "Lift up your eyes and see those coming from the north. Where is the flock that was given you, your beautiful sheep? What will you say when He appoints over you and you yourself had taught them former companions to be head over you? Will not pangs take hold of you like woman in childbirth? If you say in your heart, 'Why have these things happened to me?' Because of the multitude of your iniquity your skirts have been removed and your heels have been exposed. Can the Ethiopian change his skin or the leopard his spots? Then you also can do good who are accustomed to doing evil. Therefore I will scatter them like drifting straw to the desert wind. This is your lot, the portion measured to you from Me, declares the LORD, because you have forgotten Me and trusted falsehood. So I Myself have also stripped your skirts off over your face, that your shame may be seen. As for your adulteries and your lustful neighing, the lewdness of your prostitution on the hills in the field, I have seen your abominations. Woe to you, O Jerusalem! How long will you remain unclean?"* Israel has the assurance that the judgment of the LORD did not last forever and because of this, they continue to test the integrity of His grace.

Verses 44-52

Behold, everyone that useth proverbs shall use this proverb against thee, saying, As is the mother, so is her daughter. Thou art thy mother's daughter, that lotheth her husband

and her children; and thou art the sister of thy sisters, which lothed their husbands and their children: your mother was an Hittite, and your father an Amorite. And thine elder sister is Samaria, she and her daughters that dwell at thy left hand: and thy younger sister, that dwelleth at thy right hand, is Sodom and her daughters. Yet hast thou not walked after their ways, nor done after their abominations: but, as if that were a very little thing, thou wast corrupted more than they in all thy ways. As I live, saith the Lord GOD, Sodom thy sister hath not done, she nor her daughters, as thou hast done, thou and thy daughters. Behold, this was the iniquity of thy sister Sodom, pride, fullness of bread, and abundance of idleness was in her and in her daughters, neither did she strengthen the hand of the poor and the needy. And they were haughty, and committed abomination before Me: therefore I took them away as I saw good. Neither hath Samaria committed half of thy sins; but thou hast multiplied thine abominations more than they, and hast justified thy sisters in all thine abominations which thou hast done. Thou also, which hast judged thy sister, bear thine own shame for thy sins that thou hast committed more abominable than they: they are more righteous than thou: yea, be thou confounded also, and bear thy shame, in that thou hast justified thy sisters.

Here we see Judah following the ways of their sister Israel; hence the saying: *"As is the mother, so is the daughter."* The priestly tribe of Levites was a part of the northern kingdom, therefore Judah and Benjamin, the small southern tribes lacked good leadership and guidance, especially with regards to the teachings of the LORD, whereby if they kept them wholeheartedly, they would live within His protective shadow. What was the LORD hinting at when He said "Your mother was a Hittite, your father an Amorite and your older sister is Samaria?" First of all, these were all heathen nations that did not worship the God of Abraham, Isaac, and Jacob. Ezekiel's prophecy was against Judah. All twelve tribes are Jacob's sons, therefore the LORD referred to the divided kingdom as being sisters. Israel is here referred to as Samaria typologically.

During the reign of king Asa over the southern tribes of Judah and Benjamin, Omri was king over the northern tribes of Israel. Here is the relationship between Israel and Samaria, which is recorded in 1 kings 16:23-24: *In the thirty-first year of Asa king of Judah, Omri became king over Israel, and reigned in Tirzah. And he bought the hill of Samaria from Shemer for two talents of silver; then he built on the hill, and called the name of the city which he built, Samaria, after the name of Shemer, owner of the hill,* NKJV. Because Samaria was built on a hill the interpretation of its name also means "look out," or "watch-post." The LORD described Israel as Samaria, the older sister being the larger fraction of the divided kingdom. In reality, the older is supposed to set an example or look out for the younger, but Israel was no role model. Let's look at what the prophet Jeremiah had to say by the mouth of the Lord; an indictment against both Israel and Judah: *Then the LORD said to me in the days of Josiah the king, "Have you seen what faithless Israel did? She went up on every hill and under every green tree, and she was a harlot there. I thought, 'After she had done all these things she will return to Me'; but she did not return, and her treacherous sister Judah saw it. And I saw that for all the adulteries of faithless Israel, I had sent her away and given her a writ of divorce, yet her treacherous sister Judah did not fear; but she went and was a harlot also. Because of the lightness of her harlotry, she polluted the land and committed adultery with stones and trees. Yet in spite of all this her treacherous sister Judah did not return to Me with all her heart, but rather in deception," declares the LORD. And the LORD said to me, "Faithless Israel has proved herself more righteous than treacherous Judah. Go and proclaim these words toward the north and say, 'Return faithless Israel,' declares the LORD; 'I will not look upon you in anger. For I am gracious,' declares the LORD; 'I will not be angry forever. 'Only acknowledge your iniquity, that you have transgressed against the LORD your God and have scattered your favors to the strangers under every green tree, and you have not obeyed My voice,' declares the LORD,* 3:6-13 NASB, (see also 2 Kings 17:7-19).

Israel is referred to in a typological setting as being the older sister of Judah who failed to set a good example. Judah is then seen following the perverse footsteps of Israel; however they became worse by committing the same abominations as Sodom. 1 Kings 14:22-24 relates the story: *Judah did evil in the sight of the LORD, and they provoked Him to jealousy more than all that their fathers had done, with the sins which they committed. For they also built for themselves high places and sacred pillars and Asherim on every high hill and beneath every luxuriant tree. There were also male cult prostitutes in the land. They did according to all the abominations of the nations which the LORD dispossessed before the sons of Israel,* NASB. Sodom became an un-inhabited place for such sins, now the fate of Judah hung in the balance. It was only a matter of time before the LORD'S reprisal would be meted out. Israel's sin that caused her fall was bad; but that of Judah was much worse.

Verses 53-63

When I shall bring again their captivity, the captivity of Sodom and her daughters, and the captivity of Samaria and her daughters, then will I bring again the captivity of thy captives in the midst of them: that thou mayest bear thine own shame, and mayest be confounded in all that thou hast done, in that thou art a comfort unto them. when thy sisters, Sodom and her daughters, shall return to their former estate, and Samaria and her daughters shall return to their former estate, then thou and thy daughters shall return to your former estate. For thy sister Sodom was not mentioned by thy mouth in the day of thy pride, before thy wickedness was discovered, as at the time of thy reproach of the daughters of Syria, and all that are round about her, the daughters of the Philistines, which despised thee round about. Thou hast borne thy lewdness and thine abominations, saith the LORD. For thus saith the Lord GOD; I will even deal with thee as thou hast done, which hast despised the oath in breaking the covenant.

Nevertheless I will remember My covenant with thee in the days of thy youth, and I will establish unto thee an everlasting covenant. Then thou shalt remember thy ways, and be ashamed, when thou shalt receive thy sisters, thine elder and thy younger: and I will give them unto thee for daughters, but not by thy covenant. And I will establish My covenant with thee; and thou shalt know that I am the LORD: that thou mayest remember, and be confounded, and never open thy mouth any more because of thy shame, when I am pacified toward thee for all that thou hast done, saith the Lord GOD.

The teaching and righteous requirement of the LORD has not wavered; just as Sodom was judged by Him for their perverseness (Genesis 19:1-24), so will the house of Israel be judged. The LORD labels Israel as a typology of Samaria and Judah and Benjamin as Sodom. Both northern and southern kingdoms were judged as both tribes combined makes up the whole house of Israel; twelve sons, one flesh, yet they treated each other as though they were enemies, and these same traits are seen in the divided body of Yeshua Jesus. Doctrines and the varying forms of discipleship have builded an insurmountable wall that only the power of Yeshua will be able to destroy.

Chapter 17

Verses 1-4

And the word of the LORD came unto me, saying, Son of man, put forth a riddle, and speak a parable unto the house of Israel: and say, Thus saith the Lord GOD; A great eagles with great wings, longwinged full of feathers, which had divers colours, came unto Lebanon, and took the highest branch of the cedar: he cropped off the top of his young twigs, and carried it into a land of traffick; he set it in a city of merchants.

The LORD spoke with Ezekiel using a story format to illustrate a moral and spiritual lesson concerning the house of Israel, which He then proceeded immediately to expound. The great eagle was said to be Babylon the super power of the day. They were greatly feared because of their tactical ingenuity of laying sieges against their enemies, which created much anxiety, stress and confusion. Unable to endure this form of military operation, the people did one of two things: they either surrendered or attempted to flee.

King Nebuchadnezzar is described as a great eagle because he had a loyal, strong, and mighty army which attacked their enemies when they were most vulnerable. This was the army chosen by the LORD to be His instrument of judgment against Judah. The captain of the army laid siege on Jerusalem for many years, systematically capturing most of the residence, while others surrendered voluntarily. Nebuchadnezzar and his army is said to have come to Lebanon and took the highest branch of the cedar (verse 3b). The LORD loves to play on words and here in this conversation with the prophet, He does the same. The LORD in speaking to Ezekiel; allegorically made reference to Lebanon when describing the tranquility of the city of Jerusalem before they were captured by Nebuchadnezzar's army. During this time in history, Lebanon with its snow capped mountains had large cities that were a growing metropolis as the nation's prosperity continued because of the peaceable relationship they had with their neighbors (see Song of Solomon 4:10-15; Isaiah 60:13; Psalm 104:16-18). This was the same kind of peace and prosperity that the citizens of Jerusalem enjoyed prior to the Babylonian blockade.

The LORD continued His allegory by explaining to Ezekiel that this great eagle with great wing containing multicolored feathers: came to Lebanon and took the highest branch of the cedar. Multicolored feathers is the symbol used by the LORD in describing the best of Nebuchadnezzar's army that was made up of soldiers and generals from many nations, tribes and languages; they were the masterminds and initiators of the siege against Jerusalem, thereby taking the best of the land. The LORD goes on to say that this great army of Nebuchadnezzar took the highest branch of the cedar. Now the cedar tree is very strong and sturdy on account of its meshwork of exceedingly powerful and deep roots. This tree is also highly resistant to decay, which is a picture of the whole house of Israel and God's protective covering over them. In spite of their constant rebellion, Abba Father would never allow them to be completely annihilated by their oppressors.

Judah is described as being the highest branch of the cedar because the remaining ten tribes of the northern kingdom were already exiled by the Assyrians. It was now Judah's turn to suffer the same fate, as their sins far exceeded that of their older sister Israel. Like the cedar tree, the strength and resilience of the people living in Jerusalem at the time of the Babylonian monarchy, was not due to wise leadership, nor the great number of soldiers enlisted in their army. It was not due to their proficiency in reconnaissance or their superb skill in combat or secret intelligence outfit; it was the LORD GOD Himself who was their mighty shield of defense.

It is documented in 2 Kings 24:11-17 what actually took place: *And Nebuchadnezzar king of Babylon came against the city, and his servants did besiege it. And Jehoiachin the king of Judah went out to the king of Babylon, he, and his mother, and his servants, and his princes, and his officers: and the king of Babylon took him in the eight year of his reign. And he carried out thence all the treasures of the house of the LORD, and the treasures of the king's house, and cut in pieces all the vessels of gold which Solomon king of Israel had made in the temple of the LORD, as the LORD had said. And he carried away all Jerusalem, and all the princes, and all the mighty men of valor, even ten thousand captives, and all the craftsmen and smiths: none remained, save the poorest sort of the people of the land. And he carried away Jehoiachin to Babylon, and the king's mother, and the kings wives and his officers, and the mighty of the land, those carried he into captivity from Jerusalem to Babylon. And all the men of might, even seven thousand, and craftsmen and smiths a thousand, all that were strong and apt for war, even them the king of Babylon brought captive to Babylon. And the king of Babylon made Mattaniah his father's brother king in his stead, and changed his name to Zedekiah.* Here we see the dismantling of Judah. The cropping of the top of the young twigs was in essence referring to king Jehoiachin along with his royal family and great men of valor who were taken to Babylon.

This young king (young twig), was captured by the Babylonians. Let's see what Scripture has to say about this event, since the LORD chose the use of allegory to relay this significant story which will also reveal the correct age of Jehoiachin king of Judah at the time of his deportation. Bear in mind that in 2 Kings 24 it is stated that the king's princes were also taken. These men referred to as princes, were speaking of the king's advisors, someone with authoritative leadership, whether it be personal, military or religious. Taking these facts into consideration, let's examine 2 Chronicles 36:9-10 and cross reference it with 2 Kings 24:8-1, and 17.

2 Chronicles 36:9-11	2 Kings 24:8-10 & 17
Jehoiachin was eight years old when he began to reign, and he reigned three months and ten days in Jerusalem: and he did that which was evil in the sight of the LORD. And when the year was expired, king Nebuchadnezzar sent, and brought him to Babylon, with the goodly vessels of the house of the LORD, and made Zedekiah his brother king over Judah and Jerusalem. Zedekiah was one and twenty years old when he began to reign, and he reigned eleven years in Jerusalem.	Jehoiachin was eighteen years old when he began to reign, and he reigned in Jerusalem three months. And his mother's name was Nehushta, the daughter of Elnathan of Jerusalem. And he did that which was evil in the sight of the LORD, according to all that his father had done. At that time the servants of Nebuchadnezzar king of Babylon came up against Jerusalem, and the city was besieged. And Nebuchadnezzar king of Babylon came against the city, and his servants did besiege it. And the king of Babylon made Mattaniah his father's brother king in his stead, and changed his name to Zedekiah.

Jehoiachin was indeed eighteen and not eight at the time of his exile to Babylon. The next point needing clarification, regards Zedekiah who was Jehoiachin's uncle and not his brother as stated in 2 Kings 24. In ancient times it was customary to refer to a close family member as "brother." Fast forwarding to Ezekiel 17:13-14, where the Babylonian king made covenant with the king of Judah's seed; this statement was referring to Zedekiah whom Nebuchadnezzar appointed as an overseer, which is a better rendering than king because Nebuchadnezzar, a foreigner, had no authority to appoint kings over the people and land of Israel. Ezekiel 17:14 states that the kingdom, (speaking of Judah), would become base; in other words, made insignificant or ignoble. If Zedekiah the puppet king did as he was instructed by the king of Babylon, all would go well, if not, his fate would be no better than that of his nephew Jehoiachin. The record of 2 Kings 24 rightly states that Jehoiachin's was eighteen when he was exiled to Babylon and Zedekiah was indeed his uncle and not his brother, which is a more accurate translation of the text. The Word of God is pure (Psalm 12:6; Proverbs 30:5), therefore translation discrepancies are solely attributed to its translators.

Verses 5-6

He took also of the seed of the land, and planted it in a fruitful field; he placed it by great waters, and set it as a willow tree. And it grew and became a spreading vine of low stature, whose branches turned toward him, and the roots thereof were under him: so it became a vine, and brought forth branches, and shoot forth sprigs.

The people of Jerusalem are here called the seed of the land; they were also taken into exile and settled by the merchant port of Chebar, which means, "Great Waters." Here the people were "set as a willow tree." the LORD continues His parables, but the mysteries of His words are documented plainly in Scripture. The willow tree can be found nearby water edges where they grow abundantly. This was the settlement and new homestead given to the people of Jerusalem following their exile. Psalm 137:1-4 states: *By the rivers of Babylon, there we sat down, yea, we wept, when we remembered Zion. We hanged our harps upon the willows in the midst thereof. For there they that carried us away captive required of us a song; and they that wasted us required of us mirth, saying, Sing us one of songs of Zion. How shall we sing the LORD's song in a strange land?* These verses hint at the misery meted out to the exiles who were settled by the river Chebar which was actually a huge artificial waterway. The ethnically diverse army of the Babylonians that laid siege on the city of Jerusalem for many years, must have been impressed with the beautiful singing accompanied by the harmony of instruments, as the citizens of Jerusalem participated in festive activities to have required the poor exiles to entertainment them.

As the exiles multiplied in the land of Egypt under great duress, so they multiplied as the willow trees by the river Chebar. Humbled by their captors, they were described as *being a spreading vine of low stature whose branches* (people), were bondservants of Nebuchadnezzar king of Babylon, whom they now served with their gifts and talents. A land governed by godly leaders benefited from the LORD'S blessings and protection, and this is a proven fact throughout the Scriptures. On the converse; should that nation turn its back against the LORD their God, He graciously gives them time to repent and if no repentance is forthcoming, He turns His back against them for a season. True repentance is the key for the blessings of God to return to any nation or people who once enjoyed His favors.

Verses 7-21

There was also another great eagle with great wings and many feathers: and, behold, this vine did bend her roots toward him, and shot forth her branches toward him, that he might water it by the furrows of her plantation. It was planted in a good soil by great waters, that it might bring forth branches, and that it might bear fruit, that it might be a goodly vine. Say thou, Thus saith the Lord GOD; shall it prosper? Shall he not pull up the roots thereof, and cut off the fruit thereof, that it wither? It shall wither in all the leaves of her spring, even without great power or many people to pluck it up by the roots thereof. Yea, behold, being planted, shall it prosper? Shall it not utterly wither, when the east wind toucheth it? It shall wither in the furrows where it grew. Moreover the word of the LORD came unto me, saying, Say now to the rebellious house, know ye not what these things mean? tell them, Behold, the king of Babylon is come to Jerusalem, and hath taken the king thereof, and the princes thereof, and led them with him to Babylon; and hath taken the king's seed, and made a covenant with him, and hath taken an oath of him: he hath also taken the mighty of the land: that the kingdom might be base, that it might not lift itself up, but that by keeping of his covenant it might stand. But he rebelled against him in sending his ambassadors into Egypt, that they might give him horses and much people. Shall he prosper? Shall he escape that doeth such things? Or shall he Zedekiah break the covenant, and be delivered? As I live, saith the Lord GOD, surely in the place where the king Nebuchadnezzar dwelleth that made him king, whose oath he despised, and whose covenant he break, even with him in the midst of Babylon he shall die. Neither shall Pharaoh with his mighty army and great company make for him war, by casting up mounts, and building forts, to cut off many persons: seeing he despised the oath by breaking the covenant, when, lo, he had given his hand, and hath done all these things, he shall not escape. Therefore thus saith the Lord GOD; As I live, surely Mine oath that he hath despised, and My covenant that he hath broken, even it will I recompense upon his own head. And I will spread My net upon him, and he shall be taken in My snare, and I will bring him to Babylon, and will plead with him there for his trespass that he hath trespassed against Me. And all his fugitives with all his bands shall fall by the sword, and they that remain shall be scattered toward all winds: and ye shall know that I the LORD have spoken it.

Zedekiah was left in Jerusalem by king Nebuchadnezzar to oversee the people who remained in that city as peasant farmers. These verses relate the story of his conspiracy against the king. Zedekiah also known as Mattaniah continued as king Nebuchadnezzar's appointed leader for eleven years, then, he too, rebelled. This fatal mistake is recorded in 2 Kings 24:18-20; 2 Chronicles 36:11-13; Jeremiah 32:1-5; 34:8-22; 39:1-7; 52:1-11. Zedekiah rejected the words of the LORD by the mouth of Jeremiah the prophet, Jeremiah 21 & 37 and sought an alliance with the Pharaoh of Egypt (the second great super power or eagle). This act of treason was uncovered: *Now it came to pass in the ninth year of his reign, in the tenth month, on the tenth day of the month, that Nebuchadnezzar king of Babylon and all his army came against Jerusalem and encamped against it; and they built a siege wall against it; all around. So the city was besieged until the eleventh year of King Zedekiah. By the ninth day of the fourth month the famine had become so severe in the city that there was no food for the people of the land. Then the city wall was broken through, and all the men of war fled at night by of the gate between two walls, which was by the king's garden, even though the Chaldeans were still encamped all around against the city. And the king went by way of the plain. But the army of the Chaldeans pursued the king, and they overtook him in the plains of Jericho. All his army was scattered from him. So they took the king and brought him up to the king of Babylon at Riblah, and they pronounced judgment on him. Then they killed the sons of Zedekiah before his eyes, put out the eyes of Zedekiah, bound him with bronze fetters, and took him to Babylon,* 2 Kings 25:1-7 NKJV. Zedekiah (the vine) and his sons were captured; he witnessed their death, which was the last thing he saw; at the command of the King, he was made sightless, and this was only the beginning of Judah's heartache.

Ezekiel 17:10 refers to an eastern wind that caused much devastation. Eastern winds are known to carry hot dry air, which resulted in overwhelming crop failure. This was however a figure of speech used by the LORD, which pointed to the dire times that were ahead for Judah. Although the exiled people from Jerusalem were settled in a fruitful area by Chebar, the next seventy years would be one of great distress, sorrow and regret for living a life contrary to that of holiness, righteousness, justice and truth. The citizens of Jerusalem rejected the warnings of the prophets and now must pay the price for their lawlessness. The LORD God is not unjust; He gave favor to the godly living among the rebellious who grieved over the sins of the people.

Verses 22-24

Thus saith the Lord GOD; I will also take of the highest branch of the high cedar, and will set it; I will crop off from the top of his young twigs a tender one, and will plant it upon an high mountain and eminent: in the mountain of the height of Israel will I plant it: and it shall bring forth boughs, and bear fruit, and be a goodly cedar: and under it shall dwell all fowl of every wing; in the branches thereof shall they dwell. And all the trees of the field shall know that I the LORD have brought down the high tree, have exalted the low tree, have dried up the green tree, and have made the dry tree to flourish: I the LORD have spoken and have done it.

In Ezekiel 17:22, the Lord repeats His instructions given in Ezekiel 17:3. Using the metaphor: "taking the highest branch of the high cedar;" meaning that He would rise up a righteous man of royal lineage, who would be morally and spiritually approved by Him and separate him to do His will. This was the unfolding of a Messianic prophecy pointing to the coming of Yeshua HaMashiach; the Lord Jesus Christ. He is the Righteous Branch being exalted above all others. His scepter would be one of righteousness because He was indeed God in flesh. Only unto Yeshua Jesus can such an honor be conferred. The prophet Jeremiah declared: *Behold, the days come, saith the LORD, that I will raise unto David a righteous Branch, and a King shall reign and prosper, and shall execute judgment and justice in the earth. In His days Judah shall be saved, and Israel shall dwell safely: and this is His name whereby He shall be called, THE LORD OUR RIGHTEOUSNESS* [Jehovah Tsidkeenu]. *Therefore, behold, the days come, saith the LORD, that they shall no more say, The LORD liveth, which brought up the children of Israel out of the land of Egypt; but, the LORD liveth, which brought up and which led the seed of the house of Israel out of the north country, and from all countries whither I had driven them; and they shall dwell in their own land,* 23:7-8. These words of the Lord, speak for themselves.

In Ezekiel 17:23 the LORD God continues to infer that the coming Messiah would be like none other because He would be exalted above all earthly kings. He will be the King above all kings and Lord above all lords, from the royal lineage of David who will govern His people Israel. From this exalted and righteous King, many will live in peace for indeed He is the Prince of peace. The prophet Isaiah spoke of Him: *For a child will be born to us, a son will be given to us; and the government will rest on His shoulders; and His name will be called Wonderful Counselor, Mighty God, Eternal Father, Prince of Peace,* 9:6 NASB.

Using the same metaphorical language, the LORD continues in Ezekiel 17:24 by saying, "*And all the trees of the field* [nations of the world] *shall know that I the LORD have brought down the high tree,* [super powers] *have exalted the low tree,* [small nation of Israel], *have dried up the green tree*, [wealthy nations] *and have made the dry tree to flourish* [persecuted Israel]: *I the LORD* have spoken and have done it. In haste Mary went to Elizabeth her cousin to share the wonderful news, that she, too, was carrying a promised child. This was Mary's salutation regarding the Son of God*:* "*My soul magnifies the Lord, and my spirit has rejoiced in God my Savior. For He has regarded the lowly state of His maidservant; for behold henceforth all generations will call me blessed. For He who is mighty has done great things for me, and holy is His name. And His mercy is on those who fear Him from generation to generation. He has shown strength with His arm; He has scattered the proud in the imagination of their hearts. He has put down the mighty from their thrones, and exalted the lowly. He has filled the hungry with good things, and the rich He has sent away empty. He has helped His servant Israel, in remembrance of His mercy, as He spoke to our fathers, to Abraham and to his seed forever,"* Luke 1:46-55. The Righteous BRANCH did come as Abba Father promised and all effort to destroy Yeshua Jesus failed because no powers in the heavenly realm, or on earth, or beneath the earth could stop the prophetic fulfillment of His promise.

Chapter 18

Verses 1-4; 18-23; 27-28

The word of the LORD came unto me again, saying, What mean ye, that ye use this proverb concerning the land of Israel, saying, The fathers have eaten sour grapes, and the children's teeth are set on edge? As I live, saith the Lord GOD, ye shall not have occasion any more to use this proverb in Israel. Behold all souls are Mine; as the soul of the father, so also the soul of the son is Mine: the soul that sinneth, it shall die . . . As for his father, because he cruelly oppressed, spoiled his brother by violence, and did that which is not good among his people, lo, even he shall die in his iniquity. Yet say ye, Why? Doth not the son bear the iniquity of the father? When the son hath done that which is lawful and right and hath kept all My statutes, and hath done them, he shall surely live. The soul that sinneth, it shall die. The son shall not bear the iniquity of the father, neither shall the father bear the iniquity of the son: the righteousness of the righteous shall be upon him, and the wickedness of the wicked shall be upon him. But if the wicked will turn from all his sins that he hath committed, and keep all My statutes, and do that which is lawful and right, he shall surely live, he shall not die. All his transgressions that he hath committed, they shall not be mentioned unto him: in his righteousness that he hath done he shall live. Have I any pleasure at all that the wicked should die? saith the Lord GOD: and not that he should return from his ways, and live? . . . Again, when the wicked man turneth away from his wickedness that he hath committed, and doeth that which is lawful and right, he shall save his soul alive. Because he considereth, and turneth away from all his transgressions that he hath committed, he shall surely live, he shall not die.

In these verses the justice of God is presented, grouped and explained according to relevance. To understand the justice of God, let's see what the Apostle Paul had to say about this matter in Romans 2:1-15; *Therefore thou art inexcusable, O man, whosoever thou art that judgest: for wherein thou judgest another, thou condemnest thyself; for thou that judgest doest the same things. But we are sure that the judgment of God is according to truth against them which commit such things. And thinkest thou this, O man, that judgest them which do such things, and doest the same, that thou shalt escape the judgment of God? Or despisest thou the riches of his goodness and forbearance and longsuffering; not knowing that the goodness of God leadeth thee to repentance? But after thy hardness and impenitent heart treasurest up unto thyself wrath against the day of wrath and revelation of the righteous judgment of God; who will render to every man according to his deeds: to them who by patient continuance in well doing seek for glory and honor and immortality, eternal life: but unto them that are contentious, and do not obey the truth, but obey unrighteousness, indignation and wrath, tribulation and anguish, upon every soul of man that doeth evil, of the Jews first, and also of the Gentile; but glory, honor, and peace, to every man that worketh good, to the Jews first, and also to the Gentile: for there is no respect of persons with God. For as many as have sinned without law shall also perish without law: and as many as have sinned in the law shall be judged by the law; (for not the hearers of the law are just before God, but the doers of the law shall be justified. For when the Gentiles, which have not the law, do by nature the things contained in the law, these, having not the law, are a law unto themselves: which shew the work of the law written in their hearts, their conscience also bearing witness, and their thoughts the mean while accusing or else excusing one another).* The Lord is just, whatever mankind sows they will ultimately reap. The children will not be punished for the evil deeds of the parent neither will the parents be punished for the evil deeds of their children. Everyone will be judged individually, yet some more rigidly than others (James 3:1). There is no partiality with the LORD, He does not favor one child over the other and for this reason His justice is unbiased. This is the common theme throughout this chapter.

Verses 5-9

But if a man be just, and do that which is lawful and right, and hath not eaten upon the mountains, neither hath lifted up his eyes to the idols of the house of Israel, neither hath defiled his neighbor's wife, neither hath come near to a menstruous woman, and hath not oppressed any, but hath restored to the debtor his pledge, hath spoiled none by violence, hath given his bread to the hungry, and hath covered the naked with a garment; he that hath not given forth upon usury, neither hath taken any increase, that hath withdrawn his hand from iniquity, hath excused true judgment between man and man, hath walked in My statutes, and hath kept My judgments, to deal truly; he is just, he shall surely live, saith the Lord GOD.

These five verses present to us the justice of God with regards to righteousness. Romans 2:7 endorses: *To them who by patient continuance in well doing seek for glory and honor and immortality, eternal life.* When the Bible refers to the justice of God; it means that God is honorable in His treatment of all. The decisions that He makes regarding the children of men are true, and this should be the reciprocated pattern which mankind should follow. Micah 6:8 speaks of this principle: *He has showed you, O man, what is good. And what does the LORD require of you? To act justly and to love mercy and to walk humbly with your God,* NIV. This oracle by the prophet Micah is quite simple but profoundly true, as it embodies the attributes of the righteous as being small building blocks which leads one to eternal life.

Only through Yeshua Jesus can the Divine standards for a moral life be accomplished in us, as righteousness and justice are important attributes of Abba Father. Acts 17:29-31 clearly states: *"Being then the children of God, we ought not to think that the Divine Nature is like gold or silver or stone, an image formed by the art and thought of man. Therefore having overlooked the times of ignorance, God is now declaring to men that all people everywhere should repent, because He has fixed a day in which He will judge the world in righteousness through a Man whom He has appointed, having furnished proof to all men by raising Him from the dead,"* NASB. The LORD God our Father has given us Yeshua, our only hope of salvation. He is the one and only way to Abba Father. No image fashioned by man can intercede for the soul, only the Man Yeshua Jesus holds this authority. Psalm 135:13-18 states: *Thy name, O LORD, endureth forever; and thy memorial, O LORD, throughout all generations. For the LORD will judge His people, and He will repent Himself concerning His servants. The idols of the heathens are silver and gold, the work of men's hands. They have mouth, but they speak not; eyes have they, but they see not; they have ears, but they hear not; neither is there any breath in their mouths. They that make them are like unto them: so is every one that trusteth in them,* (see also Psalm 115:1-11).

For the seekers of truth, whether you are religious or not, go ahead and ask the LORD to prove Yeshua's Sovereignty and if you sincerely mean it; you will be mightily surprised at His response. Yeshua's personal invitation in stated in Matthew 7:7-8; Luke 11:9-13; these are His words: *"**A**sk and it will be given to you; **s**eek and you will find; **k**nock and the door will be opened to you, For everyone who **a**sk receives; and he who **s**eeks finds; and to him who **k**nocks, the door will be opened,* NIV. "Ask" is twice spelled out in these verses; therefore all we have to do is ask and keep on asking as Yeshua Jesus implores us.

Now the "Door" is Yeshua Jesus Himself: *So Jesus said to them again, "Truly, truly, I say to you, I am the door* of the sheep. All who come before Me are thieves and robbers, but the sheep did not hear them. I am the door; if anyone enters through Me, he will be saved, and will go in and out and find pleasure," John 10: 7-9 NASB. The just lives by faith knowing that they do not have to be self imposed martyrs for God; He has already tasted death for His followers and through His death they are granted eternal life. The justice of God converts the soul, thereby offering peace and eternal life to all who desires such. No rituals of flagellation, external washings, praying to the dead, and pleading with images can offer eternal life. Yeshua HaMashiach is the only way!

Verses 10-13

If he beget a son that is a shedder of blood, and that doeth the like to any one of these things, and that doeth not any of those duties, but even hath eaten upon the mountains, and defiled his neighbor's wife, hath oppressed the poor and needy, hath spoiled by violence, hath not restored the pledge, and hath lifted up his eyes to the idols, hath committed abomination, hath given forth upon usury, and hath taken increase: shall he then live? He shall not live: he hath done all these abominations; he shall surely die; his blood shall be upon him.

As we continue our examination of the justice of GOD, these few verses presents the justice of GOD upon those who miss the mark whom we call sinners. Romans 2:9 inform us: *There will be trouble and distress for every human being who does evil: first for the Jew, then for the Gentile,* NIV. Sin is described as an offence, and is a violation of the teachings of God. If one deliberately sin and continues to do so, he has frowned upon the grace of GOD and the finished work of Yeshua on the Cross. In the Old Covenant, the Lord GOD required certain sacrifices to be offered for the propitiation of sin, which simply means; the wrath of God was appeased through the blood of carefully selected unblemished animals. With the advent of our Lord and

Savior Yeshua Jesus; His blood took the place of animal sacrifices thereby appeasing the Divine justice of God for fallen humanity once and for all times. If one refuses to repent from all forms of evil; death becomes his portion by choice.

Verses 14-17

Now, lo, if he beget a son, that seeth all his father's sins which he hath done, and considereth, and doeth not such like, that hath not eaten upon mountains, neither hath lifted up his eyes to the idols of the house of Israel, hath not defiled his neighbor's wife, neither hath oppressed any, hath not withholden the pledge, neither hath spoiled by violence, but hath given his bread to the hungry, and hath covered the naked with a garment, that hath taken off his hand from the poor, that hath not received usury nor increase, hath executed My judgments, hath walked in My statutes; he shall not die for the iniquity of his father, he shall surely live.

These verses are in direct contrast to verses 10-13, which expresses the rewards of the justice of GOD. Revisiting Romans chapter two once more; we read in verses 10 and 11: *But glory, honor and peace for everyone who does good: first for the Jew, then for the Gentile. For God does not show favoritism,* NIV. The Lord rewards those who walk humbly before Him. Godly fear has nothing to do with anxiety or agitation in any form, but an intense reverence for the Lord God. Ezekiel 18:14-17 is speaking of those in whom the nine fruit of the Spirit is evident (Galatians 6:22-23). Galatians 6:24-25 give the model and qualification of living by the fruit of the Spirit: *And those who are Christ's have crucified the flesh with its passions and desires. If we live in the Spirit, let us also walk in the Spirit,* NKJV.

The rewards of the righteous are the same for Jews and Gentiles, glory will be given where glory is due and honor will be given where honor is due. 2 Corinthians 5:10 applying the NIV drives this point home: *For we must all appear before the judgment seat of Christ, that each one may receive what is due him for the things done while in the body, whether good or bad.* On the same note, Mathew 5:3-12 highlights the rewards of a pleasing life unto Abba Father: *Blessed are the poor in spirit: for theirs is the kingdom of heaven. Blessed are they that mourn: for they shall be comforted. Blessed are the meek: for they shall inherit the earth. Blessed are they which do hunger and thirst after righteousness: for they shall be filled. Blessed are the merciful: for they shall obtain mercy. Blessed are the pure in heart: for they shall see God. Blessed are the peacemakers: for they shall be called the children of God. Blessed are they which are persecuted for righteousness sake: for theirs is the kingdom of heaven. Blessed are ye, when men shall revile you and persecute you, and shall say all manner of evil against you falsely, for My sake. Rejoice, and be exceeding glad: for great is your reward in heaven: for so persecuted they the prophets which were before you.* This sums up the requirement of holiness. The Lord has placed in every one of us a conscience, which is our personal navigation of right and wrong, good or evil therefore leaving us without an excuse. His infinite mercy and grace is demonstrated in His character of being just. The sins of the father will not be the responsibility of the children who walk in the ways of the Lord. Neither will the sins of the children be assigned to the parent who walks justly before Him. Abba Father is calling the righteous: not to fit in but to stand out!

Verses 24-26

But when the righteous turneth away from his righteousness and committeth iniquity, and doeth according to all the abominations that the wicked man doeth, shall he live? All his righteousness that he hath shall not be mentioned: in his trespass that he hath trespassed, and in his sin that he hath sinned, in them shall he die. Yet ye say, the way of the Lord is not equal. Hear, now, O house of Israel; is not My way equal? Are not your ways unequal? When a righteous man turneth away from his righteousness, and committeth iniquity, and dieth in them; for his iniquity that he hath done shall he die.

Yeshua's Cross has a three-fold meaning; first it speaks of the death of the condemned; next it is the representation of trial and affliction; and lastly it speaks of Yeshua's intercession for all mankind. A hewn tree became His Cross, where He paid the final sacrifice for the unrighteousness of the Jews on the right and that of the Gentiles on the left, thereby presenting both to Abba Father through His shed blood. He is our bridge of hope whereby we are the recipients of eternal life. The justice of GOD on the unrighteous is here laid out and it correlates once more with Romans chapter 2:8-9 which states: *But for those who are self-seeking and who rejects the truth and follow evil, there will be wrath and anger. There will be trouble and distress for every human being who does evil: first for the Jew, then for the Gentile,* NIV. The righteous are those who walk in uprightness, his or her conduct is a direct reflection of the attributes of GOD in whose likeness they are created. The righteousness of God is separated by an impassable chasm; far from legalism and religious rites, rituals, and bondages of earning one's salvation. It is eternally separated from religious pit-falls and the unholy communion of idolatry and the worship of Abba Father. This form of righteousness is the true state of being approved by God, justified by faith and by the final act of Yeshua's finished work on the Cross; we are welcomed into the kingdom of GOD.

GOD is holy, and He can never allow anyone to enter His kingdom who knowingly rejects His freewill offering of salvation; for that which Yeshua Jesus did: laying down His life for His friends was a once and for all time act of His redemptive plan for us all (John 3:16; 15:13; 1 John 3:16). 1 Peter 2:3-6 and Hebrews 6:4-6 states: *If indeed you have tasted that the Lord is gracious. Coming to Him as to a living stone, rejected indeed by men, but chosen by God and precious, you also as living stones, are being built up a spiritual house, a holy priesthood, to offer up spiritual sacrifices acceptable to God through Jesus Christ. . . For it is impossible for those who were once enlightened, and have tasted the heavenly gift, and have become partakers of the Holy Spirit, and have tasted the good word of God and the powers of the age to come, if they fall away, to renew them again to repentance, since they crucify again for themselves the Son of God, and put Him to an open shame,* NKJV. The righteous who turns from his righteousness and knowingly rejects Yeshua Jesus without repenting for his folly, will never inherit the kingdom of God (1 Corinthians 6:9-10; Matthew 25:34; Psalm 1:1-6; 2 Peter 2:4-22; I Corinthians 6:9-11). Truth is freedom and to know the truth, to have tasted the saving power of God, to have walked in the ways of holiness, to have experience the grace of God, then walk away to live a wicked and immoral life utterly rejecting truth; makes one former consecration null and void. There is therefore no excuse for unrighteousness when truth has been revealed.

Verses 29-32

Yet saith the house of Israel, The way of the Lord is not equal. O house of Israel, are not My ways equal? Are not your ways unequal? Therefore I will judge you. O house of Israel, every one according to his ways, saith the Lord GOD. Repent, and turn yourselves from your transgressions; so iniquity shall not be your ruin. Cast away from you all your transgressions, whereby ye have transgressed; and make you a new heart and a new spirit: for why will ye die, O house of Israel? for I have no pleasure in the death of him that dieth, saith the Lord GOD: wherefore turn yourselves, and live ye.

So far we have reviewed the justice of GOD cross referencing Romans chapter 2:1-15 as a parallel resource from the Word of God. These final verses in Ezekiel chapter 18 addresses the justice of GOD and the morality of man. Man was never formed from the dust of the earth by the Lord to become a slave to sin. We are moral agents creating our own pathway that leads to heaven or eternal separation from God. With these facts in mind, we will now address the justice of GOD from the standpoint of morality. Romans 2:12-15 quoting once more the NIV: *All who sin apart from the law will also perish apart from the law, and all who sin under the law will be judged by the law. For it is not those who hear the law who are righteous in God's sight, but it is those who obey the law who will be declared righteous. (Indeed, when Gentiles, who do not have the law, do by nature things required by the law, they are a law for themselves, even though they do not have the law, since they show that the requirements of the law are written on their hearts, their conscience also bearing witness, and their thoughts now accusing, now even defending them.)* God's moral standing is necessary to prepare the body of Yeshua Jesus as a temple for the return of the glory of Abba Father. Therefore morality, which is a virtuous quality and conformity of walking in holiness, is well pleasing to Abba Father, Yeshua, and Holy Spirit. This is the reflection of a mature Believer bearing the fruit of the Spirit in reverence and awe of the Creator. Man is a creation and not an evolution and God holds the perfect blue print for his life. Even though man has fallen from grace and death became his portion when Adam sinned, there is still hope for the ways of the Lord are just. A soul that truly repents, will not be a castaway, but will inherit the kingdom of God. We are governed by our conscience; Holy Spirit will always bring conviction but He never condemns.

As mortals we have an advocate in the Man Yeshua Jesus. He was tempted just like us, yet without sin. The moral standard that we should live by does not cause pain or anguish; instead, it gives joy and peace in Holy Spirit. King David understood the joy of a moral life; and also the pain when he fell short; he wrote: *The law of the LORD is perfect converting the soul; the testimony of the LORD is sure, making wise the simple; the statutes of the LORD are right, rejoicing the heart; the commandment of the LORD is pure, enlightening the eyes; the fear of the LORD is clean, enduring forever; the judgments of the LORD are true and righteous altogether. More to be desired are they than gold, yea, than much fine gold; sweeter also than honey and the honeycomb. Moreover by them Your servant is warned, and in keeping them there is great reward,* Psalm 19:7-11 NKJV. The attributes of the Lord does not waver, its quantity as well as its quality are of identical value. When Jews and Gentiles repent from having violated God's teachings and turn to Him in brokenness; He will forgive. It grieves the heart of GOD when a soul willfully walks in rebellion after the truth of the gospel has been revealed, thereby choosing everlasting anguish, instead of everlasting life. Whomever we choose to serve in this life is directly linked with the kingdom in which we will spend eternity in the next. The love of God is a gift that continues giving and His teachings are inscribed in our genetic coding. If we reject Abba Father's offering of Yeshua Jesus as our Savior; who can we blame for the decisions we make? Who can we accuse for the kingdom we have chosen?

Chapter 19

Verses 1-9

Moreover take thou up a lamentation for the princes of Israel, and say, What is thy mother? A lioness: she lay down among lions, she nourished her whelps among young lions. And she brought up one of her whelps: it became a young lion, and it learned to catch the prey; it devoured men. The nations also heard of him; he was taken in their pit, and they brought him with chains unto the land of Egypt. Now when she saw that she had waited, and her hope was lost, then she took another of her whelps, and made him a young lion. And he went up and down among the lions, and he became a young lion, and learned to catch the prey, and devoured men. And he knew their desolate places, and he laid waste their cities; and the land was desolate, and the fullness thereof, by the noise of his roaring. Then the nations set against him on every side from the provinces, and spread their net over him: he was taken in their pit. And they put him in ward in chains, and brought him to the king of Babylon: they brought him into holds, that his voice, should no more be heard upon the mountains of Israel.

Ezekiel was commanded by the LORD to lament for the leaders of the whole house of Israel. The question is then asked, who is thy mother? The reply was a lioness. A lioness by nature is the protector of the pride; she hunts for food for her cubs, which are called whelps and the young lion being brought up here is metaphorically speaking of Judah. On the death bed of Jacob (Israel), he addressed his twelve sons which were more of a prophetic utterance that had an immense impact on their future. In reference to Judah, Genesis 49:8-12 records Jacob's last words: *"Judah, you are he whom your brothers shall praise; your hand shall be on the neck of your enemies; your father's children shall bow down before you. Judah is a lion's whelp; from the prey, my son you have gone up. He bows down, he lies down as a lion; and as a lion who shall rouse him? The scepter shall not depart from Judah, nor a law giver from between his feet, until Shiloh comes; and to Him shall be the obedience of the people. Binding his donkey to the vine, and his donkey's colt to the choice vine, he washed his garment in wine, and his clothes in the blood of grapes. His eyes are darker than wine, and his teeth whiter than milk,* NKJV. Here Judah is identified as the lion's whelp or cub from which Yeshua whose name means Salvation is a descendant.

The remainder of Jacob's prophetic sayings to his fourth son by his first wife Leah is Messianic in nature. Yeshua was GOD'S perfect choice to redeem Israel. He became the focal point of the *B'rit Chadashah* also known as the New Covenant between God and Israel and because of this New Covenant; Gentiles, too, will share in their inheritance. The Sovereign Ruler is Yeshua and His staff is one of supreme authority. The tribe of Judah is therefore very important on God's radar, as the redemption of Judah and the hope of the Gentiles are upheld by His word.

Although Joseph the eleventh son of Jacob was held captive in a pit then sold and taken into Egypt, the LORD was not talking about him; His words had a much deeper meaning. Ezekiel 19:4 states: ". . . *He was taken in their pit, and they brought him with chains unto the land of Egypt."* Who then was Ezekiel 19:1-9 addressing? It was speaking of an evil king of Judah known as Jehoahaz who was also called Shallum. Jehoahaz is the one being described as a *young lion*, who Pharaoh Neco of Egypt imprisoned. Although he was only twenty-three years old, he was well known among many nations for being ruthless (Jeremiah 22:8-12; 2

Kings 23:31-34). Looking back on Ezekiel 19:3, it is stated: *"And she brought up one of her whelps: it became a young lion, and it learned to catch the prey; it devoured men."* This verse alarmingly, is stating that Jehoahaz oppressed his own people to the point of death. Ezekiel 19:5 states: *Now when she saw that she had waited, and her hope was lost, then she took another of her whelps, and made him a young lion."* Remember the lioness is metaphorically speaking of the tribe of Judah.

After Pharaoh Neco had imprisoned Jehoahaz another young lion; referring to another young leader, took his place as king of Judah: his name was Jehoiakim, also known as Eliakim. 2 Kings 23:31-34 states: *Jehoahaz was twenty-three years old when he became king, and he reigned three months in Jerusalem; and his mother's name was Hamutal the daughter of Jeremiah of Libnah. He did evil in the sight of the LORD, according to all that his fathers had done. Pharaoh Neco imprisoned him at Riblah in the land of Hamath, that he might not reign in Jerusalem; and he imposed on the land a fine of one hundred talents of silver and a talent of gold. Pharaoh Neco made Eliakim the son of Josiah king in the place of Josiah his father, and changed his name to Jehoiakim. But he took Jehoahaz away and brought him to Egypt, and he died there,* NASB. More information on these two young leaders (whelps who became young lions), can be found in 2 Chronicles 36:2-5. It must be noted here that there were six men named Jeremiah mentioned in the Old Covenant. The Jeremiah mentioned in 2 Kings 23:31 was the father of Hamutal, Jehoahaz mother; he was not Jeremiah the prophet who was mightily used by the LORD to warn the tribe of Judah.

These young brothers were described as being evil as their forefathers, (2 Kings 23:32-37; 24:1-4). Jehoiakim (Eliakim) did not learn from his brother's errors in leadership and personal choices; instead of doing that which was exemplary in the sight of God, he was just as evil as Jehoahaz. Jehoiakim is here mentioned in Ezekiel as the second whelp (young leader); who gave the order for the murder of the prophet Uriah and the attempted murder of the prophet Jeremiah and his friend Baruch. Jehoiakim also burned the scrolls that were written and sent to him by Jeremiah the prophet because they denounced the king's evil occupations. The destruction of the scrolls did not however affect the fulfillment of the prophecies against him and Judah as a whole. Jehoiakim's evil ways finally caught up with him and at his death, he did not receive a stately funeral or ceremonial burial rites; instead, his body was disposed of outside the city gates of Jerusalem, (for further study see 2 Kings 24-25; 1 Chronicles 3:16-17; 2 Chronicles 36:8-9; Ester 2:6; Jeremiah 22:24-30; 24:1; 37:1; 52:31-34). Evil does not go un-noticed by the all seeing eyes of the Lord GOD. The fate of these siblings is a message that transcends time and should be a warning to all who wink at immorality and oppress those they govern because justice will be served upon them by the LORD in due season.

Verses 10-14

Thy mother is like a vine in thy blood, planted by the waters: she was fruitful and full of branches by reason of many waters. And she had strong rods for the scepters of them that bare rule, and her stature was exalted among the thick branches, and she appeared in her height with the multitude of her branches. But she was plucked up in fury, she was cast down to the ground, and the east wind dried up her fruit: her strong rods were broken and withered; the fire consumed them. and now she is planted in the wilderness, in a dry and thirsty ground. And fire is gone out of a rod of her branches, which hath devoured her fruit, so that she hath no strong rod to be a scepter to rule. This is a lamentation, and shall be for a lamentation.

To say: "*thy mother is a vine in thy blood,*" is speaking of the guilty verdict pronounced upon Jerusalem, its leaders and its people. Jerusalem was prosperous; the city had the favors of the known world under King Solomon whose shrewd trading practices made Jerusalem very rich, thus the phrase: *she was fruitful and full of branches by reason of many waters.* For this reason, very important heads of state including the queen of Sheba, came to Jerusalem to see the magnificent structures being built there, and also to visit with the king himself after hearing of his fame (1 Kings 10; 2 Chronicles 9:1-28). Solomon later fell into apostasy (1 Kings 11:1-25). The kingdom became divided shortly after his death, and some of his successors also did evil in the sight of the LORD (1 Kings 12; 2 Chronicles 10; 11). Nebuchadnezzar's army laid siege upon Jerusalem for several years. Traders were not allowed to enter the city with their wares; likewise the people could not leave to purchase goods from neighboring cities, which led to a severe food shortage (2 Chronicles 36:15-20). Eventually Nebuchadnezzar's army took the people into exile and settled them by the river Chebar, thus the phrase: *She was plucked up in fury, she was cast down to the ground* (Ezekiel 19:12).

The next portion of Ezekiel 19:12 states: *and the east wind dried up her fruit: her strong rods were broken and withered, the fire consumed them.* The east wind that dried up her fruit was an allegory describing the swiftness of Nebuchadnezzar's army to capture the citizens and seize the city of Jerusalem; raiding and destroying the temple and homes by fire, thereby completely devastating Jerusalem. Everything of value was taken and the temple was in ruins. Ezekiel 19:12 concludes: *Her strong rods were broken and withered, the fire consumed them.* This phrase referred to the king of Judah, the priest, Levites and also notable leaders who either were killed, disfigured, or imprisoned while exiled in Babylon.

Ezekiel 19:13-14 describes the exiled settlers as being *planted in the wilderness, in a dry and thirsty ground. And fire is gone out of a rod of her branches, which hath devoured her fruit, so that she hath no strong rod to be a scepter to rule.* Chebar was then a navigable canal, where the exiles from Jerusalem were settled. The "*planting of the settlers in a wilderness, in a dry and thirsty ground,*" was not directly speaking of the new home of the exiles; instead, it must be seen in correspondence and harmony with the remainder of the lamentation for Judah. Viewing the statement in its allegorical setting, meant that the exiles were in a strange land, the temple in Jerusalem being the visible presence of GOD was now destroyed and the city was stripped of all that was valuable. The exiles were now governed by taskmasters and had to do exactly as they were told or suffer greatly for their refusal. Psalm 137:1-4 quoting the NLT is worth reading once more because this was the lamentation of the people: *Beside the rivers of Babylon, we sat and wept as we thought of Jerusalem. We put away our harps, hanging them on the branches of poplar trees. For our captors demanded a song from us. Our tormentors insisted on a joyful hymn: "Sing us one of those songs of Jerusalem!" but how can we sing the songs of the LORD while in a pagan land?* Here we are given a glimpse into the mindset of the people in captivity. Their leaders were either dead or imprisoned; therefore the saying: *"she had no strong rod to be a scepter to rule."* Zedekiah the last king of Judah was not the people's choice, he was like an interim overseer who was left in Jerusalem to dictate Nebuchadnezzar's orders, as previously discussed in Ezekiel chapter 17:7-21 (for further reading, see also 2 Kings 24; 2 Chronicles 36; Jeremiah 39 and 52). Any nation that turns from the LORD will see the judgment of GOD pronounced upon it. The LORD is still however merciful and will give such a nation ample time to repent; but if they choose not to, He will send a nation more shrewd to subdue them.

Jerusalem was once a glorious and prospering city under Solomon the last king to reign over unified Israel, until he turned away from the teachings of Abba Father by building shrines and worshiping the images of his foreign wives. The message of repentance by the prophets of the LORD to the people went unheeded, therefore the LORD withdrew His blessings and the nation began a downward spiritual and economical spiral until it was completely destroyed. Rulers, priests, and noteworthy leaders, along with the majority of the citizens of Jerusalem, became utterly corrupt and rejected the LORD as their Supreme ruler. The LORD sent pestilences and other catastrophic events but the people did not turn from lawlessness; instead, they grew more defiant and perpetrated much worse evils. The very few among them who reverentially feared the LORD, falling to their knees before the Almighty in supplication, fasting, and mourning, were the small remnant that was saved. Nothing has changed; the Bible is true, there is nothing new under the sun.

Chapter 20

Verses 1-10

And it came to pass in the seventh year, in the fifth month, the tenth day of the month, that certain of the elders came to inquire of the LORD, and sat before me. Then came the word of the LORD unto me, saying, Son of man, speak unto the elders of Israel, and say unto them, Thus saith the Lord GOD; Are ye come to inquire of Me? As I live, saith the Lord GOD, I will not be inquired of by you. Wilt thou judge them, son of man, wilt thou judge them? Cause them to know the abominations of their fathers: and say unto them, Thus saith the Lord GOD; In the day when I chose Israel, and lifted up mine hand unto the seed of the house of Jacob, and made Myself known unto them in the land of Egypt, when I lifted up My hand unto them, saying, I am the LORD your God; In the day that I lifted up mine hand unto them, to bring them forth of the land of Egypt into a land that I had espied for them, flowing with milk and honey, which is the glory of all lands; then said I unto them, Cast ye away every man the abominations of his eyes, and defile not yourself with the idols of Egypt: I am the LORD your God. But they rebelled against Me, and would not hearken unto Me: they did not every man cast away the abominations of their eyes, neither did they forsake the idols of Egypt: then I said, I will pour out My fury upon them, to accomplish My anger against them in the midst of the land of Egypt. But I wrought for My name's sake, that it should not be polluted before the heathen, among whom they were, in whose sight I made Myself known unto them, in bringing them forth out of the land of Egypt. Wherefore I caused them to go forth out of the land of Egypt, and brought them into the wilderness.

In the seventh year of captivity, elders from among the people visited Ezekiel the prophet with the intention of hearing a word from the LORD. Fifty three years were yet to be fulfilled before these exiles could return to Jerusalem and the aged men who were now before the prophet, would never see the beloved city of Jerusalem again. Growing tired and weary, the elders longed to hear from the LORD, but He was displeased with them because they were responsible for the Babylonian oppression the people were now facing. In desperation they sat before Ezekiel the servant of GOD, longing to hear from the LORD, but what really was their true motive?

Knowing the intension of the hearts of these aged men, the prophet quickly informed them that the LORD had nothing favorable to say. Why did they wait for such a long time to enquire of the LORD? In the past, they abused, ridiculed and had some prophets thrown into prison. The reality of captivity now sets in; the people were facing dire hardship and were finally willing to inquire of the LORD. Had they forgotten the words of Jeremiah the prophet? Seventy years must be fulfilled in Babylon; were they trying to get out of this expressed judgment with merely a small fine? It is documented in 2 Chronicles 36:14-17: *Moreover all the chief of the priests, and the people, transgressed very much after all the abominations of the heathen; and polluted the house of the LORD which He had hallowed in Jerusalem. And the LORD God of their fathers sent to them by His messengers, rising up betimes, and sending; because He had compassion on His people, and on His dwelling place: but they mocked the messengers of God, and despised His words, and misused His prophets, until the wrath of the LORD arose against His people, till there was no remedy. Therefore He brought upon them the king of the Chaldees, who slew their young men with the sword in the house of the sanctuary, and had no compassion upon young man or maiden, old man, or him that is stooped for age: He gave them all into his hand.* The Lord will never allow oppressors to dominate His people without a cause. Seventy years was appointed for Judah's exile and no petition would reduce this sentence.

The elders sought Ezekiel with the wrong intention. They wanted to hear from the LORD but they were not willing to change, Galatians 6:7 rightly states: *Don't be mislead-you cannot mock the justice of God. You will always harvest what you plant,* NLT. In Ezekiel 20:5-10, we see the LORD reminding Judah of all He had done for them: through signs, wonders and miracles, yet they continued to rebel. Just over four centuries in Egypt, the last two in bondage and hard labor; the people cried unto the LORD; He heard and send Moses to be their deliverer. They left that land wealthy and their forefathers were eyewitnesses of the mighty power and awesome miracles of the LORD of heaven's Host in their behalf (Exodus 12:30-36); but the customs of the Egyptians followed them wherever they went hundreds of years later. For this reason the whole house of Israel sinned repeatedly against God and with each subsequent sin, the punishment of the LORD became more severe. Man has not changed; these unholy traits have followed humanity even to these modern times. Here is a thought to ponder: as the sins of the whole house of Israel grew worse, so did the punishment; what then will be the punishment of this generation whose evil ways have far surpassed that of Judah's?

Verses 11-39

And I gave them My statutes, and shewed them My judgments, which if a man do, he shall even live in them. moreover also I gave them My Sabbaths, to be a sign between Me and them, that they might know that I am the LORD that sanctify them. but the house of Israel rebelled against Me in the wilderness they walked not in My statutes, and they despised My judgments, which if a man do, he shall even live in them; and My Sabbaths they greatly polluted: then I said, I would pour out My fury upon them in the wilderness, to consume them. but I wrought for My name's sake, that it should not be polluted before the heathen, in whose sight I brought them out. Yet also I lifted up My hand unto them in the wilderness, that I would not bring them into the land which I had given them, flowing with milk and honey, which is the glory of all lands; because they despised My judgments, and walked not in My statutes, but polluted My Sabbaths: for their heart went after their idols. Nevertheless Mine eye spared them from destroying them, neither did I make an end of them in the wilderness. But I said unto their children in the wilderness, Walk ye not in the statutes of your fathers, neither observe their judgments, nor defile yourselves with their idols: I am the LORD your God; walk in My statutes, and keep My judgments, and do them; and hallow My Sabbaths; and they shall be a sign between Me and you, that ye may know that I am the LORD your God. Notwithstanding the children rebelled against Me: they walked not in My statutes, neither kept My judgments to do them; they polluted My Sabbaths: then I said, I would pour out My fury upon them, to accomplish My anger against them in the wilderness. Nevertheless I withdrew mine hand, and wrought for My name's sake, that it should not be polluted in the sight of the heathen, in whose sight I brought them forth. I lifted up Mine hand unto them also in the wilderness, that I would scatter them among the heathen, and disperse them through the countries; because they have not executed My judgments, but had despised My statutes, and had polluted My Sabbaths, and their eyes were after their father's idols. Wherefore I gave them statutes that were good, and judgments whereby they should not live; and I polluted them in their own gifts, in that they caused to pass through the fire all that openeth the womb, that I might make them desolate, to the end that they might know that I am the LORD. Therefore son of man, speak unto the house of Israel and say unto them, Thus saith the Lord GOD; Yet in this your fathers have blasphemed Me, in that they have committed a trespass against Me. For when I had brought them into the land, for the which I lifted up Mine hand to give it to them, then *they saw every high hill, and all the thick trees, and they offered there their sacrifices, and there they presented the provocation of their offering: there also they made their savour, and poured out there their drink offerings. Then I said unto them, What is the high place whereunto ye go? And the name thereof is called Bamah unto this day. Wherefore say unto the house of Israel, Thus saith the Lord GOD; Are ye polluted after the manner of your fathers? And commit ye whoredom after their abominations? For when ye offer your gifts, when ye make your sons to pass through the fire, ye polluted yourselves with all your idols, even unto this day: and shall I be enquired of by you, O house of Israel? As I live, saith the Lord GOD, I will not be enquired of by you. And that which cometh into your mind shall not be at all, that ye say, We will as the heathen, as the families of the countries, to serve wood and stone. as I live, saith the Lord GOD, surely with a mighty hand, and with a stretched out arm, and with fury poured out, will I rule over you: and I will bring you out from the people, and will gather you out of the countries wherein ye are scattered, with a mighty hand, and with a stretched out arm, and with fury poured out. And I will bring you into the wilderness of the people, and there will I plead with you face to face. Like as I pleaded with your fathers in the wilderness of the land of Egypt, so will I plead with you, saith the Lord GOD. And I will cause you to pass under the rod, and I will bring you into the bond of the covenant: and I will purge out from among you the rebels, and them that transgress against Me: I will bring them forth out of the country where they sojourn, and they shall not enter into the land of Israel: and ye shall know that I am the LORD. As for you, O house of Israel, thus saith the Lord GOD, Go ye, serve ye every one his idols, and hereafter also, if ye will not hearken unto Me: but pollute ye My holy name no more with your gifts, and with your idols.*

The Lord poured out His indictment against the whole house of Israel for their rebellion and pollution of His statutes and judgments thus deciding a painful future plagued by hardship, religious persecution and death. This evil that came upon the people could have been averted if they repented, but they continued in the ways of their ancestors. Mixing the holy with the unholy was an incompatible blend of good and evil which sealed their doom. The house of Israel had once again hit a rough spots in their loyalty to the LORD. Why then did they fall into sin to perpetrate more heinous crimes against GOD? Some calls this human propensity, but in fact, it is a battle between light and darkness; between the LORD GOD and the forces of evil and for this reason, mercy and grace was made available to all. Should mercy and grace be abused or rejected, then they are withdrawn and the judgment of God is poured out.

The house of Israel was well acquainted with the teachings of their GOD been chosen by Him to bring His glory to the nations of the earth. He calls them His firstborn and defends them in such miraculous ways, yet they choose the culture of heathens to the grief of their LORD. Deuteronomy 8:11-19 is only one of many books and verses in the Bible which sets forth the requirements of a peaceful existence for all Israel: *"Beware that you do not forget the LORD your God by not keeping His commandments, His judgments, and His statutes which I command you today, lest when you have eaten and are full, and have built beautiful houses and dwell in them; and when your herds and your flocks multiply, and your silver and your gold are multiplied, and all that you have is multiplied; when your heart is lifted up, and you forget the LORD your God who brought you out of the land of Egypt, from the house of bondage; who led you through the great and terrible wilderness, in which were fiery serpents and scorpions and thirsty land where there was no water; who brought water for you out of the flinty rock; who fed you in the wilderness with manna, which your fathers did not know, that He might humble you and that He might test you, to do you good in the end then you say in your heart, 'My power and the might of my hand have gained me this wealth.' And you shall remember the LORD your God, for it is He who gives you power to get wealth, that He may establish His covenant which He swore to your fathers, as it is this day. Then it shall be, if you by any means forget the LORD your God, and follow other gods, and serve them, I testify against you this day that you shall surely perish,* NKJV.

Israel was given a choice of life or death, yet on many occasions, they chose death, not knowing that the war that raged within them was being vomited out of the spiritual realm. The Apostle Paul reminds us in Ephesians 6:10-12: *Finally, be strong in the Lord and in the strength of His might. Put on the full armor of God, so that you will be able to stand firm against the schemes of the devil. For our struggle is not against flesh and blood, but against the rulers, against the powers, against the world forces of darkness, against the spiritual forces of wickedness in the heavenly places,* NASB. Man has unwittingly failed to recognize the dark evil forces that are constantly working against him. He struggles with the desire whether to do evil or good. These are Yeshua words recorded in Matthew 7:13-14: "*Enter through the narrow gate; for the gate is wide and the way is broad that leads to destruction, and there are many who enter through it. For the gate is small and the way is narrow that leads to life, and there are few who find it,* NASB. The easy way is not necessarily the best. Being wooed through deception and ignorance of the Word of God, many have become slaves to sin instead of being bondservants of righteousness.

As we see throughout the Holy Scriptures, the demise of a nation or people are directly associated with turning from righteousness to indulge in debauchery and every form of abominable practices that man can think of. Israel is a prime example to demonstrate to the whole world the by-products of obedience as well as disobedience. When the house of Israel did what was right, they had military success and peace, but when they refused to adhere to the established government of the kingdom of God, they experience hard times. God fearing leaders, who acknowledged and also practiced the Word of God, were blessed with His favor and those blessings also trickled down to the people. On the other hand unrighteous and evil leaders who by their rulings caused many to be immoral and lawless, brought calamity upon themselves and the people they govern. 1 Samuels 15:23 was an address to King Saul of Israel, but it is a word of warning to all: *"For rebellion is as the sin of witchcraft, and stubbornness is as iniquity and idolatry. Because you have rejected the word of the LORD, He has also rejected you from being king,"* NKJV. The rod of God's justice has continued to reach out to Israel in an attempt to get them back on the highway that leads to holiness, but instead, they have refused to totally submit to the LORD, and the same rod which is a symbol of His favor, became His rod of their judgment. As fire changes the molecular structure of a substance; so will the purging of a remnant from the twelve tribes of Israel be purified and raised from the ashes of adversity, to become firstfruits unto the LORD!

Verses 40-44

For in Mine holy mountain, in the mountain of the height of Israel, saith the Lord GOD, there shall all the house of Israel, all of them in the land, serve Me: there will I accept them, and there will I require your offerings, and the firstfruits of your oblations, with all your holy things. I will accept you with your sweet savour, when I bring you out from the people, and gather you out of the countries wherein ye have been scattered; and I will be sanctified in you before the heathen. And ye shall know that I am the LORD, when I shall bring you into the land of Israel, into the country for the which I lifted up Mine hand to give it to your fathers. And there shall ye remember your ways, and all your doings, wherein ye have been defiled; and ye shall loathe yourselves in your own sight for all your evils that ye have committed. And ye shall know that I am the LORD, when I have wrought with you for My name's sake, not according to your wicked ways, nor according to your corrupt doings, O ye house of Israel, saith the LORD GOD.

The desire of the LORD is to reconcile His people unto Himself. The prophet Zechariah spoke of the consummation of these things: *This is what the LORD says: "I will return to Zion and dwell in Jerusalem. Then Jerusalem will be called the Faithful City, and the mountain of the LORD Almighty will be called the Holy Mountain,"* 8:3 NIV. The house of Israel will not be given what they justly deserve as the LORD has said; this is His act of grace. The prophet Isaiah had visions of the days when Jerusalem and Judah would be reestablished by Almighty GOD under the scepter of Yeshua their King: *Now it shall come to pass in the latter days that the mountain of the LORD'S house shall be established on the top of the mountains, and shall be exalted above the hills; and all nations shall flow to it. Many people shall come and say, "Come, and let us go up to the mountain of the LORD, to the house of the God of Jacob; He will teach us His ways, and we shall walk in His paths." For out of Zion shall go forth the law, and the word of the LORD from Jerusalem. He shall judge between the nations, and rebuke many people; they shall beat their swords into plowshares, and their spares into pruning hooks; nation shall not lift up sword against nation, neither shall they learn war anymore,* 2:2-4 NKJV. A city on a hill cannot be hid, because they have been given the right to rule as sons and daughters with Yeshua. This however will not be the elevation of the carnal or unbelieving; it is reserved for the elect sons and daughters, who are the rightful heirs of Israel!

The LORD is all about relationship; He is the creator of the family and therefore a Father of all fathers, (see Genesis 1:26-30; 2:20-23; Psalm 68:5; Matthew 1:1-17; 6:9; 7:11; Luke 3:23-38; 11:2). Our true Father is the LORD GOD and the day is coming when we will worship Him in Sprit and in truth (John 4:23-24). At that time worship and the offering of firstfruits will be accepted, as this day will come with utter purging; a sifting and a separating of that which is holy, pure and just, because the iniquity of the house of Israel will be pardoned. Micah 7:18-20 tells us: *Who is a God like You, who pardons iniquity and passes over the rebellious act of the remnant of His possession? He does not retain His anger forever, because He delights in unchanging love. He will again have compassion on us; He will tread our iniquities under foot. Yes, You will cast all their sins into the depths of the sea. You will give truth to Jacob and unchanging love to Abraham, which You swore to our forefathers from the days of old,* NASB. God's Holy Mountain is in Jerusalem and the days are dawning when Israel will be reestablished under an everlasting banner of the Lord GOD.

Psalm 48:1-8 describes God and His relationship with His holy city, which has been a thorn in the flesh of many nations: *great is the LORD and greatly to be praised, in the city of our God, in His holy mountain. Beautiful in elevation, the joy of the whole earth, is Mount Zion on the sides of the north, the city of the great King. God is in her palaces; He is known as her refuge. For behold, the kings assembled, they passed by together. They saw it, and so they marveled, they hastened away. Fear took hold of them there, and pain, as of a woman in birth pangs, as when you break the ships of Tarshish with the east wind. As we have heard, so we have seen in the city of the LORD of hosts, in the city of our God: God will establish it forever,* NLT, (see also Isaiah 2:1-5). The LORD God has established His name in Mount Zion the city which He has chosen to reestablish His covenant with the whole house of Israel.

Verses 45-49

Moreover the word of the LORD came unto me, saying, Son of man, set thy face toward the south, and drop thy word toward the south, and prophesy against the forest of the south field; and say to the forest of the south, Hear the word of the LORD; Thus saith the Lord GOD; Behold, I will kindle a fire in thee, and it shall devour every green tree in thee, and every dry tree: the flaming flame shall not be quenched, and all faces from the south to the north shall be burned therein. And all flesh shall see that I the LORD have kindled it: it shall not be quenched. Then said I, Ah Lord GOD! They say to me, Doth he not speak parables?

Ezekiel is once more given a prophetic word for the people in the form of a simple story; this parable however caries great depth of meaning, and speaks of the woes that are yet to come upon the nation. This parable was specifically for Judah and Jerusalem, the southern kingdom; it spoke of the commencement of trouble, distress, adversity, and calamities breaking forth upon the people and the land. A severe affliction would affect old and young, rich and poor alike, which would cause great losses that could have been averted if only Judah repented. These catastrophic events would bear the signature of the LORD and all Israel would know they were being punished.

Chapter 21

Verses 1-7

And the word of the LORD came unto me, saying, Son of man, set thy face toward Jerusalem, and drop thy word toward the holy places, and prophesy against the land of Israel, and say to the land of Israel, Thus saith the LORD; Behold, I am against thee, and will draw forth My sword out of his sheath, and will cut off from thee the righteous and the wicked, therefore shall My sword go forth out of his sheath against all flesh from the south to the north: that all flesh may know that I the LORD have drawn forth My sword out of his sheath: it shall not return any more. Sigh therefore, thou son of man, with the breaking of thy loins; and with bitterness sigh before their eyes. And it shall be, when they say unto thee, Wherefore sighest thou? That thou shalt answer, for the tidings; because it cometh: and every heart shall melt, and all hands shall be feeble, and every spirit shall faint, and all knees shall be weak as water: behold, it cometh, and shall be brought to pass, saith the Lord GOD.

The grace of God extended to mankind is more than we truly realize or deserve and it continues to be revealed in these verses. Because Abba Father is acquainted with the unseen forces of evil that is constantly bombarding our thought life; He offers humanity grace and mercy that reaches out even to the vilest. From the LORD'S conversation with Ezekiel it is obvious that most of the people were rebels; resistant to His Divine authority, therefore justice had to be imposed.

Those who appeared righteous were truly hypocrites and deceivers, whose hearts were far from God.

Let's re-examine Ezekiel 18:23-26 and 32: *"Do I have any pleasure at all that the wicked should die?" says the Lord GOD, "and not that he should turn from his ways and live? But when a righteous man turns away from his righteousness and commits iniquity, and does according to all the abominations that the wicked man does, shall he live? All the righteousness which he has done shall not be remembered; because of the unfaithfulness of which he is guilty and the sin which he has committed, because of them he shall die. Yet you say, 'The way of the Lord is not fair.' Hear now, O house of Israel, is it not My way which is fair, and your ways which are not fair? When a righteous man turns away from his righteousness, commits iniquity, and dies in it, it is because of the iniquity which he has done that he dies . . . For I have no pleasure in the death of one who dies," says the Lord GOD. Therefore turn and live,"* NKJV. These verses shows that the righteous who turned away from living a holy and pure life to commit grievous wickedness will also suffer the same fate as the evil and corrupt (2 Timothy 3:1-5). We are given choices: be carnal or spiritual, righteous or unrighteous, hot or cold, for to be lukewarm is a mark of indecisiveness in which the Lord finds no pleasure.

The Lord God will not have mercy upon the righteous that turn to a riotous lifestyle, deny the Lord and consciously remain in such a state. This is what the word of God says about such people: *It is impossible for those who have once been enlightened, who have tasted the heavenly gift, who have shared in the Holy Spirit, who have tasted the goodness of the word of God and the powers of the coming age and who have fallen away, to be brought back to repentance. To their loss they are crucifying the Son of God all over again and subjecting him to public disgrace,* Hebrews 6:4-6 NIV. One might say, "But this is about Yeshua Jesus, what does this have to do with the LORD'S conversation with Ezekiel?" The truth is embedded in the fact that all the temple furnishings, sacrifices, Sabbaths, feasts and festivals, points to none other than Yeshua the Son of God in a typological setting. Whether we accept or reject the LORD'S requirements for holiness and righteousness, it does not change Abba Father's judgment upon the unrighteous, because redemption and salvation can only be acquired through His Son Yeshua Jesus who remains the same; yesterday, today, and forevermore (Hebrews 13:8). The rejection of the grace of God under these circumstances can only result in one's eternal separation from the kingdom of light and a life of everlasting peace.

Verses 8-13

Again the word of the LORD came unto me, saying, Son of man, prophesy, and say, Thus saith the LORD; Say, A sword, a sword is sharpened, and also furbished: it is sharpened to make a sore slaughter; it is furbished that it may glitter: should we then make mirth? It contemneth, [dissolve] the rod of My Son, as every tree. And He hath given it to be furbished, that it may be handled: this sword is sharpened, and it is furbished, to give it into the hand of the slayer. Cry and howl, son of man: for it shall be upon My people, it shall be upon all the princes of Israel: terrors by reason of the sword shall be upon My people: smite therefore upon thy thigh. Because it is a trial, and what if the sword contemn even the rod? It shall be no more, saith the Lord GOD.

The LORD God refers to His sword that will utterly cause His foes to be destroyed, while the rod of His Son is ready to cause all evil to melt away. The rod speaks of the Sovereignty and authority of Yeshua Jesus, and like a shepherd, His rod not only leads one to the path of righteousness, but also separates the godly from the wicked. This is where time plays a significant role, it is the most important thing that humans have been granted. Time is for man and it gives him a pattern to follow from the moment he enters this world and takes his first breath. Time governs our life here on earth to give us an opportunity to choose between light or darkness, the kingdom of God, or the kingdom of Satan. Grace and mercy is also bound by time and it gives us the opportunity to choose the kingdom we wish to spend eternity. Grace and mercy will not be needed in God's new heaven and earth because all things are perfect there, therefore, the LORD send His servants the prophets to warn His people to turn from all forms of wickedness, not desiring that any should perish so with raw display of emotions, Ezekiel struck his thigh as hard as he could as commanded by the LORD and then proceeded with a gut-wrenching cry to get the attention of the people, and the wise in heart would realize the seriousness of their predicament.

Verses 14-17

Thou therefore, son of man, prophesy, and smite thine hands together, and let the sword be doubled the third time, the sword of the slain: it is the sword of the great men that are slain, which entereth into their privy chambers. I have set the point of the sword against all their gates, that their heart may faint, and their ruins multiplied: ah! It is made bright, it is wrapped up for the slaughter. Go thee one way or other, either on the right hand, or on the left, whithersoever thy face is set. I will also smite Mine hands together, and I will cause My fury to rest: I the LORD have said it.

Next, Ezekiel forcefully and repeatedly claps his hands as instructed. This frenzied behavior was a demonstration to the elders and people in captivity that the punishment of the LORD was not only justified, it was final. There would be no escape; hard times accompanied by religious persecution in Babylon would last seventy years and not a day less. This total devastation came with a dual revelation. First of all, Ezekiel forcefully and repeatedly clap his hands (verse 14); next in verse seventeen, the LORD said, "*I will also smite Mine hands together, and I will cause My fury to rest.*" Although the army of Nebuchadnezzar totally subdued the city dwellers, and breeched large sections of the city wall, its gates, houses and temple; it was the LORD who gave them over to the king's army (2 Chronicles 26:9-15). Trouble and devastation lingered over the great city for seventy years because the presence of the LORD had departed. The GOD of Israel had removed His protective covering and released His people to the spoilers. He that had fought and won many battles for Israel; now gave them over to a heathen nation, whose gods they would be forced to worship and if they refused; they had two options to choose from: be thrown to the lions or be consumed by the flames.

Verses 18-27

The word of the LORD came unto me again, saying, Also, thou son of man, appoint thee two ways, that the sword of the king of Babylon may come: both twain shall come forth out of one land: and choose thou a place, choose it at the head of the way to the city. Appoint a way, that the sword may come to Rabbath of the Ammonites, and to Judah in Jerusalem the defenced. For the king of Babylon stood at the parting of the way, at the head of the two ways, to use divination: he made his arrows bright, he consulted with images, he looked in the liver. At his right hand was the divination for Jerusalem, to appoint captains, to open the mouth in slaughter, to lift up the voice with shouting, to appoint battering rams against the gates, to cast a mount, and to build a fort. And it shall be unto them as a false divination in their sight, to them that have sworn oaths: but he will call to remembrance the iniquity, that they may be taken. Therefore thus saith the Lord GOD; Because ye have made your iniquity to be remembered, in that your transgressions are discovered, so that in all your doings your sins do appear; because, I say, that ye are come to remembrance ye shall be taken with the hand. And thou profane wicked prince of Israel, whose day is come, when iniquity shall have an end, thus saith the Lord GOD; Remove the diadem, and take off the crown: this shall not be the same: exalt him that is low, and abase him that is high. I will overturn, overturn, overturn, it: and it shall be no more, until He come whose right it is; and I will give it to Him.

The prophet was instructed to appoint two roads where the judgment of the LORD would commence. The first one was appointed to Rabbah of the Ammonites a great city that was the inheritance of the tribe of Gad (Joshua 13:24-25). The tribe of Gad fell into idolatry by worshiping the image Milcom, an Ammonite god. Jeremiah 49:1-2 records: *Against the Ammonites. Thus says the LORD: "Has Israel no sons? Has he no heir? Why then does Milcom inherit Gad, and his people dwell in its cities? Therefore behold, the days are coming," says the LORD, "That I will cause to be heard an alarm of war in Rabbah of the Ammonites; it shall be a desolate mound, and her villages shall be burned with fire. Then Israel shall take possession of his inheritance," says the LORD,* NKJV. The LORD did not overlook the ills of the Ammonites, and they, too, would experience the judgment of the LORD.

The great valor of the Gaddites was put to the test, as well as that of the tribe of Judah who once occupied the fortified city of Jerusalem. This was not a pleasant time for Judah and intercession was too late because the LORD'S ruling had already been handed down. Through dramatization, the prophet reminds the people of their evil and idolatrous ways which led to their exile. Judah and the remaining tribes would never find lasting peace until the Prince of Peace; Yeshua Jesus, Israel's only hope return to earth and set up His Holy throne in righteousness and truth. Until such prophecies are fulfilled, the matter at hand was the fact that the LORD had given His people over to the Babylonians; His sword of reproof (Jeremiah 25:9-12; 29:10; 2 Chronicles 36:21; Daniel 9:2). There are no gray areas when the LORD speaks; when He gives His final ruling, He has nothing further to say.

While those in Jerusalem relaxed in the comfort of their fortified city unaware of their fate, the people living in Rabbah were also contented, believing that they, too, were well protected by their elite forces of Gaddites, but they, like their brethren living in Jerusalem, were also in for a mighty surprise. The Babylonians were not worshipers of the God of Israel; they were heathens who also practiced the art of witchcraft. In this instance their occult knowledge was utilized to inform the Babylonian army of the precise time to strike and who should be first. A siege was then planned by the Babylonians, which included the psychological warfare of intimidation, which heighten fear in the city as no one knew when the orders would be given to strike the ill-prepared and fearful residence of the city, thereby leaving the fate of the occupants of Jerusalem in the hands of their enemies. The walls of the city were breeched and the Babylonian army intimidated the people to the extent that those who could no longer endure the intense mind games; voluntarily surrendered instead of being killed. After the carnage was over; Chebar became the home of most of the exiles for seventy years.

Verses 28-32

And thou, son of man, prophesy and say, Thus saith the Lord GOD concerning the Ammonites, and concerning their reproach; even say thou, the sword, the sword is drawn: for the slaughter it is furbished, to consume because of the glittering: whiles they see vanity unto thee, whiles they divine a lie unto thee, to bring thee upon the necks of them that are slain, of the wicked, whose day is come, when their iniquity shall have an end. Shall I cause it to return into the sheath? I will judge thee in the place where thou wast created, in the land of thy nativity. And I will pour out Mine indignation upon thee, I will blow against thee in the fire of My wrath, and deliver thee into the hand of brutish men, and skilful to destroy thee. Thou shalt be for fuel to the fire; thy blood shall be in the midst of the land; thou shalt be no more remembered: for I the LORD have spoken it.

The reproof of the Ammonites was Milcom their god whom Israel worshiped. The judgment of the LORD was also unleashed upon the children of Amon, it was swift and unrelenting and those who were born in the land would die there. Habakkuk, who prophesied during the time of Babylonian world dominance, gives a good description of this barbaric nation also known as the Chaldeans: *"Look among the nations and watch be utterly astounded! For I will work a work in your days which you would not believe, though it were told you. For indeed I am raising up the Chaldeans, a bitter and hasty nation which marches through the breadth of the earth, to possess dwelling places that are not theirs. They are terrible and dreadful; their judgment and their dignity proceed from themselves. Their horses also are swifter than leopards, and more fierce than evening wolves. Their chargers charge ahead; their cavalry comes from afar; they fly as the eagle that hastens to eat. They all come for violence; their faces are set like the east wind. They gather captives like sand. They scoff at kings, and princes are scorned by them. They deride every stronghold, for they heap up earthen mounds and seize it. Then his mind changes, and he transgresses; he commits offense, ascribing this power to his god,"* 1:5-11 NKJV. The Babylonians were indeed brutal men who subdued the residence of Jerusalem and Ammon.

Zephaniah 2:8-11 gives some more insight into the LORD's rebuke against the children of Ammon: *"I have heard the taunting of Moab and the reviling of the sons of Ammon, with which they have taunted My people and become arrogant against their territory. Therefore as I live,"* declares the LORD of hosts, the God of Israel, *"Surely Moab will be like Sodom and the sons of Ammon like Gomorrah a place possessed by nettles and pits, and a perpetual desolation. The remnant of My people will plunder them and the remainder of My nation will inherit them. This they will have in return for their pride, because they have taunted and become arrogant against the people of the LORD of hosts. The LORD will be terrifying to them, for He will starve all the gods of the earth; and all the coastlands of the nation will bow down to Him, everyone from his own place,"* NASB. The gods of the Ammonites became a stumbling block for the children of Israel and the LORD did not take this lightly. The Ammonites reproof would come upon them suddenly because they introduced the children of Israel to witchcraft; a crime punishable by death. The LORD God is aware of the sin traps of the heathens that caused His people to go astray and for this reason His reprisal was not immediate. Abba Father gave His elect time to repent, but instead, they choose suffering over peace and quietness.

Chapter 22

Verses 1-16

Moreover the word of the LORD came unto me, saying, Now, thou son of man, wilt thou judge, wilt thou judge the bloody city? Yea, thou shalt shew her all her abominations. Then say thou, Thus saith the Lord GOD, The city sheddeth blood in the midst of it, that her time may come, and maketh idols against herself to defile herself. Thou art become guilty in thy blood that thou hast shed; and hast defiled thyself in thine idols which thou hast made; and thou hast caused thy days to draw near, and art come even unto thy years: therefore have I made thee a reproach unto the heathen, and a mocking to all countries. Those that be near, and those that be far from thee, shall mock thee, which art infamous and much vexed. Behold, the princes of Israel, every one were in thee to their power to shed blood. In thee have they set light by father and mother: in the midst of thee have they dealt by oppression with the stranger: in thee have they vexed the fatherless and the widow. Thou hast despised Mine holy things, and hast profaned My Sabbaths. In thee are men that carry tales to shed blood: and in thee they eat upon the mountains: in the midst of thee they commit lewdness. In thee have they discovered their father's nakedness: in thee have they humbled her that was set apart for pollution. And one hath committed abomination with his neighbour's wife; and another hath lewdly defiled his daughter in law; and another in thee hath humbled his sister, his father's daughter. In thee have they taken gifts to shed blood; thou hast taken usury and increase, and thou hast greedily gained of thy neighbours by extortion, and hast forgotten Me, saith the Lord GOD. Behold, therefore I have smitten Mine hand at thy dishonest gain which thou hast made, and at thy blood which hath been in the midst of thee. Can thine heart endure, or can thine hands be strong, in the days that I shall deal with thee? I the LORD have spoken it, and will do it. and I will scatter thee among the heathen, and disperse thee in the countries, and will consume thy filthiness out of thee. And thou shalt take thine inheritance in thyself in the sight of the heathen, and thou shalt know that I am the LORD.

These are very serious allegations stacked up against the house of Israel. The nation could not deny these charges, for in doing so they would be calling God a liar! The sins that stood out above the rest, were those of a sexual nature: 1 Corinthians 6:18-20 applying the NASB earnestly reproves mankind: *Flee immorality. Every other sin that a man commits is outside the body, but the immoral man sins against his own body. Or do you not know that your body is a temple of the Holy Spirit who is in you, whom you have from God, and that you are not your own? For you have been bought with a price: therefore glorify God in your body.* Sins of a sexual nature, unlike others, are committed against one's body. If a person commits fornication or adultery, he or she has committed sin against his or her own body; there is no "paying back" where sexual sins are concerned.

This was the indictment of the LORD against all of Israel; they were:

- o Murderers
- o Idolaters
- o Leaders abusing their authority by giving orders for assassinations
- o Children dishonoring their parents
- o Neglecting emigrants, orphans and widows

- Desecration of the things of God
- Disregard for the Sabbaths
- Deliberately lying resulting in the death of another
- Members of secret societies and sacrificing to pagan gods
- Indecent, indulging in unrestrained perversion
- Having intercourse with a woman during menstruation
- Having intercourse with their mother or father's wife
- Wife swapping (swingers)
- Having intercourse with their son's wife
- Having intercourse with their sisters or half sisters
- Ordering murder for hire
- Charging high interest rates for loans
- Gaining wealth through dishonest dealings
- Rejecting God as their Creator

These were the LORD'S observation of the sins of the house of Israel and history continues to repeat itself. The sins that the LORD was against thousands of years ago are still in effect. Isaiah 2:6-12 states: *For You have forsaken Your people, the house of Jacob, because they are filled with eastern ways; they are soothsayers like the Philistines, and they are pleased with the children of foreigners. Their land is also full of silver and gold, and there is no end to their treasures; their land is also full of horses, and there is no end to their chariots. Their land is also full of idols; they worship the work of their own hands, that which their* own fingers have made. People bow down, and each man humbles himself; therefore do not forgive them. Enter in the rock, and hide in the dust, from the terror of the LORD and the glory of His majesty. The lofty looks of man shall be humbled, the haughtiness of men shall be bowed down, and the LORD alone shall be exalted in that day. For the day of the LORD of hosts shall come upon everything proud and lofty, upon everything lifted up and it shall be brought low, NKJV.

The morality of mankind has declined in such a way that only the return of the Righteous Ruler: Yeshua Jesus, can bring restoration. It is no longer eleven fifty nine on the clock of God; it is already midnight. The bowl of man's sin is now full and the judgment of God is about to be poured out. As man continues to reject God as his creator; the heavens shout forth His glory and the unmistaken wonders of life on earth continues to bear witness of it, whether we acknowledge it or not.

This is not all gloom and doom; there is hope. The Apostle Paul gives us this advice recorded in 2 Corinthians 6:14-18 and 7:1, appropriately paraphrased by the New Living Translation: *Don't team up with those who are unbelievers. How can righteousness be partner with wickedness? How can light live in darkness? What harmony can there be between Christ and the devil? How can a believer be a partner with an unbeliever? And what union can there be between God's temple and idols? For we are the temple of the living God. As God said: "I will live in them and walk among them. I will be their God, and they will be My people. Therefore, come out from among unbelievers, and separate yourselves from them, says the LORD. Don't touch their filthy things, and I will welcome you. And I will be your Father, and you will be My sons and daughters, says the LORD Almighty." . . . Because we have these promises, dear friends, let us cleanse ourselves from everything that can defile our body and spirit. And let us work toward complete holiness because we fear God.* Man has no excuse for rejecting the teachings and statutes of the LORD. To knowingly refuse to adhere to godly instructions will not delay or abort the judgment of God. Chaos is the order of the day when men act immorally and without any form of self control. Immorality is not an inherited trait, it is learned and successive generations have followed this aimless path to self-destruction. The word of God does not lie; Galatians 6:7-8 clearly states: *Do not be deceived, God is not mocked; for whatever a man sows, that he will also reap. For he who sows to the flesh will of the flesh reap corruption, but he who sows to the Spirit will of the Spirit reap everlasting life,* NKJV. Israel suffered greatly because of immorality, if the LORD judged His people Israel, He will also judge this present generation; we have a mandate to break this cycle.

Verses 17-22

And the word of the LORD came unto me, saying, Son of man, the house of Israel is to Me become dross: all they are brass, and tin, and iron, and lead, in the midst of the furnace; they are even the dross of silver. Therefore thus saith the Lord GOD; because ye are all become dross, behold, therefore I will gather you into the midst of Jerusalem. As they gather silver, and brass, and iron, and lead, and tin, into the midst of the furnace, to blow the fire upon it, to melt it; so will I gather you in Mine anger and in My fury, and I will leave you there, and melt you. Yea, I will gather you, and blow upon you in the fire of My wrath, and ye shall be melted in the midst thereof. As silver is melted in the midst of the furnace, so shall ye be melted in the midst thereof; and ye shall know that I the LORD have poured out My fury upon you.

The Lord likens the impurity of the house of Israel as unto dross. This glorious nation which belongs to the LORD had corrupted themselves with the evil practices of the heathens. This was more than mere curiosity; it was blatant sin. Israel, a monotheistic nation chosen to bring the glory of God to the Gentiles, failed to realize that they are built upon a unique foundation. In Ezekiel 22:18, the house of Israel was likened unto five metals: brass and tin, iron, lead, and silver. The LORD then repeats Himself in Ezekiel 22:20 by saying: *"I will gather you in the midst of Jerusalem. As they gather silver, and brass, and iron, and lead, and tin, into the midst of the furnace."* The LORD introduces a dichotomy by changing the order of the metals, which meant that He was also changing the message. Let's define each metal individually from its Hebraic root and metaphorical settings because they teach two distinctive and very important lessons. Keep in mind that the Hebrew word used for *dross* has several meanings which includes: *refuse, apostatize, backslider, go back,* and *turn away.*

Ezekiel 22:18	Ezekiel 22:20
The house of Israel became the dross of these metals unto the LORD in the middle of the furnace	Men gather these metals in the middle of the furnace to blow the fire upon it, in order to melt it
Tin – Divided	Silver - Price
Brass – Filthiness	Brass - Filthiness
Iron – To pierce	Iron – To pierce
Lead – To pulverize	Lead – To pulverize
Silver - Price	Tin - Divided

Here is the interpretation: the group on the left is Israel; Abba Father found them to be **filthy** (bronze), in other words sin laden. They were **divided** (tin) into a northern and southern kingdom following a revolt after King Solomon's death; therefore, this meant that He was addressing all twelve tribes. They were **pierced** (iron), which is to say; they suffered for their sins and idolatry, they were then **pulverized** (lead): crushed, defeated and dispersed into the nations, which was the **price** (silver) they paid for their sins. The LORD said His people had become dross unto Him; metaphorically stating that they were backsliders who had abandon their heritage by turning away from the teachings of the LORD to follow after strange gods. The prophet Isaiah spoke by the mouth of the LORD this oracle: *"Thus says the LORD, the King of Israel, and his Redeemer, the LORD of hosts: I am the First and I am the Last; besides Me there is no God. And who can proclaim as I do? Then let him declare it and set it in order for Me, since I appointed the ancient people. And the things that are coming and shall come, let them show these to them. Do not fear, nor be afraid; have I not told you from that time, and declared it? You are My witnesses. Is there a God besides Me? Indeed there is no other Rock; I know not one."* Those who make an image, all of them are useless, and their precious things shall not profit; they are their own witnesses; they neither see nor know, that they may be ashamed. . . He burns half of it in the fire; with this half he eats meat; he roasts a roast, and is satisfied. He even warms himself and says, "Ah! I am warm, I have seen the fire." And the rest of it he makes into a god, his carved image. He falls down before it and worships it, prays to it and says, "Deliver me, for you are my god," 44:6-9 and 16-17 NKJV. Israel had abandoned their GOD, but He, being in covenant with them, would never utterly leave or forsake His heritage.

The LORD then switches around the order of the metals in the second message in Ezekiel 22:20; to silver, brass, iron, lead, and tin; then referred to *"they,"* as He continued to dialogue with Ezekiel (see column on the right). To say "they," infers that He was addressing both Jews and Gentiles who would participate in a sacrificial offering. First of all; to *blow the fire upon it, to melt it*: is speaking of the type of persecution; the first was affliction (brass/filthiness or sin), the second was separation (tin/to divide), the third was persecution (iron/to pierce), the fourth dispersion (lead/to pulverize), and the fifth repatriation (silver/ to redeem); this was the dross removing process. After these things were accomplished, the house of Israel would be re-gathered in the *"midst"* of Jerusalem, where the eyes of the nations of the world would be focused.

Here is yet another revelation; the Hebrew word used for *"midst"* is **Tawech** [8432], it conveys the following meaning: to sever or separate as we see in the understanding of the meaning of "tin." **Tawech** not only mean that which is naturally divided; it metaphorically and figuratively alludes to two types of division. The first referring to the veil of the Temple, while the second figuratively speaking of the voluntary act of one giving up the soul, which takes us to the interpretation of the column on the right and the second message.

Isaiah 53 is a Messianic prophesy that records Abba Father's final act of love for both Jews and Gentiles by offering His Son Yeshua HaMashiach; His Passover Lamb. Isaiah's oracle states: *Who has believed our report? And to whom has the arm of the LORD been revealed? For He shall grow up before Him as a tender plant, and as a root out of dry ground. He has no form of comeliness; and when we see Him, there is no beauty that we should desire Him. He is despised and rejected by men, a Man of sorrows and acquainted with grief. And we hid, as it were, our faces from Him; He was despised, and we did not esteem Him. Surely He has borne our griefs and carried our sorrows; yet we esteemed Him stricken, smitten by God, and afflicted. But He was wounded for our transgressions, He was bruised for our iniquities; the chastisement of our peace was upon Him, and by His stripes we are healed. All we like sheep have gone astray; we have turned every one, to his own way; and the LORD has laid on Him the iniquity of us all. He was oppressed and He was afflicted, yet He opened not His mouth; He was led as a lamb to the slaughter, and as a sheep before the shearers is silent, so He opened not His mouth. He was taken from prison and from judgment, and who will declare His generation? For He was cut off from the land of the living; for the transgression of My people He was stricken. And they made His grave with the wicked but with the rich at His death, because He had done no violence, nor was any deceit in His mouth. Yet it pleased the LORD to bruise Him; He has put Him to grief. When You make His soul an offering for sin, He shall see His seed, He shall prolong His days, and the pleasure of the LORD shall prosper in His hand. He shall see the labor of His soul, and be satisfied. By His knowledge My righteous Servant shall justify many, for He shall bear their iniquities. Therefore I will divide Him a portion with the great, and He shall divide the spoil with the strong, because He poured out His soul unto death and He was numbered with the transgressors, and He bore the sin of many, and made intercession for their transgression,* NKJV. Yeshua was the Passover Lamb, thus fulfilling Abba Father's promise that His Son would be a once and for all time sacrifice for sin. The *midst,* not only described a physical location, in the city of Jerusalem, but also conveys figuratively, the passion of Yeshua: **Tawech**, the giving up of His soul viewed by both Jews and Gentiles! Ironically this occurred on Passover in the Hebrew month Nissan, which is also known as the month of redemption!

In Ezekiel 22:20 (see column on the right), silver is mentioned first; it is the **price** of redemption for the sins or **filthiness** (brass) of the people. Yeshua was **pierced** (iron) and **pulverized** (lead), at the end of His suffering the veil of the Temple split in two **divided** (tin), demolishing the separation that through Him, the permanent and new High Priest; men would come boldly to the Mercy Seat where the grace of Abba Father now becomes his covering. Psalm 22:13-22 also speaks prophetically of Yeshua's sufferings: *They gape at Me with their mouths, like a raging and roaring lion. I am poured out like water, and all My bones are out of joint; My heart is like wax; it has melted within Me. My strength is dried up like a potsherd, and My tongue clings to My jaws; You have brought Me to the dust of death. For dogs have surrounded Me; the congregation of the wicked has enclosed Me. They pierced My hands and My feet; I can count all My bones. They look and stare at Me. They divide My garments among them, and for My clothing they cast lots. But You, O LORD, do not be far from Me; O My strength, hasten to help Me! Deliver Me from the sword, My precious life from the power of the dog. Save Me from the lion's mouth and from the horns of the wild oxen! You have answered Me. I will declare Your* *name to My brethren; in the midst of the assembly I will praise You,* NKJV. The four gospels of the New Covenant also corroborates with accounts of the Old Covenant of Yeshua's suffering; Matthew 27: 27-44; Mark 15:16-32; Luke 23:26-43 and John 19:1-37.

The Apostle Paul also a Jew was inspired to pen these words: *For other foundation can no man lay than that is laid, which is Jesus Christ. Now if any man build upon this foundation gold, silver, precious stones, wood, hay, stubble; every man's work shall be manifest: for the day shall declare it, because it shall be revealed by fire; and the fire shall try every man's work of what sort it is. If any man's work abide which he hath built there upon, he shall receive a reward. If any man's work shall be burned, he shall suffer loss: but he himself shall be saved; yet so as by fire. Know ye not that ye are the temple of God, and that the Spirit of God dwelleth in you? If any man defile the temple of God, him shall God destroy; for the temple of God is holy, which temple ye are,* 1 Corinthians 3:11-17. Another important aspect that could have been overlooked is the fact that Yeshua's finished work as the final sacrifice for sin also fulfilled His prayer to the Father. Holy Spirit, the Ruach HaKodesh of God came to dwell in us and upon His arrival He commenced erecting a spiritual Temple and when He is finished, we will be established as ONE NEW MAN; a permanent dwelling place for the Godhead.

In Ezekiel 22:19 the LORD gathers the house of Israel in Jerusalem; the Hebrew word used here is **Qavats** [6908], among its meaning: is to assemble or to congregate in a single location. The LORD explicitly said, *"The midst of Jerusalem."* In verse 20 however, the same word *"gather"* is used but the Hebrew word here is **Qvutsah** [6910], remarkably this word is only used once in the Cannon of Scriptures, which surprisingly is Ezekiel 22:20. This word conveys the meaning to collect or to fill completely until it overflowed. During the Pesach, also known as the Passover celebrations, the city of Jerusalem became the focal point as Jews from all over gathered there to commemorate their flight from slavery and bondage in Egypt.

This explains why the Hebrew word **Qvutsah** (to gather), is only used once in Scripture because of the uniqueness of that Pesach or Passover. It was the day that brought animal sacrifices to a permanent cessation. Yeshua Jesus fulfilled the sacrificial offering of animals; He, being the perfect and final sacrifice for the sins of all (Hebrews 10:1-18). This was also the day when the veil of the Temple was breached creating an opening from top to bottom thereby instating Yeshua as High Priest; which brought to an end the sacrificial duties of the earthly high priest. No longer would he be required once every year to enter the Most Holy Place (Holiest of all) to offer sacrifice for his sin and that of the people, (for further reading see, Matthew 27:51; Mark 15:38; Luke 23:45, Hebrews 4:14-16).

The entire city of Jerusalem was crammed with Jews to observe the Pesach (Passover) and became eye witnesses of the glorious power of Almighty GOD as He enthroned His Son as King and High Priest. The word **Qvutsah** thus describes the vast number of people in the city of Jerusalem at the time when Yeshua was crucified; this being the preparation of a special Sabbath; an eight day celebration known as the Pesach (Passover)! During this unique celebration, Yeshua became the Redeemer of all mankind; the perfect Passover Lamb of GOD.

To summarize: Ezekiel 22:20; Yeshua became our Redeemer, paying the ultimate price with His life (silver = price paid), for the sins of all mankind (brass = filthiness). He was wounded for our transgressions, (iron = pierce). He was stricken, smitten, afflicted, and bruised for our iniquities; the chastisement of our peace was laid upon Him, and by His stripes we are healed (lead = pulverize). This Yeshua did and as He willingly gave up His Spirit; the veil of the Temple was torn in two from top to bottom (tin = divided). Yeshua (Jesus the Messiah); therefore united the house of

Israel as one nation again as well as affording a relationship with the Gentiles who would call Him Savior and Lord.

Verses 23-31

And the word of the LORD came unto me, saying, Son of man, say unto her, Thou art the land that is not cleansed, nor rained upon in the day of indignation. There is a conspiracy of her prophets in the midst thereof, like a roaring lion ravening the prey; they have devoured souls; they have taken the treasure and the precious things; they have made her many widows in the midst thereof. Her priest have violated My law, and have profaned Mine holy things: they have put no difference between the holy and the profane, neither have they shewed difference between the unclean and the clean, and have hid their eyes from My Sabbaths, and I am profaned among them. Her princes in the midst thereof are like wolves ravening the prey, to shed blood, and to destroy souls, to get dishonest gain. And her prophets have daubed them with untempered morter, seeing vanity, and divining lies unto them, saying, Thus saith the LORD GOD, when the LORD hath not spoken. The people of the land have used oppression, and exercised robbery, and have vexed the poor and needy: yea, they have oppressed the stranger wrongfully. And I sought for a man among them, that should make up the hedge, and stand in the gap before Me for the land, that I should not destroy it: but I found none. Therefore I have poured out Mine indignation upon them; I have consumed them with the fire of My wrath: their own way have I recompensed upon their heads, saith the Lord GOD.

Prophet, priests, princes, and those with delegated authority, are criticized for oppressing the poor. A special warning was levied against the prophets and priests who profaned the judgments of the LORD, by oppressing the poor and accumulating unjust wealth to lavish upon themselves. Prophets were rebuked for lying and giving prophesies for gain, as they destroyed the souls of men by causing many to turn from the LORD God and back to sin. This was a great evil that was upon the land and Abba Father withheld His blessings. The chief rulers, which included the priests, were condemned for violating the teachings of God, which they further compounded by their contemptible irreverence for that which is sacred. The Sabbaths of the LORD were not adhered to and everyone did as they pleased.

The LORD turns His focus on the appointed leaders (princes), whom He describes as being devouring wolves; shedding blood thereby destroying souls. A wolf is a predator that singles out its victim and at the opportune moment, seize to gains control. The King James Version uses the word "*destroy,*" in Ezekiel 22:27 of our study. The Hebrew word transliterated "destroy," is **Avad** [6]; and it is different from "*destroy*" **Shachath** [7843] used in 22:30. The word **Avad** is describing the sudden loss of wealth, rank reputation and happiness of a nation; it speaks of its ruin that comes without warning, plunging a people to the near brink of extinction due to starvation. These devastating occurrences are the direct sinister results planned by those in leadership.

Again the LORD addresses the prophets, accusing them of delivering messages out of their own hearts (untempered). These are the LORD'S words to His true prophet Jeremiah: *I have heard what the prophets said, that prophesy lies in My name, saying, I have dreamed, I have dreamed. How long shall this be in the hearts of the prophets that prophesy lies? yea, they are prophets of the deceit of their heart; which think to cause My people to forget My name by their dreams which they tell every man to his neighbour, as their fathers have forgotten My name for Baal. The prophet that hath a dream, let him tell a dream; and he that hath My word, let him speak My word faithfully. What is the chaff to the wheat? saith the LORD. Is not My word like as a fire? Saith the LORD; and like a hammer that breaketh the rock in pieces? therefore, behold, I am against the prophets, saith the LORD, that steal My words every one from his neighbour. Behold, I am against the prophets, saith the LORD, that use their tongues, and say, He saith. Behold*

I am against them that prophesy false dreams, saith the LORD, and do tell them, and cause My people to err by their lies, and by their lightness; yet I sent them not, nor commanded them: therefore they shall not profit this at all, saith the LORD, 23:25-32, (for further reading, see also Jeremiah 14:14-15; Matthew 7:22-23). It is dangerous to prophesy lies in the name of the LORD, because it is an injustice and utter wickedness. The LORD'S goes on to address the natives of the land who oppressed, robbed, and distressed their neighbors and those in need of their financial support; especially foreigners. The LORD also looked among them to see if there was any He could use to defend the disenfranchised so that He would not destroy the land, but He found none; all were corrupt.

This takes us to the second use of the word *"destroy"* spoken of in Ezekiel 22:30, here the Hebrew word used is **Shachath** [7843]; it speaks of the nature of the crime and its prescribed punishment. This, too, would cause destruction. The first use of the word described the destruction caused by corrupt leaders, **Avad** [6]; while its second use **Shachath** [7843], described the destruction which is the direct result of the evils perpetrated by the heads of the business communities. The vial of the LORD'S judgment was about to be poured out without warning and the instigators of lawlessness would be personally rewarded by the LORD GOD Himself!

Chapter 23

Verses 1-21

The word of the LORD came again unto me, saying, Son of man, there were two women, the daughters of one mother: and they committed whoredoms in Egypt; they committed whoredoms in their youth: there were their breasts pressed, and there they bruised the teats of their virginity. And the names of them were Aholah the elder, and Aholibah her sister: and they were Mine, and they bare sons and daughters. Thus were their names; Samaria is Aholah, and Jerusalem Aholibah. And Aholah played the harlot when she was Mine; and she doted on her lovers, on the Assyrians her neighbours, which were clothed with blue, captains and rulers, all of them desirable young men, horsemen riding upon horses. Thus she committed her whoredoms with them, with all them that were the chosen men of Assyria, and with all on whom she doted: with all their idols she defiled herself. Neither left she her whoredoms brought from Egypt: for in her youth they lay with her, and they bruised the breasts of her virginity, and poured their whoredoms upon her. Wherefore I have delivered her into the hand of her lovers, into the hand of the Assyrians, upon whom she doted. These discovered her nakedness: they took her sons and her daughters, and slew her with the sword: and she became famous among women; for they executed judgment upon her. And when her sister Aholibah saw this, she was more corrupt in her inordinate love than she, and in her whoredoms more than her sister in her whoredoms. She doted upon the Assyrians her neighbours, captains and rulers clothed most gorgeously, horsemen riding upon horses, all of them desirable young men. Then I saw that she was defiled, that they took both one way, and that she increased her whoredoms: for when she saw men portrayed upon the wall, the images of the Chaldeans portrayed with vermilion, girded with girdles upon their loins, exceeding in dyed attire upon their heads, all of them princes to look to, after the manner of the Babylonians of Chaldea, the land of their nativity: and as soon as she saw them with her eyes, she doted upon them, and sent messengers unto them into Chaldea. And the Babylonians came to her into the bed of love, and they defiled her with their whoredom, and she was polluted with them, and her mind was alienated from them. So she discovered her whoredoms, and discovered her nakedness: then My mind was alienated from her, like as My mind was alienated from her sister. Yet she multiplied her whoredoms, in calling to remembrance the days of her youth, wherein she had played the harlot in the land of Egypt. For she doted upon their paramours, whose flesh is as the flesh of asses, and whose issue is like the issue of horses. Thus thou calledst to remembrance the lewdness of thy youth, in bruising thy teats by the Egyptians for the paps of thy youth.

Once again the LORD speaks to Ezekiel regarding Israel and Judah. In this chapter He refers to them in terms that are less than flattering. He calls Israel "Aholah" and Judah "Aholibah;" being daughters of one mother. This expression is much deeper than merely saying they were sisters. In Ezekiel 16:45-63, Israel was called Samaria, while Judah was called Sodom, both names of chief cities. Here in chapter twenty-three the disappointment of the LORD with both groups was expressed with the use of much more debased names Aholah and Aholibah, as a reflection of His utter disgust. It must be noted here that there are slight variations in the spelling of these names in some versions of the Bible. Aholah is spelled "Oholah" and Aholibah as "Oholibah," however they are one in the same.

Judah (Aholibah) is also called Jerusalem, but in chapter sixteen Sodom. Why did the Lord change their name? Could the change in identity be due to the fraction of the nation into two kingdoms? For further study see 1 Kings 11 & 12. Both Israel and Judah were found guilty of adultery with the heathen nations although they were betrothed unto the LORD. Betrothal or engagement held the same degree of sanctity as marriage, and to become bedfellows with heathens was seen as whoredom. The temple also called the Tent of Meeting was GOD'S visible presence among His people, yet they lusted after the gods of other nations. For this reason Israel is called Aholah, which is translated "her tent," "in her tent," or 'her own tent;" a reflection of her stubbornness and rebellion.

The reason for the unflattering name given to the ten tribes of the northern kingdom, is explained in 1 Kings 12:27-33: Jeroboam king of Israel said: *"If these people go up to offer sacrifices in the house of the LORD at Jerusalem, then the heart of this people will turn back to their lord, Rehoboam king of Judah." Therefore the king asked advice, made two calves of gold, and said to the people, "It is too much for you to go up to Jerusalem. Here are your gods. O Israel, which brought you up from the land of Egypt!" And he set up one in Bethel, and the other he put in Dan. Now this thing became a sin, for the people went to worship before the one as far as Dan. He made shrines on the high places, and made priests from every class of people, who were not of the sons of Levi. Jeroboam ordained a priest on the fifteenth day of the eight month, like the feast that was in Judah, and offered sacrifices on the altar. So he did at Bethel, sacrificing to the calves that he had made. And at Bethel he installed the priests of the high places which he had made. So he made offerings on the altar which he had made at Bethel on the fifteenth day of the eight month, in the month which he had devised in his own heart. And he ordained a feast for the children of Israel, and offered sacrifices on the altar and burned incense,* NKJV. It is stated in verse twenty-eight of the above citation that the King made two golden calves to worship; breaking the first commandment (Exodus 20:1-6).

Jeroboam king of Israel knew the requirements of the LORD, yet he had golden calves made which he presented to the people to worship as the gods who rescued them from Egypt. The king's reason for this devious plan was motivated by fear. He believed the people would revolt and reinstate Rehoboam king of Judah over all Israel, if they made the journey to the city of Jerusalem to worship and offer sacrifices to the LORD. This proved that Jeroboam was a selfish and insecure man; his evil devises were a success because the people remained in their home town and worshiped the golden calves. This was good news to this evil king but it would become a snare unto him and those he governed. The northern kingdom was guilty of breaking the first commandment and in defiance turned from the GOD of their forefathers to worship images.

Israel abandoned Jerusalem as their central place of worship where the only true temple of GOD was located. King Jeroboam influenced the ten northern tribes to rebel against the LORD by committing a grave abomination; bowing themselves and worshipping the golden calves they created. Through the intercession of Moses; the wrath of God was abated the first time the people made a calf of gold to worship as god (Exodus 32:1-14); but this time the LORD punished them. The northern kingdom designed their own temple and in so doing they rejected the LORD God their Sovereign Ruler. The pejorative name "Aholah," was given to Israel by the LORD as this name fitted the crime they had committed. The LORD God now informs Jeroboam of His displeasure and the punishment he would receive along with the people (see 1 Kings 13:1-5; 14:4-16). King Jeroboam was given sufficient time to repent, but he chose not to. The sins of the northern kingdom were reprehensible, but those of the southern kingdom were much more degrading.

Verses 22-35

Therefore, O Aholibah, thus saith the Lord GOD; Behold, I will raise up thy lovers against thee, from whom thy mind is alienated, and I will bring them against thee on every side; the Babylonians, and all the Chaldeans, Pekod, and Shoa, and Koa, and all the Assyrians with them: all of them desirable young men, captains and rulers, great lords and renowned, all of them riding upon horses. And they shall come against thee with chariots, wagons, and wheels, and with an assembly of people, which shall set against thee buckler and shield and helmet round about: and I will set judgment before them, and they shall judge thee according to their judgments. And I will set My jealousy against thee, and they shall deal furiously with thee: they shall take away thy nose and thine ears; and thy remnant shall fall by the sword: they shall take thy sons and thy daughters; and thy residue shall be devoured by the fire. They shall also strip thee out of thy clothes, and take away thy jewels. Thus will I make thy lewdness to cease from thee, and thy whoredom brought from the land of Egypt: so that thou shalt not lift up thine eyes unto them, nor remember Egypt any more. For thus saith the Lord GOD; Behold, I will deliver thee into the hand of them whom thou hatest, into the hand of them from whom thy mind is alienated: and they shall deal with thee hatefully, and shall take away all thy labour, and shall leave thee naked and bare: and the nakedness of thy whoredoms shall be discovered, both thy lewdness and thy whoredoms. I will do these things unto thee, because thou hast gone a whoring after the heathen, and because thou art polluted with their idols. Thou hast walked in the way of thy sister; therefore will I give her cup into thine hand. Thus saith the Lord GOD; Thou shalt drink from thy sister's cup deep and large: thou shalt be laughed to scorn and had in derision; it containeth much. Thou shalt be filled with drunkenness and sorrow, with the cup of astonishment and desolation, with the cup of thy sister Samaria. Thou shalt even drink it and suck it out, and thou shalt break the sherds thereof, and pluck off thine own breasts: for I have spoken it, saith the Lord GOD. Therefore thus saith the Lord GOD; Because thou hast forgotten Me, and cast Me behind thy back, therefore bear thou also thy lewdness and thy whoredoms.

While the name given to the northern tribe intimated that they built their own abominable temple; the name given to Judah was a grief unto the LORD because He called the people of the southern kingdom "Aholibah" meaning, "My Tent is in her" that is to say, the presence of the LORD was there. Israel was to be blamed for the grave sins that Judah committed later on, because the ten tribes of the northern kingdom did not set a godly example for the southern tribe comprised of Judah and Benjamin. The time would come when the sins of both the northern and southern kingdom would be purged by Josiah king of Judah (2 Kings 23:6-21) who was instrumental in the spiritual reformation of the nation (2 Chronicles 35). Following the death of Josiah, many kings ruled the southern tribes who were both good and evil, however, GOD had a final plan for a just and pure King whom He would raise up in the last days; and His name would be called the BRANCH.

The prophet Isaiah said: *"There shall come forth a Rod from the stem of Jesse, and a Branch shall grow out of his roots. The Spirit of the LORD shall rest upon Him, the Spirit of wisdom and understanding, the Spirit of counsel and might, the Spirit of knowledge and of the fear of the LORD. His delight is in the fear of the LORD, and He shall not judge by the sight of His eyes, nor decide by the hearing of His ears; but with righteousness He shall judge the poor, and decide with equity for the meek of the earth; He shall strike the earth with the rod of His mouth, and with the breath of His lips He shall slay the wicked. Righteousness shall be the belt of His loins, and faithfulness the belt of His waist,* Isaiah 11:1-5 NKJV. This was a prophecy about Yeshua Jesus, for there was no one else on earth that could fulfill such requirements. Until these things were fulfilled in the New Covenant (*B'rit Chadashah*). The LORD would punish His leaders and people; not because He desired perfection but that He longed to see His people uphold true holiness. Israel and Judah were punished for knowingly breaking the teachings of the LORD that would have made them stand out as a holy nation. It was now Judah's turn to be rebuked.

Judah (Aholibah) tumbled headlong into the ditch of sin opened by their sister of the northern tribes Israel (Aholah); and in their descent, took far more heinous abominations along with them. 2 Kings 23:1-15 applying the NIV gives us a peek into Judah's crimes and the measures King Josiah had taken to cleanse the land: *Then the king called together all the elders of Judah and Jerusalem. He went up to the temple of the LORD with the people of Judah, the inhabitants of Jerusalem, the priests and the prophets all the people from the least to the greatest. He read in the hearing all the words of the Book of the Covenant, which had been found in the temple of the LORD. The king stood by the pillar and renewed the covenant in the presence of the LORD to follow the LORD and keep His commands, statutes and decrees with all his heart and all his soul, thus confirming the words of the covenant written in this book. Then all the people pledged themselves to the covenant. The king ordered Hilkiah the high priest, the priests next in rank and the doorkeepers to remove from the temple of the LORD all the articles made for Baal and Asherah and all the starry hosts. He burned them outside Jerusalem in the field of the Kidron Valley and took the ashes of Bethel. He did away with the idolatrous priests appointed by the king of Judah to burn incense on the high places of the towns of Judah and on those around Jerusalem those who burned incense to Baal, to the sun and moon, to the constellations and all the starry hosts. He took the Asherah pole from the temple of the LORD to the Kidron Valley outside Jerusalem and burned it there. He ground it to powder and scatter the dust over the graves of the common people. He also tore down the quarters of the male shrine prostitutes that were in the temple of the LORD, the quarters where women did weaving for Asherah. Josiah brought all the priests from the towns of Judah and desecrated the high places, from Geba to Beersheba, where the priests had burned incense.*

He broke down the gateway at the entrance of the gate of Joshua, the city governor, which was on the left of the city gate. Although the priests of the high places did not serve at the altar of the LORD in Jerusalem, they ate unleavened bread with their fellow priests. He desecrated Topheth, which was in the Valley of Ben Hinnom, so no one could use it to sacrifice their son or daughter in the fire of Molek. He removed from the entrance to the temple of the LORD the horses that the kings of Judah had dedicated to the sun. They were in the court near the room of an official named Nathan-Melek. Josiah then burned the chariots dedicated to the sun. He pulled down the altars the kings of Judah had erected on the roof near the upper room of Ahaz, and the altars Manasseh had built in the two courts of the temple of the LORD. He removed them from there, smashed them to pieces and threw the rubble into the Kidron Valley. The king also desecrated the high places that were east of Jerusalem on the south of the hill of Corruption the ones Solomon king of Israel had built for Ashtoreth the vile goddess of the Sidonians, for Chemosh the vile god of Moab, and for Molek the detestable god of the people of Ammon. Josiah smashed the sacred stones and cut down the Asherah poles and covered the sites with human bones. Even the altar at Bethel, the high place made by Jeroboam son of Nebat, who had caused Israel to sin even that altar and high place he demolished. He burned the high place and ground it to powder, and burned the Asherah pole also (for further studies see 2 Chronicles 34).

These revelations given to Ezekiel concerning the lifestyle of his brethrens were an eye opener as they proved to the prophet that the LORD had not forsaken His people; they were bent on living their lives as they pleased. They saw other nations having great pleasure and delight without restraint or accountability and yearned to be like them but one day, they too, would be punished. The LORD was therefore taking the prophet back in time to prove that He was a GOD of justice, and that He did not punish without a cause.

Verses 36-49

The LORD said moreover unto me; Son of man, wilt though judge Aholah and Aholibah? Yea, declare unto them their abominations; that they have committed adultery, and blood is in their hands, and with their idols have they committed adultery, and have also caused their sons, whom they bare unto Me, to pass for them through the fire, to devour them. Moreover this they have done unto Me: they have defiled My sanctuary in the same day, and have profaned My Sabbaths. For when they had slain their children to their idols, then they came the same day unto My sanctuary to profane it; and, lo, thus have they done in the midst of Mine house. And furthermore, that ye have sent for men to come from far, unto whom a messenger was sent; and, lo, they come: for whom thou didst wash thyself, paintedest thy eyes, and deckedst thyself with ornaments, and satest upon a stately bed, and a table prepared before it, whereupon thou hast set Mine incense and Mine oil. And a voice of a multitude being at ease was with her: and with the men of the common sort were brought Sabeans from the wilderness, which put bracelets upon their hands, and beautiful crowns upon their heads. Then said I unto her that was old in adulteries, Will they now commit whoredoms with her, and she with them? Yet they went in unto her, as they go in unto a woman that playeth the harlot: so went they in unto Aholah and unto Aholibah, the lewd women. And the righteous men, they shall judge them after the manner of women that shed blood; because they are adulteresses, and blood is in their hands. For thus saith the Lord GOD; I will bring up a company upon them, and will give them to be removed and spoiled. And the company shall stone them with stones and dispatch them with their swords; they shall slay their sons and their daughters, and burn up their houses with fire. Thus will I cause lewdness to cease out of the land, that all women may be taught not to do after your lewdness.

And they shall recompense your lewdness upon you, and ye shall bear the sins of your idols: and ye shall know that I am the Lord GOD.

Israel was defiled, but Judah took defilement to another level; all because she followed in the footsteps of the poor example of her sister Israel. The ten northern tribes of Israel were subdued and taken into slavery by the Assyrians (2 Kings 17:1-6, 23; 18:9-12). Judah, instead of turning from the very sins that caused the exile of the northern tribes, committed sins that were worse. The Temple of the LORD being located in Jerusalem gave the residence a false sense of peace and security, but they were dead wrong, not knowing that when judgment was pronounced by the LORD, nothing would subvert His punishment. How could they serve the gods of the heathens, offering their children up for sacrifice; then without fear go to the Temple and offer the holy required sacrifices and worship the LORD? The sanctuary became defiled and the unauthorized use of the holy incense and oils were the final straw.

Not only did Judah worship the gods of the heathens they also dress like them. They were narcissistic, wore heavy makeup for the eyes and adorned embellishments to enhance their appearance. They wore bracelets and beautiful tiaras given to them as gifts by the Sabeans who were Arabs that worshiped the goddess of rain, fertility, death and doom. The Sabeans also worshiped the sun, moon and other heavenly bodies and now they were bed-fellows of Israel (Aholah) and Judah (Aholibah); no wonder the LORD used these derogatory names to describe them. While the house of Israel was busy mingling with the heathens to the point where it was impossible to differentiate between them and the Sabeans; GOD had a plan. The whole house of Israel was having a good time reveling and worshiping with idolaters, but unbeknown to them, the LORD was stirring the Babylonians; a mixed barbaric nation who was described as being more righteous than Judah; what a travesty.

Chapter 24

Verses 1-14

Again in the ninth year, in the tenth month, in the tenth day of the month, the word of the LORD came unto me, saying, Son of man, write the name of the day, even of this same day: the king of Babylon set himself against Jerusalem this same day. And utter a parable unto the rebellious house, and say unto them, Thus saith the Lord GOD; Set on a pot, set it on, and also pour water into it: gather the pieces thereof into it, even every good piece, the thigh, and the shoulder; fill it with the choice bones. Take the choice of the flock, and burn also the bones under it, and make it boil well, and let them seethe the bones of it therein. Wherefore thus saith the Lord GOD; Woe to the bloody city, to the pot whose scum is therein, and whose scum is not gone out of it! Bring it out piece by piece; let no lot fall upon it. For her blood is in the midst of her; she set it upon the top of a rock; she poured it not upon the ground, to cover it with dust; that it might cause fury to come up to take vengeance; I have set her blood upon the top of a rock, that it should not be covered. Therefore thus saith the Lord GOD; Woe to the bloody city! I will even make the pile for fire great. Heap on wood, kindle the fire, consume the flesh, and spice it well, and let the bones be burned. Then set it empty upon the coals thereof, that the brass of it may be hot, and may burn and that the filthiness of it may be molten in it, that the scum of it may be consumed. She hath wearied herself with lies, and her *great scum went not forth out of her: her scum shall be in the fire. In thy filthiness is lewdness: because I have purged thee, and thou wast not purged, thou shalt not be purged from thy filthiness any more, till I have caused My fury to rest upon thee. I the LORD have spoken it: it shall come to pass, and I will do it; I will not go back, neither will I spare, neither will I repent; according to thy ways, and according to thy doings, shall they judge thee, saith the Lord GOD.*

The LORD gave Ezekiel explicit instructions to document the exact date memorializing the siege of Jerusalem by the Babylonian army. Jerusalem, a walled city, was about to become a roofless prison for its dwellers; enforced by a secondary wall built around it by their enemies. This secondary wall became not only a prison for its occupants, but it created great anxieties and a sense of doom for those living there. Jerusalem was literally cut off from the outside world; food was in short supply and most of the panicked stricken residents surrendered peacefully to the king's army.

Ezekiel was instructed by the LORD to document the ninth year, tenth month and tenth day of the month; the date of the commencement of Nebuchadnezzar's blockade on the city of Jerusalem. This information is also mentioned in 2 Kings 25:1-3 and Jeremiah 52:4-6; this was the very day that the LORD spoke to Ezekiel concerning the siege. Therefore the hand of the Lord was already upon Ezekiel before the exile of the city dwellers. It is stated that Ezekiel warned the people in the city of the eminent invasion of Nebuchadnezzar's army on the very day of the siege. Using prophetic role play Ezekiel dramatized the downfall of Jerusalem, but many did not take his warning seriously; including the leaders.

Jerusalem was set ablaze and the people were in a state of extreme agitation and confusion, commotion and deep distress, as the Babylonians slaughtered the residence without mercy. With the destruction occurring in the city by the Babylonian army, the LORD spoke to Ezekiel reassuring him that his life would be spared. This priest would be among the remnants that would be taken to Babylon unscathed in the midst of all the chaos, as the LORD had chosen him to be His voice among the exiles that would be settled by Chebar. Is this the action of a cruel God? He loves His people so much that He strategically place Jeremiah in Jerusalem, Daniel and others in the kings' palace, and Ezekiel with the exiles at Chebar; preserving for Himself a remnant that would be saved and turn to the LORD their GOD, (see Psalm 102; Joel 2:32; Romans 9:25-33).

The arch enemy of all mankind also attempted to capitalize upon the plight of the people by seizing this opportunity to use Nebuchadnezzar for his own devious scheme, which was much more than the enslavement of Judah. Satan would use Judah's exile to contaminate the holy seed because this is Yeshua's tribe! This fallen Cherub desired to totally erase Judah's identity through inter-marriage and adaptation to a new language and culture. As the LORD used Nebuchadnezzar to bring about judgment upon His people, the fallen Cherub seized the opportunity to take advantage of it. If a generation is forty years, then eighty years in Babylon would affect the language, culture and customs of the people beyond recognition; especially those born in Babylon. Is this one of the reasons why the Babylonian exile of the tribe of Judah was appointed for only seventy years? The book of Daniel proves that he and others of distinguished birth among the exiles were selected for passive and ethnic cleansing.

If Nebuchadnezzar could change in totality the behavior patterns of the tribe of Judah he could also slowly but methodically change their identity. The book of Daniel 1:3-8 vividly brings out this point: *Then the king ordered Ashpenaz, chief of his court officials, to bring into the king's service some of the Israelites from the royal family and the nobility young men without any physical defect, handsome, showing aptitude for every kind of learning, well informed, quick to understand, and qualified to serve the king's palace. He was to teach them the language and literature of the Babylonians. The king assigned them a daily amount of food and wine from the king's table. They were to be trained for three years, and after that they were to enter the king's service. Among those who were chosen were some from Judah: Daniel, Hananiah, Mishael and Azariah. The chief official gave them new names: to Daniel the name Belteshazzar; to Hananiah, Shadrach; to Mishael, Meshach; and to Azariah, Abednego. But Daniel resolved not to defile himself with the royal food and wine, and he asked the chief official for permission not to defile himself this way,* NIV. Look at the list of qualifications required for those selected to participate in the king's systematic elimination of cultural identity:

- Young men without physical defect
- Handsome
- Showing aptitude for every kind of learning
- Well informed
- Quick to understand and qualified to serve the king
- Taught the language and literature of the Babylonians
- Dietary changes from kosher to non-kosher
- The assumption of Babylonian names to obscure their lineage.

Furthermore, to validate the belief that a passive ethnic cleansing was a part of Satan's diabolical plan, notice only choice young males were selected for this tutelage; first of all for reproductive purposes through inter-marriage. Next, it would be an extremely difficult task to brainwash the older more seasoned exiles who were well seasoned in their cultural heritage, customs, religious beliefs and language. Although the day of reckoning had come and the sins of Judah justly punished, their sifting was far from being over. In the end, the LORD in His unfathomable love and wisdom would unveil an awesome and glorious plan for His people (Jeremiah 50:17-20). Whatever the plans of the LORD to discipline His children, we can be sure that the scheming of Satan will also be in the midst.

Verses 15-27

Also the word of the LORD came unto me, saying, Son of man, behold, I take away from thee the desire of thine eyes with a stroke: yet neither shalt thou mourn nor weep, neither shall thy tears run down. Forbear to cry, make no mourning for the dead, bind the tire of thine head upon thee, and put on thy shoes upon thy feet, and cover not thy lips, and eat not the bread of men. So I spake unto the people in the morning: and at evening my wife died; and I did in the morning as I was commanded. And the people said unto me, Wilt thou not tell us what these things are to us, that thou doest so? Then I answered them, The word of the LORD came unto me, saying, Speak unto the house of Israel, Thus saith the Lord GOD; Behold, I will profane My sanctuary, the excellency of your strength, the desire of your eyes, and that which your soul pitieth; and your sons and your daughters whom ye have left shall fall by the sword. And ye shall do as I have done: ye shall not cover your lips, nor eat the bread of men. And your tiers shall be upon your heads, and your shoes upon your feet: ye shall not mourn nor weep; but ye shall pine away for your iniquities, and mourn one toward another. Thus Ezekiel is unto you a sign: according to all that he hath done shall ye do: and when this cometh, ye shall know that I am the Lord GOD. Also, thou son of man, shall it not be in the day when I take from them their strength, the joy of their glory, the desire of their eyes, and that whereupon they set their minds, their sons and their daughters, that he that escapeth in that day shall come unto thee, to cause thee to hear it with thine ears? In that day shall thy mouth be opened to him which is escaped, and thou shall speak, and be no more dumb: and thou shalt be a sign unto tem; and they shall know that I am the LORD.

Ezekiel was a loving husband by these words of the LORD. The LORD tells His servant that his wife was about to die. Ezekiel was instructed not to express grief or lament over her death as this would be a sign unto the people that just as the prophet did not express grief publicly, He, the LORD, would not express any deep mental anguish because of their captivity, and neither should they mourn when their sons and daughters were killed by the Babylonians. No traditional mourning practices should be observed; for the LORD had prohibited it. This was a sign to Judah of the seriousness of their crimes against the LORD and also the gravity of their punishment.

The sanctuary located in Jerusalem was desecrated by the Babylonians (2 Kings 25:8-21); but Judah is described as a little sanctuary of the LORD, (Genesis 49:10; Psalm 114:1-2), because from this tribe Yeshua Messiah would come into this world as a Deliverer. For seventy years Judah would be purged; this was their sentence for hundreds of years of taking a deliberate and careless sinful path. Ezekiel was now made speechless; he could not mourn for the death of his wife and neither could he respond to the cries of his brethren; a direct indication that the LORD had nothing to say to them. The LORD sent His servants the prophets to the people on many occasions, but instead of obeying their instructions, they had them stones, killed, or thrown into prison, they refused to listen to the voice of the LORD through His servant, and now His lips were sealed; Ezekiel being the expressed sign of His intention. What the LORD had decreed by the mouth of His prophets for hundreds of years had now come to fruition (see Amos 2:4-16).

This rebellion would come to a final end in the future and Judah will once again be the LORD'S sanctuary, and Israel the glory of His Sovereignty! Acts 7:44-50, quoting the NKJV makes this an undeniable truth: *"Our fathers had the tabernacle of witness in the wilderness, as He appointed, instructing Moses to make it according to the pattern that he had seen, which our fathers, having received it in turn, also brought with Joshua into the land possessed by the Gentiles, whom God drove out before the face of our fathers until the days of David, who found favor before God and asked to find a dwelling for the God of Jacob. But Solomon built Him a house. However, the Most High does not dwell in temples made with hands, as the prophet says: 'Heaven is My throne, and earth is My footstool. What house will you build for Me? Says the LORD, or what is the place of My rest? Has My hand not made all these things?"* And 2 Corinthians 6:16 states: *And what agreement hath the temple of God with idols? For ye are the temple of the living God; as God hath said, I will dwell in them, and walk in them; and I will be their God, and they shall be My people.*

The prophet Jeremiah also spoke by the mouth of the Lord: *Behold, the days come, saith the LORD, that I will make a new covenant with the house of Israel, and with the house of Judah: not according to the covenant that I made with their fathers in the day that I took them by the hand to bring them out of the land of Egypt; which My covenant they break, although I was a husband unto them, saith the LORD: but this shall be the covenant that I will make with the house of Israel; After those days, saith the LORD, I will put My law in their inward parts, and write it in their hearts; and will be their God, and they shall be My people,* 31:31-33. There is hope; the spiritual sanctuary of God will be cleansed and made pure for Yeshua Jesus. The desecrations of the natural temple led to its destruction; the desecration of the spiritual temple led to its defilement. We have seen the sufferings of Israel and Judah in our study of the book of Ezekiel because they rejected God and His plan of redemption for them. The LORD is the ever present I AM therefore, what He has done in the past, He will do yet again.

As we seek truth we will find it and volumes two and three of this work will undoubtedly draw one closer to the LORD as more marvelous revelations about Yeshua Jesus, His brethrens the Jews, and the engrafted Gentiles is unsealed. If the LORD so chooses to reveal the hidden truths in His Word, it is a sign unto all that the end of things as we know it is quite near. Abba Father will do whatever it takes to seek and save those who are undecided, agnostic, secular, or unbelieving. If this is not love then in the reality of our existence we will continue to search for something to fill the void in our soul. The Way, the Truth, and the Life is not a twelve step program, but a Person name Yeshua Jesus the Messiah, He will fill every void and give us the gift of everlasting life and peace.

www.ingramcontent.com/pod-product-compliance
Lightning Source LLC
Chambersburg PA
CBHW070737170426
43200CB00007B/552